D1601677

Celtic and Early Christian Wexford

Celtic and Early Christian Wexford

AD 400 to 1166

Edward Culleton

FOUR COURTS PRESS

Set in 10.5 on 12.5 point Ehrhardt for
FOUR COURTS PRESS
Fumbally Lane, Dublin 8, Ireland
e-mail: info@four-courts-press.ie
and in North America for
FOUR COURTS PRESS
c/o ISBS, 5804 N.E. Hassalo Street, Portland, OR 97213.

A catalogue record for this title
is available from the British Library.

ISBN 1–85182–515–0

Printed in Great Britain
by MPG Books, Bodmin, Cornwall

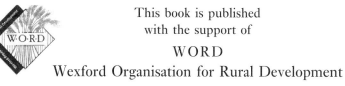 This book is published
with the support of

WORD

Wexford Organisation for Rural Development

Comhairle Chontae Loch Garman

are pleased to be associated
with this publication

Wexford County Council

Contents

III

CO. WEXFORD, A PLACE OF CHANGE

APPENDICES

List of illustrations

CREDITS

Photographs Duchas: 1, 3-6, 8, 15-17; Edward Culleton: 2, 11-13; Ken Hemmingway: 7, 14; National Museum of Ireland: 9a; Brian Lynch, Bord Fáilte: 9b; Peter Harbison: 10a; Pádraig Ó hÉailidhe: 10b

Figures Dorothy Kelly: 1; Joseph Hunt: 2; Ordnance Survey: 3.

Maps Matthew Stout

List of abbreviations

Ann. Clon.   *The Annals of Clonmacnoise*, D. Murphy (ed. and trans.), Dublin, 1896.

AFM   *The Annals of the Kingdom of Ireland by the Four Masters*, J. O'Donovan (ed. and trans.), 7 vols, Dublin, 1851.

Ann. Inisfallen   *The Annals of Inisfallen*, S. Mac Airt (ed. and trans.), Dublin, 1951.

Ann. Loch Cé   *The Annals of Loch Cé: A Chronicle of Irish Affairs from AD 1014-1590*, W. M. Hyannis (ed. and trans.), London, 1871.

Ann. Tig.   *The Annals of Tigernach*, W. Stokes (ed. and trans.), *Revue celtique*, 1895, 1896, 1897, and reprinted (as 2 vols) Lampeter, 1993

AU   *The Annals of Ulster to AD 1131*, S. Mac Airt and G. Mac Niocaill (ed. and tran.), Dublin 1983.

B. Arm.   Book of Armagh.

B. Lein.   Book of Leinster.

MD   *The Martyrology of Donegal*, J. O'Donovan, J.H. Todd and W. Reeves (ed. and trans.), Dublin, 1864.

MG   *The Martyrology of Gorman*, W. Stokes (ed. and trans.), Henry Bradshaw Society, London, 1895.

MO   *The Martyrology of Óengus, the Culdee*, W. Stokes (ed. and trans.), Henry Bradshaw Society, London, 1905, reprinted Dublin, 1984.

MT   *The Martyrology of Tallaght*, R.I. Best and H.J. Lawlor (ed. and trans.), Henry Bradshaw Society, London, 1931.

OS   Ordnance Survey.

Spellings of Irish names follow Professor F.J. Byrne in *Irish kings and high kings*, 1973.

Preface

This book explores the changes in the landscape, religion and political situation in the area now called Co. Wexford in the period 400-1166. The first date has been chosen because it signifies the beginning of the conversion of the pagan, Celtic inhabitants to Christianity. The second date marks the departure of Diarmait Mac Murchada to seek foreign aid to recover his kingdoms of Uí Cheinnselaig and Leinster.

I realize that to write a history of a period covering over 750 years is an ambitious undertaking, made no less difficult by the lack of, or the tendentiousness of, the available information. Even the title that should be applied to this period is disputed. Should it be Early Medieval or Early Christian? I have opted for the latter, given that much of the book is devoted to the history of Christianity in the county.

While this period appears remote to the modern mind it is well to remember that developments then still have a significant bearing on Co. Wexford today. Take the landscape, previously fairly heavily forested, which became dotted with ráths, monasteries and churches, traces of which are still numerous in the countryside. The Gaelic estates of the later period became the precursors of the present-day townlands, while many modern place-names, although somewhat altered over the centuries, also date to this period.

In religion, paganism was replaced by Christianity, but not in the easy manner or short time often portrayed. The Church suffered its own vicissitudes; religious practice was sometimes apathetic and Church organization inefficient; yet the names of the early Wexford missionary saints are still commonly used as first names to this day. Politically, the small independent *tuatha* gradually lost power which then became centralized in one family, in Wexford's case, the Mac Murchada, in Ferns. Their territory, carved out over centuries, was the forerunner of the modern diocese and most of the county.

One of the most pleasant aspects about writing this book was the unstinted cooperation and help I experienced from many experts. Some read and commented on early drafts of various chapters, others gave me previews of their forthcoming papers or directed me to important sources of information, or enlightened me on obscure historical points. These included Monsignor Patrick Corish, Billy Colfer, Charles Doherty, Conleth Manning, Nollaig Ó Muraíle, Dónall Mac Giolla Easpaig, Michael Ryan, John Bradley, Peter Harbison, Nicholas Furlong, Próinséas Ní Chatháin, Pádraig Ó Riain, Tadgh O'Keeffe, Elizabeth Fitzpatrick, Michael O'Connell, Fiachra Ó Lionáin and the late Frank Mitchell. Adrian Phillips, Doris Molloy, Anna Kinsella and Joseph Culleton also helped in various ways.

Translations from Latin texts were done by John Dunleavy and from the French by Emily Hourican. John Hunt's translation of the Latin Life of St Munnu was given to me by his son-in-law, Tom Williams. Brian Gilsenan and Celestine Rafferty helped with proof-reading. The maps were expertly drawn by Matthew Stout. Illustrations were supplied by Ken Hemmingway, Brian Lynch of Bórd Fáilte, Dúchas, Michael Moore, the National Museum, Billy Colfer, Joseph Hunt and Dorothy Kelly. The library staff in the Royal Irish Academy, Trinity College, the Royal Society of Antiquaries of Ireland and Wexford County Library facilitated me at all times. Rory Murphy introduced me to several Early Christian sites in north Wexford.

To all the aforementioned, to the Wexford Organization for Rural Development and to Wexford County Council for their financial support, and to my family for their help and forbearance, I offer my heartfelt thanks.

Celtic and Early Christian Wexford –
an overview

To gain an understanding of the history of this period necessarily involves an examination, not only of the functioning of the early Church, but also of the political, social and economic milieu in which it operated. The period covered is over 750 years. It goes without saying that great changes must have taken place over such an extended period of time, not alone in the Church but also in secular society. For this reason I thought it useful to provide an overview in the hope that the general reader will be encouraged to follow the story in greater detail in the body of the text.

The history of the area covering the present Co. Wexford began to be written down only in the eighth century. Previously, all events and family histories were recorded orally, with all the distortions which followed such a method. The written records are not contained in any single document but must be painstakingly put together from the slight references in the annals, in the Lives of the saints and from the genealogies of the different branches of the ruling families. All these were written down much later and usually to serve a particular purpose such as to enhance the importance of a family like the Mac Murchada, or the glory of a saint such as Aidán (Máedóg). It is difficult to establish the true facts of history at any period, but even more difficult when so few records, which themselves may be biased, are available.

Early accounts, then, are a blend of some facts together with genealogy, mythology and fabulous Lives of the saints, mostly of a propagandist nature. Given these reservations and the inventiveness of earlier historians it is no wonder that accounts of the early history of Co. Wexford have varied widely. In recent times, however, several notable scholars, such as Doherty, Byrne, Ó Corráin, Sharpe and Smyth, working from original documents, have pieced together various parts of this historical jigsaw.

The Celts

Different groups of people had been settling in the area since at least 6,000 BC. The last to arrive were the Celts. According to O'Rahilly (1940) the earliest Celtic people were the Fotharta, who took over much of Leinster but were eventually confined to small areas in Carlow and Wexford, the later baronies of Forth in both counties.

The next group of Celts to arrive was the Brigantes, an important tribe in northwest England. It has erroneously been stated that another group, the Menapii, settled in the Wexford area. This group, in fact, settled further north, as can be seen from Ptolemy's second-century map of Ireland. The Brigantes occupied much of south Leinster but, like the Fotharta, were eventually confined to the Slieve Margy area of Laois and to Bargy in south Wexford, to which they gave their name. The Benntraige of Bantry barony may also have been Brigantes.

Their conquerors were the Uí Cheinnselaig, a branch of the Laigin, who gave their name to Leinster. They proved to be the strongest and most enduring of all.

These Iron Age groups of Celts left few tangible traces in Co. Wexford, apart from hillforts at Ballybuckley (Bree) and Courthoyle (Newbawn) and promontory forts at Pollshone, Nook, Baginbun (Ramstown), Templetown and possibly Saltee Island Great. In Celtic mythology the river Slaney is named after a Brigantes warrior called Sláine. Finn Mac Cumhaill is reputed to have had a dwelling near Hook Head and to have defeated the king of Leinster in a battle at Camaross. Another member of the Fianna, Conan, gave his name to Duncannon.

The Celts were pagans and apparently worshipped several gods, including Lugh. His festival of Lughnasa was celebrated until recent times on Fraughan Sunday at several hilltops in Co. Wexford, including Caher Rua's Den, Carrigbyrne and Ballyleigh Hill. The druids were the highly educated priests of the Celts, even though they did not have writing. Everything, including their laws, history, genealogy and poetry, had to be committed to memory and recited orally. On Ptolemy's map Carnsore Point is named 'Hieron Akron', which is Greek for Holy Cape, indicating that it was a druidic centre of major significance.

Christianity was introduced into the area around AD 400, probably from Britain. At this time most of the present Co. Wexford was controlled by the Uí Barriche. But the Uí Cheinnselaig were gradually encroaching from the north and eventually conquered the whole area. The county was divided into eight or nine distinct population groups or *tuatha*, a term which eventually became synonymous with the territories they occupied. In the south were the remnants of the Uí Barriche, Fotharta and Síl Brain, while the rest was divided among Uí Cheinnselaig family groups, who also controlled adjoining parts of Carlow and Wicklow. For several hundred years the county's political history was dominated by power struggles among the Uí Cheinnselaig for the kingship of their own territory and by them for the kingship of Leinster. Eventually, a branch descended from Onchu, known as the Síl nOnchon, asserted control in the person of Diarmait Mac Máel na mBó.

The Uí Cheinnselaig provided several kings of Leinster, among them Brandubh, of the Uí Felmada branch, who was associated with the foundation of the monastery of Ferns. He was killed in 605, but his direct descendant, David, The O' Morchoe, lives in Co. Wexford. The most powerful Uí Cheinnselaig kings of Leinster were Diarmait Mac Máel na mBó (1052-70) and his great grandson, Diarmait Mac Murchada (1126 or 1131-71), who invited the Normans to Ireland to help him regain his kingdoms from which he had been deposed.

Society and economy

Irish society during the Early Christian period was highly stratified. Apart from the kingly families there were the nobles and the commoners. The latter category, who were free, consisted of professional people such as poets, historians, genealogists and lawmakers, farmers and artisans such as wrights and masons. Below these were the unfree tenants, serfs and slaves.

The basic unit of society was the extended family or kin group, descended from a common great-grandfather, although later it became confined to a common grandfather. This unit owned most of the land, but each kin member held his own individual farm. However, it seems that by the ninth century the kin group no longer functioned as a unit, each family becoming completely independent of the group. There were strict laws governing disposal of land, which had to have the approval of the kin. The Church also held a vast amount of land, donated as gifts to particular monasteries and churches. The professional classes held land in recognition of their services to the king.

The land was mainly used for cattle rearing and a man's status was determined by the number of animals he owned. Cattle raiding seems to have been endemic and was regarded as a young man's sport.

The better off in society lived within circular enclosures known as ráths which varied in size according to a person's status and wealth. In Co. Wexford the sites of around six hundred ráths have been identified. Towards the end of the period such enclosures seem to have gone out of fashion.

Clientship to the nobility formed the basis of the economic system. A lord might contract to advance either cattle or land to a client on which he received interest in the form of food rent and service, including the military kind. Thus, the more clients a man had beholden to him the greater his power and status in society.

Life was not always easy and the Annals record a long list of famines, plagues and diseases of man and beast. It has been suggested that the great plagues of the sixth and seventh centuries were responsible for the large influx of young men into the monasteries.

The progress of Christianity
After its introduction into this highly class-conscious society, Christianity seems to have spread fairly rapidly, despite the opposition of the pagan druids. In the late fifth and early sixth centuries the missionary saints, Ibar, Abbán, Munnu and Aidán, better known as Máedóg, founded monasteries at Beggerin, Adamstown, Taghmon and Ferns.

The early church organization was based on the *tuatha*, with a bishop over each territory. This would have given eight or nine bishops to the area encompassed by Co. Wexford.

The laity were served by secular priests, whom they had to maintain. Within a few centuries the countryside appears to have been dotted with churches, some attached to a large mother church, some private and some belonging to the monasteries. These churches, many of which were, in fact, large ecclesiastical centres, were usually surrounded by a circular or oval bank of earth, like the ráths. They varied greatly in size; among the largest in dimension were Ferns (450 x 300 metres), Kilmokea (330 x 260 metres), Clongeen (300 metres approx.), Killegney (250 metres approx.) and Temple-shanbo (250 metres approx.). Many of the smaller sites varied between sixty and ninety metres in diameter. Using a standard set of criteria, almost one hundred Early Christian sites have been identified in the county.

The monasteries gradually became wealthy through grants of land and other gifts. In the beginning the monks had led a strictly regulated contemplative life, but this began to break down in the eight century. To combat this decline a movement known as the Céli Dé, 'the servants of God,' came into being. One of the leaders was St Maelruan of Tallaght, whose influence extended into the Screen, Ballinaleck and Ardcandrisk areas as shown by the church and holy well dedications to him. The wealth of the monasteries attracted envious eyes, Irish as well as Viking, leading to many attacks and even warfare between the monasteries. In 817 Ferns and Taghmon fought a battle in which 400 people were reportedly killed. The Vikings attacked Beggerin in 821 and Ferns in 835 and 921. In 828, 835 and 921 they attacked Taghmon. By the tenth century, however, they had formed a settlement at Wexford which eventually grew into a town. This became a trading port which gave a stimulus to agricultural production in the hinterland.

The monasteries appear to have ceased to function as such by the tenth century, apart from Ferns, which being the seat of the Uí Cheinnselaig, survived as a religious, educational and economic centre. At the synod of Rathbreasail in 1111, which was convened to reform the Irish Church, Ferns became the seat and the name of the newly-formed diocese. From that period also the Church began to introduce the parish as the basis of church organization.

To help in the twelfth-century reform of the Irish Church religious orders were brought into Ireland from abroad. At Ferns Diarmait Mac Murchada granted property and income to the canons regular of St Augustine to establish St Mary's abbey, around 1160. Its ruins are preserved as a national monument.

It is now thought that the monasteries may not have been as important in the life of the people as was originally believed and that it was mostly the secular clergy who ministered to the laity throughout the Early Christian period. Even then, such ministration seems to have been largely for the better-off in the highly stratified Gaelic society. The functions which the priest was obliged to perform in return for his keep were baptism, Mass, confession and prayers for the sick and the dead.

Over the centuries from the arrival of Christianity until the departure of Diarmait Mac Murchada many changes had taken place within Irish society. By the twelfth century the social and economic set up depicted in the law tracts, if it ever existed as such, was long gone. The kin group had largely broken down and the *tuatha* had lost their independence. Power was now concentrated in the king. Thus, Diarmait Mac Murchada reigned supreme in Uí Cheinnselaig, surrounded by his court like any feudal lord.

Surnames had come into use by the eleventh century and many families gave their names to their estates. These estates corresponded to the *baile* or later townland, several of whose family names are preserved in the modern townland names such as Ballybrazil, Ballybrennan and Ballyregan.

The church, too, had undergone significant changes. With the secularization of the monasteries religious life had declined in Ireland, as in Europe as a whole. But Ferns had survived to become the seat of the newly established diocese and parishes were beginning to be formed on the well-defined Gaelic estates.

Developments in Ireland then, including Uí Cheinnselaig, were little different to those in Britain and mainland Europe except in name and perhaps in scale.

I

The environmental, economic and social background

Historical events and processes take place against a background of particular environmental, economic and social conditions. This chapter sketches the background against which Christianity was introduced and in which it developed in Ireland and Co. Wexford between the years 400 and 1166.

As a habitation for man Co. Wexford has been favoured by nature with fertile soils, a moderate climate and flat to undulating or hilly topography. Situated in the extreme southeast corner of the country, the area has always been relatively isolated from the rest of the country. Reinforcing this isolation was the vast bulk of the Blackstairs mountains on the northwest, with its lower slopes covered in thick forest. South of these mountains the Waterford estuary formed a further barrier. On the east and south coasts the Irish Sea, while facilitating trade and travel with Britain and Continental Europe, also cut the area off from inland.

The varied landscape
On a broad scale the Wexford landscape falls into several distinct topographic areas (Map 1).

A lowland plain, which is mainly below eighty metres in elevation, occupies most of the county. It stretches from Gorey in the north to Kilmore in the south and from there to the Waterford estuary in the west and occupies a large area centring on the Slaney valley in central Wexford. The rocks underlying this plain are mainly shales and slate which are between 600 to 400 million years old. There are also some limestone and sandstone rocks in places.

Volcanic hills were formed when small underwater volcanoes pushed molten material up to the surface over 400 million years ago. This solidified to form hard rocks which resisted breakdown by weathering agents. And so today they form a line of volcanic hills running from Duncannon in the southwest to Kilmichael Point on the northeastern border of the county. The most prominent of these hills are at Carrigbyrne, Bree, Vinegar Hill and Tara Hill.

The shale hills to the west such as Slievecoiltia and those to the northwest were formed during a period of mountain building which took place around 400 million years ago. The mountains were formed at this time, too, as a massive dome, over 300 metres high, was created along the northwest boundary of the county. Into this flowed molten magma from deep down in the earth's crust. This magma then solidified to form the whitish granite of the Blackstairs mountains, with its peaks at Mount Leinster and Caher Rua's Den. Away in the southeast of the county a coarse pinkish granite emerged to form the promontory of Carnsore Point.

The 'kame and kettle' topography of the Screen-Blackwater area forms a unique feature on the Wexford landscape. It is composed entirely of sand and gravel deposited by an ice sheet which pushed in from the Irish Sea around 25,000 years ago. Between the sand hills (kames) are many small lakes (kettles).

The soil distribution pattern

The land is the great producer of crops which sustain the human race. Before the introduction of artificial fertilizer to enhance growth, the natural fertility of the soil was of supreme importance and in this regard Co. Wexford has been particularly fortunate. Apart from the more elevated areas and steeper slopes the whole county is covered by material deposited during the Ice Age which now forms the parent material of the soils. During the last glacial episode, which lasted from 25,000 to around 15,000 years ago, a glacier moving down the Irish Sea pushed onto the low ground along the east coast, where it laid down a thick mantle of material which it had incorporated from the sea bed. At an earlier period an ice sheet had advanced into Co. Wexford from the Irish midlands, crossing the lower slopes of the Blackstairs mountains. The material deposited by this ice sheet was mainly derived from the underlying shale bedrock over which it passed but invariably contained debris of other rock types as well.

The various types of glacial deposits significantly influenced the kind of soil which formed in any area. Other factors which played a part were climate, vegetation, topography, time and man himself. Map 2 shows the principal soil types in the county and their drainage characteristics (for a detailed description and maps see *Soils of county Wexford* by Gardiner and Ryan, 1964). That soil type had a major influence on the settlement pattern in the Early Christian period, as reflected in the greater number of ráths in particular areas (see pages 61 and 63, below).

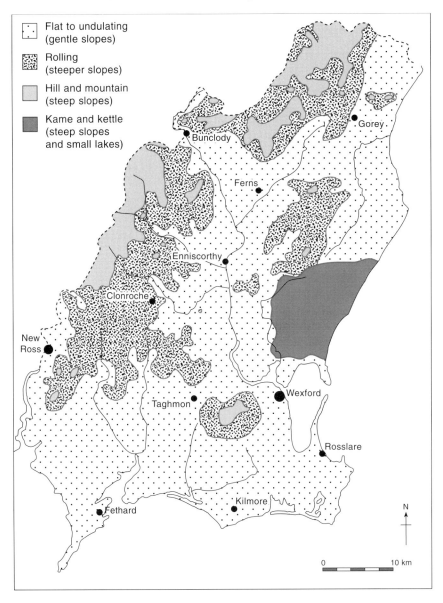

Legend:

- Flat to undulating (gentle slopes)
- Rolling (steeper slopes)
- Hill and mountain (steep slopes)
- Kame and kettle (steep slopes and small lakes)

Gorey

Bunclody

Ferns

Enniscorthy

Clonroche

New Ross

Wexford

Taghmon

Rosslare

Kilmore

Fethard

N

0   10 km

Map 1 The topography of Co. Wexford ranges from the granite mass of the Blackstairs mountains to the shale hills of northwest Wexford and volcanic outcrops such as Vinegar Hill to the flat, glacial till-covered lowlands of the south.

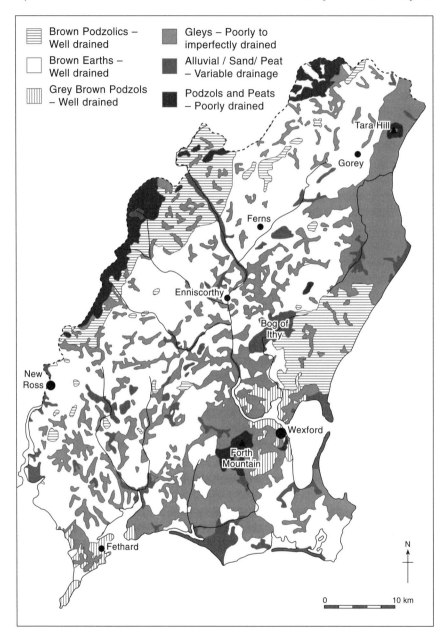

Brown Podzolics –
Well drained

Brown Earths –
Well drained

Grey Brown Podzols
– Well drained

Gleys – Poorly to
imperfectly drained

Alluvial / Sand/ Peat
– Variable drainage

Podzols and Peats
– Poorly drained

Tara Hill

Gorey

Ferns

Enniscorthy

Bog of
Ithy

New
Ross

Wexford

Forth
Mountain

Fethard

N

0   10 km

Map 2 The different types of soil in the county resulted from the inter-
action of climate, topography and living organisms with the underlying
parent material over many thousands of years. In the last few thousand
years man's activities have also influenced the pattern of soil formation.

Climate

Co. Wexford has a favourable climate for man and his crops and livestock. Compared to the rest of the country it enjoys a somewhat lower average annual rainfall, longer periods of bright sunshine, longer frost-free periods and higher mean annual temperatures. However, the climate becomes slightly less favourable away from the coast. Annual rainfall varies within the county from around 800 mm along the east and south coasts to around 1200 mm near the Blackstairs mountains. Hours of sunshine at Rosslare vary from 1.75 in January to 6.50 in June; mean annual temperature at Enniscorthy can range from around 40°F in January to around 60°F in July

Man and the landscape

The earliest evidence for human habitation in Co. Wexford comes from the Mesolithic or Middle Stone Age, around 7000 years ago (Culleton, 1984, 3). At that time the county would have been covered in thick forest, apart from the very wet areas. With the introduction of farming around 6000 years ago the type of land cover gradually changed as the forest was cut down to make farmland. By the opening of the Early Christian period around AD 400, Co. Wexford would have been a mosaic of forest, grassland, cultivated areas, moorland and heathery mountain. Apart from cutting down the forest human activity had other effects on the landscape. For example, at Garradreen, Taghmon, evidence of soil erosion following deforestation around 500 was found (Culleton and Mitchell, 1976, 120-3). It is not possible to give the extent of the different categories of land cover for this period. However, later sources such as place-names and charters give us some clues to its variety (this is so particularly for the early centuries of the new millennium, that is, after AD 1000). Many of the early place-names have been preserved in modern townland names. But that does not mean that the informing element in the name ever referred to the total area of the townland, which, in any case, has probably changed over the centuries (see p. 179 below). Hence, while giving us very valuable information they do not convey the actual extent of the area denoted in the name.

One of the most frequently found elements in place-names in the county refers to grassland or pasture as indicated by the prefix clon-, from the Irish *cluain*, meaning meadow. Poorer type grassland, which was used for summer grazing, is usually shown by the element bol-, boley, or bool-, from the Irish *buaile*. Several place-name elements indicate wet or marshy land. For example, the prefix *ask*; which is a slight variation of the Irish *easc*, meaning quagmire, annagh from the Irish *eannach* meaning marsh, and curra from the Irish *corrach* meaning bog, as well as the English place-names Moor, Moortown and Moorfields are self-explanatory. Forest cover is shown by the element 'kill', from the Irish *coill* meaning wood, as distinct from the ecclesiastical connotation of church. Commonage was once extensive in the county and remnants are shown on the six-inch Ordnance Survey maps.

Perhaps the most enduring evidence of man's activities on the landscape during the Early Christian period comes from the number of ráths and ecclesiastical sites which dot the countryside. Ráths were the homesteads of the nobles and farmers and consisted of a circular enclosure, usually around thirty metres in diameter. Within the enclosure were located the dwelling house and outhouses. The size and number of ramparts indicated the status of the occupant. Three were specified for an overking, two obviously indicated a king of a *tuath*.

By the twelfth century and probably much earlier farmers no longer lived in ráths but in single, scattered farmsteads, not unlike at the present time, or in small clusters of farmhouses. Around the farm buildings was the infield; further out lay large open fields, mostly in pasture but interspersed here and there with several adjacent strips of cultivated land. A good example of this type of strip farming layout, possibly dating back to the Early Christian period, is found at Churchtown, on the promontory of Hook Head (OS six-inch sheet 54). But ráths, although deserted and overgrown, would still have been a familiar sight to the inhabitants of the county. What significance they attached to them at that time is hard to say, but, given the level of superstition of the time and the fear of interfering with them which has persisted until recent times, it is likely that they were held in some awe and left undisturbed.

Around 600 ráth sites have been located in Co. Wexford, of which about 150 remain intact (Moore, 1996, 28). As if emphasizing the continuity of landscape occupation during the previous millennia for its Early Christian inhabitants, megalith features such as portal tombs (dolmens), standing stones and stone alignments, as well as various types of mounds, for example, tumuli, barrows and stone cairns, dotted the landscape. Other prehistoric remains included hillforts at Ballybuckley and Courthoyle and coastal promontory forts – Pollshone, Nook, Ramstown, Templetown and possibly Saltee Island Great.

Enclosure of certain areas with fences was widespread. The brehon laws had stipulated four types of fences (Ó Corráin, 1983, 247). These were a ditch, a stone fence, an oak and a post-and-wattle fence. The latter two types of fences were of a temporary nature; the oak type was for fencing around woodland, while the post- and-wattle type was for protecting tillage crops and possibly for other restricted areas such as waterholes or ponds for cattle. The ditch and stone fences were obviously of a more permanent nature. The ditch had to be three feet wide at the top, two in the middle and one at the bottom. The earth from the ditch was thrown up to form a bank about three feet in height. The stone fences would obviously have been similar to those of today and would have been constructed in Co. Wexford only where the glaciers left numerous medium-sized boulders strewn on the land, as at Bunclody, Carrigbyrne and Carne.

The ditch and bank type fence, on the other hand, would have been used in most parts of the county. A references to ditches is found in the Forest Charter of Ross and Taghmon (Orpen, 1934, 55): 'And from Rathmochelath to the ditch which goes along the main road which comes from the castle of Ros, and is the ditch between my preserve and the land of Thomas Boscher, near Benbroil, which the Irish usually call Deriardcoleman, and along the said ditch as far as the valley which leads down to Crouath.' Even today remnants of these ditch and bank structures may be found. For example, Swan (1972-3, 80-7) mentions a large bank separating the manor and medieval parish of Rosslare from the medieval parish of Kilscoran. This bank may possibly have separated two earlier Gaelic estates. Colfer (pers. comm.) has also found some examples in southwest Wexford. If we accept that these fences mark original territorial boundaries, we have direct field evidence of such boundaries going back to Early Christian times. It seems likely that individual family farms had such a type of boundary fence, which served, not only to delineate the territory, but also to prevent trespass of animals which was often a cause of legal action in the period. As will be seen later, ecclesiastical enclosures, many also surrounded by an earthen bank, became a familiar sight on the landscape as Christianity spread throughout the county.

The Wexford woodlands

The earliest description of woods in the county is by Giraldus Cambrensis (Scott and Martin, 1978, 41) who described Diarmait Mac Murchada's retreat before the Irish forces descending on Ferns in 1169 'with his followers within an area not far from Ferns which was sealed off on all sides by very thick forests, steep mountains, rivers and bogs ... Here, with Fitzstephen's help, he set about felling trees, made the woods impenetrable from all sides with fallen trees and logs joined together ...' This was obviously part of the Duffry or Dubhtire, so called because of its covering of dense forest. The strategic importance of these woods in protecting Ferns was well recognized.

The Dunbrody abbey charter granted between 1207 and 1213 refers to woods, plains, meadows, pasture, mills, marshes and bogs (Hore, iii, 37). This charter also contains a reference to a wood which Hore describes as stretching from where 'the abbey stands down to the river on the north and over to Dunbrody Castle in the east, and which was in being when Robert Leigh wrote his Ms in 1684'. That large oak trees were growing in the area is shown by the description of a lay brother, Alan, 'who took up his dwelling in a certain hollow oak and there made his abode during the time of his sojourn' (Hore, iii, 45). This brother had been sent from Buildwas in Wales to inspect the area which was being offered to the abbey by William Marshal. The foundation charter of Tintern abbey, dated to 1200, also contains a reference to forests as follows: 'And let the said Abbey with all its tenements be outside the forest and altogether without the regard of the forestry … And let them have pasture throughout all my forests' (Hore, ii, 22-3).

By far the most enlightening information on the extent of the forest in south Wexford is found in the forest charter of Earl Richard Marshal dated to 1232 or 1233. This document gives the boundaries of the great forests stretching from the Slaney at Ferrycarrig to the Corock river and from Longraige to the Barrow and thence northwards to Lacken Hill. Lands of the earl outside those limits were deforested 'for the good of my soul and the souls of my descendants' (Orpen, 1934, 54). 'Deforested' here may have meant taking it out of legal protection and not maintaining it solely as a hunting preserve for the lord. The actual density of trees in these forests is not known for certain, since the term 'forest' seems to have been used in a legalistic sense. It is likely that the tree density varied and that many areas of farmland were located within the forest.

An idea of the complex pattern of land in twelfth-century Co. Wexford is given in Diarmait Mac Murchada's charter to Ferns abbey around 1160. This charter describes the lands as "being in wood, in plain, in meadows, in pastures' and ' in waters, in mills, in roads and paths, in moors and marshes' (Hore, vi, 180). There is no doubt that large areas of Co. Wexford, particularly the river valleys of the Slaney, Urrin, Boro and Bann, were heavily wooded. Since trees grow naturally unless disturbed by man through tree felling, or through disease, as happened in the second half of the twentieth century when elm trees were practically wiped out, woodlands had probably persisted for centuries in these areas.

The economic background

The Irish economy in the late pagan–Early Christian period was based entirely on agriculture, particularly cattle. In the period preceding the advent of Christianity to Ireland agricultural production was rising as a result of climatic improvement and use of better tillage implements, particularly the plough. Cattle production was the dominant activity. It has been suggested (McCormick, 1995, 33-7) that agriculture was given a further fillip by the introduction of dairy farming at around the same time as Christianity arrived in Ireland. Values of land, the honour price of people and fines for breaking the law were calculated in terms of the milch cow, which was equivalent in value to one ounce of silver (Kelly, 1997, 58). A female slave was often valued at three milch cows.

Early in the period, land was jointly owned by a kin group which consisted of all male descendants of a common great-grandfather. However, members of the kin group actually farmed independently, apart from cooperating in the use of oxen, ploughs and mills for grinding cereal grain. Male members could also own land privately, which they could dispose of in consultation with the kin group. Eventually the kin group was reduced to male descendants of a common grandfather.

The land was owned mainly by the nobles who, in turn, rented it, together with cows or steers (oxen), to their farmer clients. A person's status in society was related to the number of clients he held. Rent was paid in food and service. Given the dependence on cattle, outbreaks of disease could cause high mortality in the herd, leading to starvation among the population. Apart from cattle, sheep, pigs and goats also formed part of the economy, as well as hens, geese, ducks, doves and bees.

Arable farming was widely practised, particularly in areas of suitable climate such as Co. Wexford. The principal crops grown were wheat, barley, rye and oats. Peas, beans, cabbage and onions were also grown. For fruit, apples and plums trees were grown. The Life of St Aidán describes the saint sowing barley seed, grinding wheat in the mill and planting fruit trees (see p. 105, below). To increase crop yields, farmyard manure or dung from a dunghill in the farmyard was spread on the land.

The monasteries were also engaged in farming. Donation of land by wealthy patrons meant that, in time, the monasteries became owners of great amounts of land. At their height they are thought to have owned about one-third of the land of Ireland.

As more land was deforested and as agriculture slowly developed, surpluses of goods accrued, particularly to kings and monasteries. To dispose of these, local markets were set up and controlled by the kings and abbots of the monasteries. As pointed out by Doherty (1980, 70), in the absence of coinage in the Early Middle Ages, goods changed hands mostly by way of gift-exchange, reciprocity or distribution. This led to a strengthening of the king's power and wealth and also to increased wealth for a monastery, which in turn led to the development of small towns.

No doubt the monasteries of Ferns and Taghmon benefited from such markets. Ferns may even have been minting its own coin in the eleventh century (Dolley quoted in Doherty, 1980, 82).

Roads and passes

Central to all the activity involved in farming – access to mills and markets, attendance at church, military movements and trade between towns and villages – was a network of roads. It is difficult to visualize the extent of the road system in Co. Wexford in the pre-Norman period. That roads were well established is evident from the obligation imposed by the brehon laws on those whose lands bordered such roads to maintain them properly. Seven classes of roads are listed in Cormac's Glossary, which is dated to the ninth century (O'Donovan, 1868).

The Irish annals are full of descriptions of marching armies plundering, taking hostages and stealing cows. Monks seem to have been continually travelling between monasteries and, on a smaller scale, the people bringing grain to the mills and returning with flour would have needed a network of roads. Market places would also have been served by roads. Place-names with the word *augh*, meaning a ford, indicate a road of some sort and several examples are found for this period in Co. Wexford – for example, Aughfad (Accefade), Aughermon (*Admoinger*); several others are no longer identifiable.

Also, as pointed out by Ó Lochlainn (1940, 465) the Normans found 'a country apparently so well provided with roads that they had little difficulty in moving bodies of heavily clad mailed warriors north, south, east and west without the preliminary military work of making roadways'. Probably the most important road to touch on Wexford was the Slighe Chualann, one of the five main roads leading from Tara. Ó Lochlainn (1940, 473) gives the following route for this road – Dublin, Tallaght, Saggart, Rathcoole, Kilteel, Ballymore Eustace, Dunlavin, Baltinglass, Rathvilly, Tullow, Leighlinbridge, Goresbridge (Belach Gabhrain), Ullard, Graig, St Mullins, Ross, Rosbercon and Waterford. This would have provided access through the thick forest to the south of the Blackstairs mountains. It could also possibly have linked up with the road mentioned in the Forest Charter which led from the ráth of either Creaken or Knockmullin to a main road running from New Ross west of Arnestown to St Mullins (Orpen, 1934, 55). This charter also lists a road running from Wexford to Clonmines, which is joined by another, probably minor road, running from Ferrycarrig through Newbay to join the main road at Sceetar.

In the *Song of Dermot and the Earl*, Mac Murchada is said to have come to Bannow 'by direct road' to meet the newly arrived Normans (Scott and Martin, 1978, 37). This indicates that there must have been some kind of route in existence, possibly made centuries earlier to link up the monasteries of Ferns and Taghmon.

Many roads may have originated as cattle tracks. The Irish word for road is *bóthar*, *bó* being the Irish word for a cow. An eighth-century document on land classification states that 'a cow track giving access to a cattle pad, or a remote piece of land or a highway' adds a yearling calf to its value (Mac Niocaill, 1971, 85). Lucas (1985, 59) states that 'many present day roads follow the line of toghers (causeways) which preceded them as a means of communication in the face of topographical difficulties'. He goes on to list all the toghers for Co. Wexford in the *Civil survey* of 1654 (Simington, 1953).

Roads are briefly referred to in the charter of Dunbrody abbey as follows: a) from near Campile to Taghmon, the old road leading over Tinnock Hill and on to Burkestown; b) from Bannow to Ballyvaroge (Hore, iii, 38).

Co. Wexford was always afforded a fair measure of security by the mountains and forests to the north and west, the Barrow river and the Waterford estuary in the southwest and the seas to the south and east. Although it did not prevent Ruairi O'Connor and his allies from reaching Ferns on a few occasions, access was limited to passes through the Blackstairs mountains, one between Clonegal and Bunclody, the other through Sculloge Gap, and, on the lower ground to the Pass of Poulmounty, north of New Ross.

The growth of the Norse town of Wexford led to an increasing trade with its hinterland. Trade entails transport of goods which, in turn, requires roads. Hence, the limited pre-Viking network system already in existence would have had to be considerably expanded and improved to cater for the increasing demand. There is no doubt that several roads linked Wexford town to its hinterland. Hadden (1968) has made a very plausible case for 'trails' to the south, southeast, west and north of the county. These trails would have been used to carry agricultural produce such as hides and meat into the Norse town in exchange for wine, silks, slaves and even grain.

Bealach or ballagh denotes a road through a pass and several examples of this word survive in place names in the county. These are located in the following places:

Ballagh – Newbawn
Ballagh and Ballagh Burrow – Rosslare
Ballagh – Tomhaggard
Ballaghablake – Castlebridge
Ballaghboy – Leskinfere (Clogh)
Ballinvalley – Kilmuckridge, meaning 'baile an bhealaigh', the place of the road
Ballaghkeen – Bealach caoin, meaning 'smooth passage' was the name of a barony, and the title 'The Ballagh' is now given to an area near Oulart.

The Norse word for road or path is *gate*, of which there are several examples in the county – for instance, Bunargate, Libgate, Mountaingate.

The social background
The basic divisions of society were between the nobility and the commoners such as the professional classes, farmers and craftsmen. These people were free and their basic family unit was the kin group. The unfree classes consisted of serfs, servants and slaves.

The nobles belonged to the families of the ruling septs. Each sept had its own defined area of jurisdiction known as a *tuath* and each competed for the kingship of Uí Cheinnselaig. In extent the *tuatha* corresponded to the later baronial divisions within the county. For most of the Early Christian period the following septs were in possession:

Non-Uí Cheinnselaig septs: Uí Bairrche (Bargy), Fotharta (Forth), Benntraige (Bantry), Síl Brain (Shelburne)

Uí Cheinnselaig septs: Síl Máeluidir (Shelmalier), Uí Dega (Gorey), Uí Felmada (Ballaghkeen), Ó Brain? (Scarawalsh), Síl Chormaic, Síl nÉladaig, Síl nOnchon.

The fortunes of the noble families waxed and waned over the centuries, and warfare between them was not unknown as evidenced by the battle between Ferns and Taghmon in 817 (see p. 138, below). Towards the end of the period their influence diminished as the regional kings such as Diarmait Mac Máel na mBó and later Diarmait Mac Murchada became more powerful.

Among the professionals, the *filidh* (poets) always occupied a prestigious place in Celtic and later Irish society, being responsible for preserving the ancient traditions, genealogy and history of the tribe. Poets wielded immense power, and satire from them was greatly feared. Originally they were also the lawmakers, but early in the historic period the lawyers and others formed their own castes. Each major family had its own coterie of learned men, for example, the Ó Doráin were hereditary lawyers to the Uí Cheinnselaig.

Another professional group consisted of the poet-historians. These were not historians in the modern sense of trying to understand the past. Rather their function was to glorify their lords by exaggerating, or if necessary inventing, the origins, genealogy and valorous deeds of their forebears. This led to many distortions of the record of historical events, making it difficult for modern scholars to distinguish fact from fiction. The origin of the foundation of the monastery of Ferns is a case in point (see p. 134, below).

Farmers were of two classes – an *ocaire* with a small farm, and a *boaire* with a larger farm. The *ocaire* probably did all the farm work with the help of his family and also in cooperation with other small farmers. The rent to his lord was paid in food and services. The *boaire* was of a higher status but also had to pay rent to his lord to whom he was in clientship.

Craftsmen, who were held in high regard, included woodworkers such as mill-, wheel- and shipwrights, carpenters, furniture makers, fine metal workers and workers in stone. Smiths were accorded the highest esteem of all. A famous craftsman mentioned in Irish legend is the Gobán Saor who was reputed to have built a church for St Abbán, and for St Aidán he erected 'a church with wondrous carvings and brave ornaments, so that there was not the like of it, and no one in his time surpassed this Gobán in wright's craft' (Plummer, 1922, ii, 182).

The unfree classes were the serfs who were bound to the land and changed hands in line with ownership, servants who worked on the land and who could possibly be free to change employers and slaves who were made do the heaviest manual work on the farm and in the kitchen.

Hazards and hardships

People in Early Christian Ireland were sometimes at the mercy of the most horrific conditions. The most severe and probably the most frightening, because they had no known cause, were the plagues which reached here from abroad. The Annals of the Four Masters record a plague in 543 which, reportedly swept away one-third of the human race. This was followed by another incidence in 548. It has been suggested that around this time there may have been a major volcanic eruption or that a comet may have struck the earth. As a result the sky was clouded over by dust or vapour, which caused widespread famine and plague. An even worse plague struck in the mid- 660s. The Annals of the Four Masters record that great mortality arose in Ireland, in August, in Magh Itha, in Fotharta. In a note in the Annals O'Donovan gives this as Forth, in south Wexford, but Hogan (1910, 522) places it around Limerick, near Gorey. This plague then spread throughout the rest of the country. It seems that many churches were abandoned at this time.

Another plague, around 700, which lasted for three years, was so bad that the Annals of Ulster record that 'man ate man'. Plagues or pestilence were also recorded for 917 (Ann. Clon.), 987 (AFM), 1017 and 1093 (Ann. Inisfallen) and 1095 (Ann. Loc Cé).

Famine, often related to severe weather conditions which wiped out the corn crop or caused the deaths of most of the cattle, has been recorded for the years 663 (AFM), 670 (AU), 919 (Ann. Inisfallen), 963 (AFM), 993 (AU), 1005 (Ann. Inisfallen.) and 1048 (AFM). In 1109 mice ate up all the corn in certain territories (AFM). This probably included Co. Wexford, which, because of its suitable climate, would have been a corn-growing area.

The following extracts from the Annals of Ulster give some idea of the range of hardships and calamities to which the people were exposed:

670   Great famine, great snowfall
680   A most severe leprosy
684   Great mortality of children
685   Great windstorm
700   Famine and pestilence prevailed in Ireland for three years, so that man ate man

764   An abnormally great drought, a bloody flux through Ireland
917   Snow and extreme cold and unnatural ice, so that chief rivers and
         lakes were passable
993   Great mortality of people, cattle and bees
1047   Great snowfall from December to March, caused deaths of many
         people, and cattle and sea beasts and birds
1116   Great pestilence: hunger was so widespread, both among Laigin
         and Munstermen that it emptied churches and forts and states.

Other constant hazards were warfare and raiding although these would
never have involved the mass of the people (see pp 45-57, below).

2

Pagan Celtic Wexford

By the time of Christ the Celts were well established in Ireland. They had spread initially from central Europe and eventually extended to most of western Europe, including Spain and Britain. The story of their cultural takeover of Ireland is still a matter of discussion among scholars. Did they come as invaders or as groups or tribes who were assimilated into the existing population? Whatever the answers it is agreed that their way of life and their language had become dominant in Ireland by the first century AD.

The earliest documentary evidence for the distribution of Celtic tribes in Ireland comes from a map produced by Ptolemy, a Greek cartographer living in Alexandria in Egypt in the second century. This map places the Brigantes, who were a major group in northwest England, in the Co. Wexford area (Map 3). The Brigantes would probably have been part of the Laigin who gave their name to the province of Leinster. Two branches of the Laigin, the Uí Bairrche and Uí Cheinnselaig, were to play important roles in the history of the county. The Uí Bairrche were originally more powerful and controlled south Leinster until ousted by the Uí Cheinnselaig. Orpen (1894, 124) mistakenly placed the Menapii in this general area, an error which he subsequently rectified (1913-6, 51). But the error has persisted: a Wexford ship has been called 'Menapia' as has a street and a public house.

It is interesting to note that St Ibar of Beggerin was descended from a branch of the Uí Bairrche in Co. Down, known as the Uí Echach Uladh.

An ancient tale in Keating's *History of Ireland* (ed. Dinneen, 1908, iii, 215) tells how the Picts landed at Inbhear Sláine (Wexford harbour). But both sides of the harbour were occupied by chiefs from Britain who were called the Tuatha Fidga. Even worse, these carried poison weapons which inflicted wounds that were invariably fatal. However, a druid of the Fir Bolg devised the following remedy against the Tuatha Fidga:

> The milk of one hundred and fifty white and hornless cows to be thrown into a pit in the midst of a field where you have been wont

to fight these people, and then challenge them to meet you in battle on the same ground; and let every man of your people that shall receive a wound, bathe himself in the pit, and he shall be healed from his poisoned wound.

Together the Picts and the Fir Bolg challenged the Tuatha Fidga to battle, and, protected by the healing properties of the milk, routed them. This

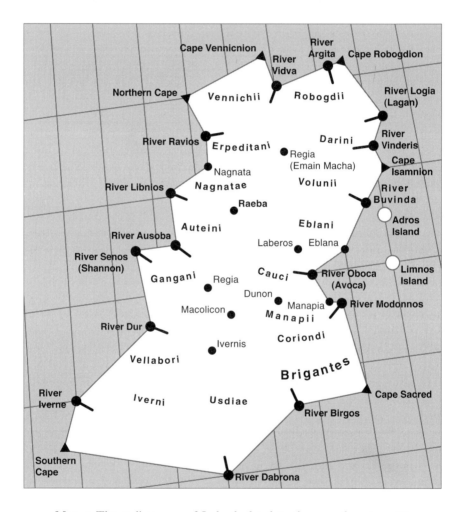

Map 3 The earliest map of Ireland, dated to the second century AD, was made by a Greek cartographer named Ptolemy, who lived in Alexandria. He derived his information from the accounts of merchants and seamen who had traded westwards to the edge of the known world.

event was said to have taken place at Ard Lemnacht, which was later called Forth Mountain, outside Wexford town.

Traces of the Celts

The Celts left precious few traces of their presence in the area now called Co. Wexford (Map 4). The most comprehensive accounts of Iron Age or Celtic Wexford are given by Stout (1987, 26-30) and Moore (1996). However, few of the sites mentioned by them can be dated with any degree of certainty.

Promontory forts are probable relics of the Iron Age. Five such forts were located around the coast on seaward-jutting promontories, where precipitous cliffs on the seaward side and deep ditch-and-bank fortifications on the land side made for a safe and effective stronghold. These were at Glen (Pollshone), Nook, Ramstown (Baginbun), Templetown and Great Saltee Island, although this may be the remains of an eroded ringfort. Inland, at Ballyleigh, near Pollmounty, an area up to one and a half acres in extent has been enclosed by a nearly circular drystone wall of granite boulders. Known as the Ráth of Tork, this was the site of a festival at Lughnasa which was celebrated on the last Sunday of July up to fairly recent times. Tork or torc means king or lord; hence this is likely to have been a royal seat. The site is at over 150 metres elevation and was possibly a Celtic hillfort. Moore (1996, 25) describes two hillforts from the county, one at Ballybuckley, Bree, measuring around 130 metres in diameter; the other around 110 metres across, at Courthoyle, Newbawn. These large enclosures, situated in strategically elevated and defensible positions, may have been places of refuge in turbulent times or even locations for holding ceremonies or rituals for large congregations. They were built in the Late Bronze Age and the Early Iron Age. Stout also mentions two probable Iron Age pins from the county, now in the National Museum, one with the head of a mountain goat or ibex, the other with an omega head, the last letter of the Greek alphabet.

Roche (1985-6) discovered two stone heads in a farmyard at Gibberwell, Duncormick, which may be Celtic. Stout (1987, 30) has described them as 'slightly larger than life-size ... Their main features are a rounded head with flat face, a slit mouth, wedge-shaped nose and pointed oval eyes with minimal brows.' The cult of the head has been found all across Iron Age Europe but it also survived into the medieval period as evidenced by the heads on a number of Romanesque churches such as Clone, near Ferns.

Celtic legends

Co. Wexford is not without its share of Celtic lore and legend. Probably the most famous relates to the naming of the Slaney river and Wexford harbour. In the *Lebor Gabála Érenn: The book of the taking of Ireland* (Macalister,

1938) Sláine is portrayed as the captain of an invading Fir Bolg force which landed at the river mouth, then known as Port Coelrenna, meaning 'the place of the narrow point' (the Fir Bolg may be roughly equated with the Celts who began coming to Ireland around 500 BC). In honour of his conquest of southeast Ireland the river was called Sláine. Remarkably it has borne his name for over 2000 years, only now slightly changed to Slaney.

Mac an Bhaird (1991-3, 14) suggests that the name Coelrenn may be derived from a group called the Cuirenrige, named after Cuirenn, brother of Eochaidh Find Fuath nAirt, supposed ancestor of the Fotharta. The name change would have been from Port Cuirenn to Port Coelrenn to Port Coelrenna. He then tentatively puts forward the idea that the Cuirenrige may, in fact, be the Koriondai of Ptolemy's map, but this is very doubtful.

Although the name 'Loch Garman' is now applied to the town and county of Wexford, it once applied only to the harbour area. The mythological origin of the term and of the great expanse of water is given in the *Dinnshenchas*, an ancient compilation which purports to explain the sources of the placenames of Ireland. The explanation for Loch Garman is given in the *Vision of Cathair Mor*, a poem of fifty-one stanzas written by Eochadh Eolach Ó Ceirín in the twelfth century (Gwynn, 1913, iii, 168-83). During the reign of Cathair Mor as king of Tara (AD 120-3) a great *feis* was held every year at Samhain (Hallow'een). Once, when the king and his guests had over-indulged themselves and lay sleeping, one of Cathair Mor's retinue named Garman Garb (Garman the Rough) stole the queen's gold diadem. He made his way to Inbhear Sláine where he was overtaken by Cathair Mor's soldiers at the 'spring' of Coelrenn. But the spring, in protest at his presence, burst forth in anger and covered the whole harbour area. Garman was drowned and from that time the name Loch Garman clung to the bay. An alternative explanation was that Garman Glas (the Grey) was buried there and when his grave was dug the lake burst forth and submerged the surrounding lands.

Finn Mac Cumhaill, the legendary leader of the Fianna band of warriors, is reputed to have had a dwelling place near Hook Head (*Book of Leinster*, Best et al., 1954-83). It was to this place that Breasal Belach, king of Leinster, came to enlist Finn's help against the high king who was coming to levy the Boruma tribute on the Leinstermen. This tribute had supposedly been imposed on them by the Uí Néill kings of Meath for an ancient insult. The story goes that the king of Leinster married the daughter of an Uí Néill king but later fell in love with her sister. He then incarcerated his wife, pretended she was dead, and married her sister. The first wife eventually escaped. When the sisters learned the truth they both collapsed and died. For this dishonour to his family the Uí Néill king imposed the tribute. In reality it was a pretext for waging war on Leinster. Finn, being himself a Leinsterman, agreed to fight against the high king. The battle was fought at Cama-

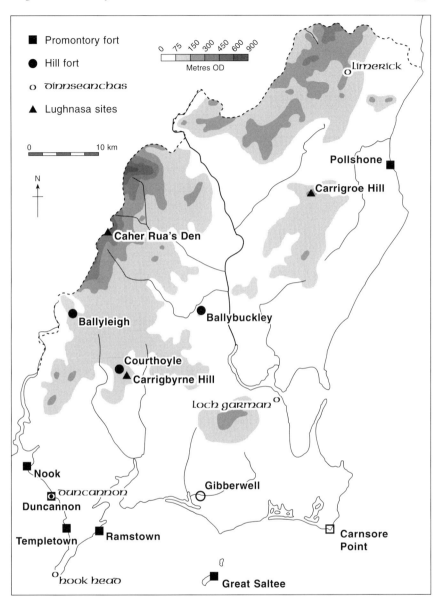

■ Promontory fort

● Hill fort

o ɔıɴɴseaɴchas

▲ Lughnasa sites

0 75 150 300 450 600 900
Metres OD

0   10 km

N

o Lımeᴚıck

Pollshone ■

▲ Carrigroe Hill

▲ Caher Rua's Den

● Ballyleigh

● Ballybuckley

● Courthoyle
▲ Carrigbyrne Hill

Loch gaᴚman o

■ Nook

o ɔuɴcaɴɴoɴ
Duncannon

Gibberwell
○

☑ Carnsore
Point

■   ■ Ramstown
Templetown

o hook heaɔ

■ Great Saltee

Map 4 Few traces of the Celts are found in Co. Wexford. Promontory forts at Glen, Pollshone, Nook, Ramstown and Templetown may have served as Celtic strongpoints, as well as the hillforts at Ballybuckley and Courthoyle. The pagan festival of Lughnasa (Hallow'een) was celebrated at several elevated sites.

ross and the victorious Leinstermen, with the help of Finn and his followers, left nine thousand of the enemy dead on the battlefield.

According to the Book of Lecan, another member of the Fianna, Conán
Maol Mac Mórna, may have given his name to Duncannon, the dún or fort
of Conán.

Limerick, in the parish of Killinierin, was also associated with Finn Mac
Cumhaill (Hore, vi, 651). Finn, supposedly, was given the land known as
Formall na Fhian by Breasal Belach.

The religion of the Celts

The Celts were pagans whose priests were the druids; the word 'druid' perhaps, comes from *dru wid-s*, meaning 'one with knowledge of the oak' (Ní
Chatháin, 1979-80, 211). As priests, the druids function was to mediate
between the 'otherworld' and the world of the people. These druids left no
written documents and the early writers, being Christian and anxious to
obliterate all traces of paganism, did not write down any descriptions of their
rites or religious beliefs. For information on them we must turn to some
Continental writers.

Strabo, a Greek traveller (54 BC -25 AD) stated that the druids were the
most just of men, they taught that men's souls and the universe are inde-
structible. Julius Caesar (102-44 BC) also stated that the Celtic Gauls
believed that 'the soul did not die but passed into another body,' that is, was
reincarnated. That they believed in sun worship is shown by the words of
St Patrick in his *Confessio* (de Paor, 1992, 108) 'For the sun is that which
we see rising daily at His command, but it will never reign, nor will its
splendour last forever. And all those who worship it will be subject to griev-
ous punishment.' They performed human sacrifices. How common this ritual was we do not know, but archaeological evidence indicates that it was
practised in Ireland as elsewhere (Raftery, 1994, 199).

Life at that time was lived in an entirely rural environment and landscape features, such as mountains and rivers, were regarded as manifesta-
tions of the supernatural order and therefore to be revered. Some rivers,
including the Shannon and the Boyne, were regarded as divine. Certain trees
such as the oak were considered sacred. Some groves of trees were sacred
and were used for ritual druidic purposes. Spring wells were also important
to the druids. The Life of St Patrick (de Paor, 1993, 169) describes how
druids honoured and made votive offerings to a well near Castlebar, Co.
Mayo. But goodness was reckoned in an ability to perform wonderful deeds
rather than in any moral sense.

The druids were one of the three learned classes in Ireland, the others
being the bards and the *filidh*. They were trained specialists in their pagan
religion, and acted as judges in disputes and as advisors to the kings, which

made them politically important. They had their own schools which meant that pre-Christian Ireland had a strong tradition of learning and a core of highly educated individuals. In fact, the Church often had great difficulty in combating them in debate. Co. Wexford may have had one such pagan centre, if not of learning, at least of fame as a sacred area. This is shown by the Greek name, Hieron Akron, meaning 'Holy Cape,' given to Carnsore Point on Ptolemy's map of Ireland. This southeastern point of Wexford is relatively close to the island of Anglesey, in north Wales, which Tacitus, the Roman writer, described as a druidic centre (Grant, 1956). It is possible that close communications existed between the two centres in the pre-Christian period.

Some of the powers attributed to the druids also recur in the Lives of the saints. An incident in the Life of Munnu of Taghmon shows how the saint's cloak could make the wearer invisible to his enemies. Moling of St Mullins, like the druids, could cause shape-changing to confuse his opponents.

From stories passed down orally and recorded several centuries later we know that the Celts in Ireland had several gods. They appear to have treated them not so much as divinities like the gods of Greece and Rome, but as having supernatural or magical powers. Lugh was one of the most powerful gods and his name is commemorated in the festival of Lughnasa.

Lughnasa festival sites in Co. Wexford

The festival of Lughnasa was one of the four great festivals of the Celtic year and was reputedly founded by Lugh in honour of his foster-mother, Tailtiu. In Christian times the festival became associated with the harvest and was celebrated on the Sunday nearest to the first of August. The festival was a popular assembly of the people, usually on heights but also at wells, lakes and rivers. The definitive book on Lughnasa was written by Máire Mac Néill (1962) and the following abbreviated accounts of Wexford sites are base on it.

Caher Roe's Den, Blackstairs Mountain: On the last Sunday of July, known locally as Mountain Sunday, one of the longest-lasting of popular assemblies was held at this spot and on the bare plateau of the summit above it, which is called the Meeting Place. Until the middle of the twentieth century the day and the outing were well known to the country people on both the Wexford and Carlow sides of the ridge and in the adjoining parts of Co. Kilkenny. In his book *No hurling at the dairy door* Billy Rackard (1996, 6) gives a vivid description of the event as it would have been around 1915, with crowds of people flocking to the mountain by cart and bicycle, and traders advertising their wares.

Carrickbyrne Hill: On the second Sunday of July crowds of people from the surrounding countryside used to visit the hill. The day was known as

Rock Sunday and Fraughan Sunday and even carried with it the custom of eating new potatoes for the first time, so we need have no hesitation in regarding it as a Lughnasa festival. The earlier date may have been chosen here because of the wider celebrity and drawing power of the assembly at Caher Roe's Den. The pastimes at Carrickbyrne, as at other assembly-places, were dancing singing, contests of athletic skill and fraughan-picking.

Carrigroe Hill, Ferns: On the last Sunday of July, known as Fraughan Sunday, people went to the hill to pick the berries. The custom was dwindling by the 1940s, but people could remember the days when large crowds went there. On top of the hill there is a cleft rock called the Giant's Bed; a middle-aged woman in 1942 remembered having been told by her father that flowers were placed in the Giant's Bed on Carrigroe on the last Sunday of July long ago.

Ballyleigh Hill (not Pollmounty Hill as given by Mac Néill): On the last Sunday of July, known as Fraughan Sunday, crowds of holiday-makers and berry-pickers resorted to the hill and spent the afternoon hours enjoying themselves. In the evening they gathered in the valley farmhouses where the country fiddlers had come to play, and dancing, singing and storytelling passed the night. A large dry stone granite walled enclosure (1. 5 acres), known as the ráth of Tork, is situated on top of the hill.

Holy Well, Donaghmore: In 1840 O'Donovan (Ordnance Survey Letters, Wexford) learned that a 'pattern' had been held there on the last Sunday of July until about twenty years before. He said that none remembered that it was held in honour of a saint. Father Shearman, who made enquiries in 1871, learned a little more. The last Sunday of July was known as Domhnach Chrom Dubh, and according to a man of ninety three years, the oldest native of the place, the patron saint was called 'Owen Eodoch' about whom very little more could be elicited. It is regrettable that Father Shearman did not give more precise phonetic indications of the name.

St Davin's Well, Kildavin, Murrintown: In 1840 O'Donovan (Ordnance Survey Letters, Wexford) reported that until twenty two years earlier a patron had been held at the well on the first of August, which was believed to be St Davin's day. He also said that there was still a vivid tradition of the saint but, unfortunately, he did not record for us of what that tradition consisted. The day of the patron, the nearness to the mountain, the vivid tradition all suggest a Lughnasa survival. Except for this parish dedication, St Davin seems to be unknown. It is remembered vaguely that a patron was held about the end of July on Forth Mountain.

Ogham stones

A form of writing called ogham is thought to cross the Late Iron Age–Early Christian chronological divide. This earliest writing in Irish probably dates from the fourth century AD and continued in use for special purposes until the eighth century. It was based on the Latin alphabet then current in western Europe, the letters being represented by varying numbers of strokes or notches carved along the edges of stones of suitable shape and texture.

Ogham stones were used to commemorate important personages and the inscription always gives the name of the person and sometimes describes him as 'son' or 'grandson' of another famous person. In several places his ancestral sept or territorial group is named.

Four ogham stones have been found within the county – at Cotts (Broadway), Great Saltee Island, Killabeg (Monagear) and St Brecaun's church, Hook Head.

Cotts: This ogham stone was described by Macalister (1945, i, 48) as being of red granite (from Carnsore Point), four feet one inch above ground, one foot ten inches broad, one foot seven inches thick, sunk one foot six inches in the ground. The inscription IARNI was carved on the stone. An excavation by Macalister revealed no trace of a burial.

Great Saltee Island: This ogham stone was stated by Macalister (1945, i, 48) to have been discovered by Standish Mason in 1925, and that it was later stolen, but the thieves, frightened by a gale, threw it into the sea from which it was subsequently recovered. When Macalister saw it in 1937, it was in the possession of the parish priest of Piercestown. It is now in the County Museum, Enniscorthy. A note attached to it, written in Irish by the noted Wexford antiquarian Fr Joseph Ranson, claims that this is not correct, but that Fr Thomas O'Byrne, parish priest of Piercestown, took it from the island and that it fell into the sea by accident but was later recovered. Macalister deciphered the lettering as follows: LONAMNI AVI BARI.

Killabeg: Macalister (1945, i, 49-50) has the following description of an ogham stone in this townland: 'A standing stone, six feet three inches by three feet, by one foot eight inches: The dexter angle of the principal face once bore an ogham inscription, but it has all been chipped away, leaving only the tip of an M, three feet one inch above the ground. The marks left by the processes of destruction are quite unmistakable. A cross, one foot five inches high and one foot two inches across the arms, which expand outwards, was cut on the principal face of the stone after the destruction of the inscription: it encroaches upon some of the new surface produced by the fractures.' Inscribing a cross on an ogham stone may have been a way of christianizing a pagan monument.

St Brecaun's church, Hook Head: In 1845 part of an ogham stone was found on the shore near the ruins of this church. A second part was found about 1930 (Macalister, 1930, 52-5). The inscription reads: SEDANI MAQQI CATTABBOTT AVVI DERCMASOC. Translated into English this reads 'Of

Setanios, son of Cathdub, grandson (or descendant) of Dermasoc'. According to Macalister Der Mosach was the son of Cathair Mor, a Leinster king who is supposed to have ruled all Ireland in the second century AD. Excavations at the site of the church in 1987 uncovered another fragment of the stone (Breen, 1988, 31).

3

Politics, rulers and raiders, 400-1166

The period 400-1166 saw many changes in the political situation in Co. Wexford. These resulted from the ousting of the Uí Bairrche by the Uí Cheinnselaig, from internal power struggles among the ruling Uí Cheinnselaig, from interference from neighbouring rulers and from the attacks and later settlements of the Vikings.

At the opening of the historical period, that is in the fifth century when writing first began in Ireland, the country was divided into about one hundred and fifty small kingdoms or *tuatha*. These have been defined by Ó Corráin (1972, 29) as 'the primary political units of early Ireland, a small local kingdom ruled by the lowest grade of king' (Map 5). By the eighth century the *tuatha* were losing power as more powerful kings such as those of the Uí Cheinnselaig established themselves.

Over the *tuatha* and groups of small kingdoms was the king of all Leinster. Leinster itself was composed of the two lesser kingdoms of the northern Laigin, known as *Laigin tuathgabair* and the northern Laigin known as *Laigin deasgabair*. Several families, including the Uí Cheinnselaig, laid claim to the kingship of Leinster.

The political history, then, of Co. Wexford for this period is dominated by power struggles for the kingship of Uí Cheinnselaig and by them for that of all Leinster. But the Church, as a major source of wealth and power, also became involved in the politics of the period. This is clearly illustrated in the struggle for control of the monastery of Ferns in the ninth century (see p. 138, below).

The names of the Uí Cheinnselaig kings of Leinster and the branches to which they belonged, taken from Ó Corráin, 1971, 7-39, are given in Appendix 1 while those of the kings of Uí Cheinnselaig are listed in Appendix 2.

THE NON-UÍ CHEINNSELAIG SEPTS

Uí Bairrche

The Uí Bairrche were of British origin, being a branch of the Brigantes, who themselves were part of a larger group called the Laigin (Smith, 1982, 19). Leinster and Lleyn in Wales bear their name. Mac an Bhaird (1991-3, 9) goes so far as to suggest that the Brigantes located by Ptolemy in south Wexford may have been the earliest group of the Laigin to settle in Ireland.

Around the middle of the fifth century the Uí Bairrche appear to have been in control of large parts of Wexford and Carlow, with the neighbouring Fotharta acting as their allies. According to Byrne (1973, 137) the king list for the late fourth and early fifth centuries, contained in an archaic poem, named two Uí Bairrche rulers of South Leinster, Muiredach Mo Snithech and Moenach. Muiredach is listed as 'king of Ireland' in one genealogical tract. In another poem, *The Testament of Cathair Mor*, Cathar, an early fifth-century king of Leinster, leaves his weapons to Daire Barrach, alleged ancestor of the Uí Bairrche.

Early rivalry between the Uí Bairrche and the Uí Cheinnselaig is recorded in the *Vita tripartita* (Stokes 1887, ii, 342-3) when Óengus Mac Meic Ercal of the Uí Bairrche slew Crimthann Mac Énna Cheinnselaig, king of the Uí Cheinnselaig, in 483, in revenge for banishment of his people by the Uí Cheinnselaig. Despite pressure from the encroaching Uí Cheinnselaig, the Uí Bairrche were still powerful in south Wexford up to the second half of the sixth century. The Life of St Munnu describes how Guaire Mac Eoghain, seeking the kingship of Uí Cheinnselaig, plundered the Uí Bairrche and drove off their flocks and herds. The Uí Bairrche of south Wexford are again mentioned in 1041 when they backed an Uí Muiredaig claimant from north Leinster for the kingship of Leinster. They were attacked by Diarmait Mac Máel na mBó's brother, Domnall Reamhar, but he was pursued, defeated and killed by Murchad Mac Dúnlainge at Lorum, Co. Carlow (Ó Corráin, 1970-1, 29).

The Fotharta

Like the Uí Bairrche, the Fotharta were also probably associated with the Brigantes, perhaps, as Smith (1982, 19) suggests, as mercenaries to the Uí Bairrche. The position of Brigid shows the close connection between the Fotharta and the Brigantes, and hence also with the Uí Bairrche. St Brigid belonged to the Kildare branch of the Fotharta but, as her name implies, Brigid was proto-Irish for Briganti, a pagan goddess of the Brigantes.

Groups of the Fotharta, which means 'alien people', were found scattered throughout Leinster. They were found closely aligned with the Uí Bairrche in south Wexford and in Carlow. In the Life of Munnu of Taghmon, a

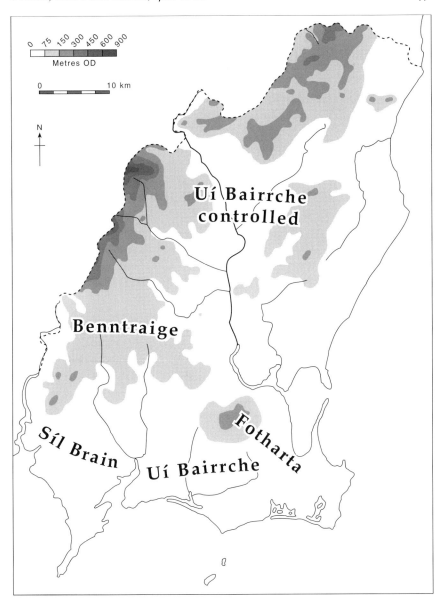

Map 5 At the beginning of the Early Christian period, around AD 400, the Uí Bairrche controlled south Leinster, including the area later to become Co. Wexford. Other tribes such as the Benntraige, Fotharta and Síl Brain would have been subject to them.

prince of the Fotharta is mentioned as being trained in the monastery there (Plummer 1910, ii, p. xxi).

The south Wexford Fotharta were known as Fotharta an Chairn (*Cairn* [= heap] refers to the large number of rounded granite boulders at Carnsore Point and the surrounding area) and the Carlow branch as Fothairt Fea. Both branches gave their names to the baronies of Forth in Wexford and Carlow. In the early historic period the Fotharta territory in south Wexford stretched as far as Taghmon. This is shown by the fact that it was one of their chiefs, Dimma, who gave Munnu the land on which to found his monastery.

By the eleventh century they had taken the name of Ua Lorcáin (Larkin). The Ua Lorcáin were also associated with the Ua Tuathail of Uí Muiredaig, located around Castledermot, Co. Kildare. In 1024 we find Máel Morda Mac Lorcáin as king of Uí Cheinnselaig. But it is not possible to know to which branch of the Fotharta he belonged as no genealogical record has been found for him. Máel Morda was slain by Uí Faeláin in 1024 and was succeeded by his son, Tadc Mac Lorcáin, who died 'on his pilgrimage' in Glendalough in 1030 (Ó Corráin, 1971, 18). Tadc's son, Ruaidre, was blinded by Diarmuit Mac Máel na mBó in 1036 to prevent any challenge to the kingship.

Byrne (1987, 28) states that Diarmait Mac Murchada installed an Ua Lorcáin, who had been displaced from the kingship of Uí Muiredaig, in the lordship of Fotharta an Chairn. This later ensured Ua Lorcáin's support of Mac Murchada's attempt to regain his kingdom.

Other non-Uí Cheinnselaig septs
The Síl Brain, who gave their name to the barony of Shelburne, may have been a branch of the Loígis, another alien people in Leinster; Co. Laois is named after them. Another alien tribe, the Benntraige, gave their name to the barony of Bantry in west Wexford. They were also located around Bantry, Co. Cork. Neither of these groups appears to have played a prominent part in the history of the period under discussion. Bantry eventually came under the control of the Clann Coscraigh, a branch of the Uí Felmada (Byrne, 1987, 25).

Originally from the Kildare area the Uí Enechglaiss were forced towards the coast around Arklow sometime after the sixth century. Their territory, which stretched south as far as the Inch river in north Wexford, was not part of Uí Cheinnselaig and hence remained in the Dublin-Glendalough diocese after Co. Wexford was shired in 1210.

Another group, Cinél Flaitheamhain, mentioned in Ó hUidhrin's poem (see p. 195, below), also seems to have been located in north Wexford, but little is known about its history.

THE RISE OF UÍ CHEINNSELAIG

The Uí Cheinnselaig are descended from a common ancestor, Énna Cenn-selach, literally meaning 'dirty head', reputedly so-called from covering his head with the gore of his fallen enemies.

At the opening of the historical period we find them based in the Rathvilly area of Co. Carlow (Smyth, 1982, 62). From there they began to expand down the Slaney valley, through Bunclody, into Co. Wexford. By the end of the sixth century they were exerting pressure on the Uí Bairrche of south Wexford. In the following centuries they came to dominate completely the region now known as Co. Wexford, although some of the older groups such as the Uí Bairrche, Fothartha, Benntraige and Síl Brain retained their ancient territories (Map 6). By at least the end of the eighth century they were in control of Ferns, and by the eleventh century they had made it their headquarters. The genealogies of the various branches are given in the Book of Leinster (ed. Best et al., 1954-83) and in O'Brien (1962). The minor branch of the Uí Dega established themselves in north Wexford, while the Uí Felmada, Síl Cormaic and Síl Máeluidir took over central Wexford. Eventually two other branches of Uí Cheinnselaig became powerful, the Síl nÉladaig and Síl nOnchon. The latter family eventually became dominant, taking over the kingship not only of Uí Cheinnselaig but of Leinster and Norse Dublin. From this branch, too, came Diarmait Mac Murchada.

Electing a king

The changing pattern of kings and ruling families in Early Christian Wexford is perhaps best understood by looking at the rise and fall of particular segments of the Uí Cheinnselaig separately.

To succeed to the kingship certain qualifications were specified in ancient Irish law. The potential king must belong to the same royal *derbhine* as a previous king. The *derbhine* was a family of four generations in the male line, the great grandfather, the grandfather, the father and the son. Succession as the king was by election from eligible members of the royal *derbhine*. In addition to the correct lineage the claimant had to be without physical blemish and to be of sound mind. Hence the common practice of eliminating potential claimants by maiming or blinding.

Succession was seldom easy. It must be remembered that polygamy was allowed under Irish law and the children of each wife were deemed equal in law, thus giving a large number of claimants. Ó Corráin (1971, 27-8), in a study of regnal succession in the Uí Cheinnselaig, found that thirty-eight kings succeeded their father, six of them directly. There are ten instances of succeeding grandsons and two succeeding great grandsons. Of the balance, five kings are of unknown antecedents, six fall totally outside any *derbhine* and eight others are outside the the direct line.

The ceremony of inauguration of a king was carried out by the hereditary *file* calling out the name and title of the king-to-be, who was then formally presented with a hazel wand. Each kingdom had its own inauguration site in an elevated position, with a sacred tree or trees and an inauguration stone.

Keating (Dinneen, 1908, iii, 15) stated that 'On Leac Mic Eochada the lord of Uí Cheinnselaig was inaugurated, and it was Mac Eochada who inaugurated him'. Orpen (1911, 270-1) suggested that Leac Mhic Eochada may have been located at Loggan, in north Wexford. According to Fitzpatrick (1997, 66) 'the identification of the site Leac Mhic Eochada remains speculative, but the association of Clann Eochada with the Loggan district, and their stated role as inaugurators of the chiefs of Uí Cheinnselaig, may offer some support to Orpen's suggestion'. There has always been a strong tradition in the area that the mound at Loggan was the inauguration site (Rory Murphy, pers. comm.). The mound itself consisted of a glacial deposit of sand and gravel which was removed in 1970. Several Bronze Age cist burials were discovered there in the last century (Culleton, 1984, 40).

Keating has also given the following description: 'On Cnoc an Bhogha Mac Murchada was inaugurated; and it was Ó Nualláin who inaugurated him; his steed and trappings for Ó Nualláin; O Deoradháin (Doran) was his brehon and Mac Eochadha his ollamh in poetry.'

Knockavocka is a low hill overlooking Ferns, the Mac Murchada capital, and, as stated by Fitzpatrick (1997, 63) the Irish name, Cnoc an Bhogha, approximates to its anglicized form of Knockavocka. It has a large shale boulder measuring 1.50 by 1.20 metres. Knockavocka only became the inauguration site of the Mac Murchada in the twelfth century (pers. comm. Nicholas Furlong).

It has also been suggested that Ardamine, which is thought to be Ard Ladrann where St Aidán landed, was an inauguration site for a branch of the Uí Cheinnselaig. The mound there is now a motte, but it was not unusual for the Normans to remodel an earlier mound for their own ends.

The Uí Dega

The Uí Dega, who occupied a part of north Wexford centred on Killinierin, were related to the Uí Cheinnselaig. They gave their name to the deanery of Oday. Ardamine (Ard Ladrann) appears to have been one of their royal sites. However, this area had been taken over by the Síl Chormaic, a branch of the Uí Cheinnselaig, before 722. In the twelfth century it was ruled by the Ó hAodha. Another branch of the Uí Déga was located in Ossory.

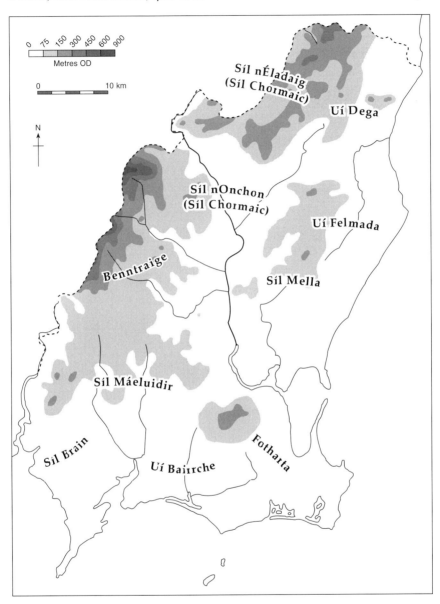

Map 6 By around AD 900 the Uí Cheinnselaigh were in control of the area. Different branches of the family, such as the Síl Máeludir, Síl Chormaic and Uí Felmada, ruled certain parts, while the older occupants, the Uí Bairrche, Fotharta, Benntraige and Síl Brain, still clung on to their territories.

The Síl Máeluidir

This branch of Uí Cheinnselaig, descended from Crimthann, another son of Énna, established itself in south central Wexford. Their territory later became known as the barony of Shelmalier (Síl Máeluidir) West. Their first king of Uí Cheinnselaig was Bran (709-12). An internal struggle within the branch resulted in a battle in 712 in which Bran and his son were killed by Cu Changelt, who then became king. Other Síl Máeluidir kings of Uí Cheinnselaig were Laidcnend (717-27), Censelach (769-70), Cathal (809-19) and Cairpre (819-44) (Ó Corráin, 1971, 11).

In the eighth and early ninth centuries the Síl Máeluidir were involved in several battles with the Síl Chormaic for the kingship of Uí Cheinnselaig and the monastery of Ferns, with all its rich possessions. In 769 Dub Calcaig of Síl Chormaic was slain by Censelach of Síl Máeluidir in a battle at Ferns. He himself was killed by Etarscel of Síl Chormaic, who then held the kingship until 809. In 783, the Síl Máeluidir tried again, resulting in a 'war' between the abbot of Ferns, a member of Síl Chormaic, and his steward, one of the Síl Máeluidir. By 809 Cathal of the Síl Máeluider was king of Uí Cheinnselaig, but Ferns monastery lay within the control of the Síl Chormaic. This situation was intolerable to the Síl Máeluidir who led the forces of the monastery of Taghmon against Ferns. In this *bellum* (war) 400 people were killed. But the Síl Máeluidir were soon to have other problems as the Viking attacks began in Wexford, and other branches of the Uí Cheinnselaig strove for power.

The Uí Felmada

This branch of Uí Cheinnselaig descended from Fedelmid or Fedilimid, son of Énna Cheinnselaig. They were a powerful family and provided five early kings of Leinster. The most powerful was Brandubh (meaning black raven). This Brandubh reputedly confirmed the land to St Aidán on which he built his monastery at Ferns. The Uí Felmada ruled two subkingdoms in Uí Cheinnselaig, Uí Felmada Tuaid, based around Rathvilly, Co. Carlow, and Uí Felmada Theas in Ballaghkeen, in east central Wexford. In the twelfth century the Uí Felmada still ruled this area but had changed their name to Ua Murchada. The descendants of this family still live in Co. Wexford, the present incumbent of the Gaelic title, The O'Morchoe, being David.

The Síl Chormaic

This branch, descended from Crimthann, son of Énna Cennsalaig who died in 483, was destined to provide a line of kings whose descendants survive to this day as the Mac Murrough Kavanaghs. They had established themselves in north Wexford by 722 as Colcu is styled king of Ard Ladrann (Ardamine) in that year. Colcu's son, Áed Mend Mac Colgan, became not only ruler of

Uí Cheinnselaig but king of Leinster from 734 to 738. He was the last of the Uí Cheinnselaig to hold that position till the eleventh century. The Annals of Ulster record Áed Mend's death in a hand-to-hand fight with Áed Allan, king of the Uí Néill, at the battle of Ath Senaig or Uchbad, at Ballyshannon, near Kilcullen, Co. Kildare, in 738. Another of Colcu's sons, Bresal, became abbot of Ferns and died in 744. Despite the attempts by the Síl Máeluidir, the descendants of the Síl Chormaic held on to the economically and strategically important abbey until 1171. By the eighth century the Síl Chormaic were coming under pressure, not alone from the Síl Máeluidir to the south but also from the rising power of the Síl nÉladaig to the north. This seems to be the reason why they began to move westwards into the territory of Uí Dróna. This area, which they eventually dominated, later became the barony of Idrone in Co. Carlow.

Rian, the progenitor of the Uí Riain (later Ryan), was a tenth-century ruler of the Uí Drón lands. Muiredach Mac Riain, the last Síl Chormaic king of Uí Cheinnselaig, was slain by the Vikings at the battle of Bithlann in 978. During the ninth century the Síl Chormaic split into two segments, the Síl nÉladaig and the Síl nOnchon.

The Síl nÉladaig
The first mention of the Síl nÉladaig is in 732 when their king of Uí Cheinnselaig, Elothach Mac Faelchon, was slain by Áed Mend Mac Colgan. Their next king of Uí Cennsalaig was Echthigern Mac Guaire who was slain in 853 by Bruatar Mac Aeda. According to Ó Corráin (1971, 14) 'the defeat and death of Echthigern Mac Guaire may have been the climax of a segmentary strife resulting from an attempt of the Síl Chormaic to regain the kingship'. The Síl nÉladaig provided several Uí Cheinnselaig kings, the last definite holder being Donnchad Mac Taidg, who was deposed in 965, although his successor, Máel Ruanaid Mac Domnaill, may also have belonged to the Síl nÉladaig.

The Síl nÉladaig gave their name to Shillelagh, Co. Wicklow.

The Síl nOnchon
This important branch of the Uí Cheinnselaig is descended through Faeláin, a sixth-century king of the sept, through Onchu, whose line becomes Síl nOnchon and eventually Mac Murchada. The rise of this branch has been traced by Ó Corráin (1971, 7-39) and the following account is mainly taken from his published work.

The Síl nOnchon first came to prominence when Tadc Mac Diarmata became king of south Leinster in 858. Tadc's claim to the kingship was through Faeláin the grandfather of Onchu, who lived six generations earlier. Tadc's reign lasted until 865 when he was slain by his kinsmen. The next king of the Síl nOnchon line was Tadc's brother Cairpre, who reigned from 869 until he too was slain in 876. Cairpre's son Cinaed reigned from 922 until killed by the Vikings in 935. The Síl nOnchon again held the kingship from 938 until 953 through Cellach Mac Cinaeda, slain in battle by the Osraige in 947, and his son, Echthigern, who in turn was killed by his nephews in 953. From then until the arrival on the scene of Diarmait Mac Máel na mBó in 1032 the kingship was held by various branches of the Uí Cheinnselaig. At one period it was even held by the Ua Lorcáin, a non-Uí Cheinnselaig tribe with branches in south Wexford, Carlow and Kildare. It is possible that the Ua Lorcáin were by now part of the Uí Cheinnselaig through marriage.

The rise of the Mac Murchada

Diarmait Mac Máel na mBó's father, Donnchad, had killed Áed Mac Echthigern, *tanaise* of Uí Cheinnselaig, in the oratory at Ferns in 1003. Áed obviously posed a threat to Diarmait's ambitions. Áed's brother Coipre (died 974) had been coarb at the monastery of Cluain Mor Máedóg (Clonmore), Hacketstown, Co. Carlow, which was the power base of the faction opposing Diarmait.

Diarmait Mac Máel na mBó was a ruthless and ambitious man who quickly established himself as king of Uí Cheinnselaig and in 1042 as king of Leinster. He involved his son, Murchad, in the affairs of his kingdom and it was from this Murchad that the name Mac Murchada is derived.

In 1070 the family of Diarmait's brother, Domnall Reamhar, slain in 1041, began to display ambitions for the Uí Cheinnselaig kingship. Diarmait took hostages from Domnall's descendants but that did not prevent conflict between the various segments, who were often assisted by outside forces from Munster, Osraige or Meath who feared the rising power of Diarmait.

Eventually, Donnchad Mac Murchada, grandson of Diarmait Mac Máel na mBó, gained the kingship of Uí Cheinnselaig in 1089 and, despite opposition, retained it until slain by Domnall Ó Briain of Munster in 1115. Ó Briain's allies on this occasion were the Norse of Dublin. According to Giraldus Cambrensis (Scott and Martin, 1978, 67) after the battle they buried Donnchad Mac Murchada with a dog, an insult that long rankled with his descendants and eventually cost the Norse dearly. The Mac Murchada, however, retained the kingship of Uí Cheinnselaig.

UÍ CHEINNSELAIG CONFLICTS WITH OTHER RULERS

The southern Uí Néill

Both the Uí Néill based in Meath and the Laigin laid claim to the prestigious kingship of Tara. This resulted in many forays into each other's territory before the border was finally fixed at the Liffey. The northern Laigin were mainly involved but were sometimes assisted by the Uí Cheinnselaig.

598   Brandubh Mac Echach of Uí Cheinnselaig, king of Leinster, defeated the UíNéill at Dunbolg, Co. Wicklow.
605   Brandubh Mac Echach and the Laigin were defeated by the Uí Néill.
626   Crundmael Mac Ronán of Uí Cheinnselaig fought an indecisive battle with the Uí Néill.
628   Domnall, high king of the Uí Néill, ravaged all Leinster.
738   Áed Mend Mac Colgan of Uí Cheinnselaig was defeated by the Uí Néill at Ath Senaig or Uchbad, at Ballyshannon, near Kilcullen, Co. Kildare. Áed Mend was killed in hand-to-hand fighting with Áed Allan, king of Uí Néill.
780   Cairpre Mac Laidcnen of Uí Cheinnselaig fought with the Northern Laigin against the Uí Néill invasion of the province. In the battle, fought at Kilcock, Co. Kildare, the Uí Néill were victorious.

The northern Laigin
In the mid-eight century the ruling Uí Dúnlainge family of north Leinster separated into three segments – the Uí Donchada, Uí Faeláin and the Uí Muiredaig. In south Leinster the Uí Cheinnselaig, despite internal struggles, reigned supreme. All these dynasties laid claim to the high kingship of Leinster with varying degrees of success.

The Osraige
The kingdom of Osraige corresponded largely to the present diocese of the same name and stretched along the southern borders of Leinster and Munster. For this reason it became embroiled in the affairs of both provinces, particularly from the eighth century onwards. In 690 Bran had defeated them but in 761 they killed Dongal Mac Laidcnen, king of Uí Cheinnselaig in battle.

The Osraige king, Cerball Mac Dúnlainge, had designs on the high kingship of Leinster through a falsely concocted pedigree. In 879 he defeated the Uí Cheinnselaig at Foulkarath, Co. Kilkenny. This seems to have been a major battle as 200 men were reported lost, either through wounds or by drowning in the river Nore.

In the tenth century the Osraige again tried to claim the kingship of Leinster. In 947 Cellach Mac Cinaeda, king of Uí Cheinnselaig was slain in battle by the Osraige. In 974 Domnall Mac Cellaig was slain in a battle with the Osraige. Finally, in 1036 the Osraige achieved their ambition of the kingship of Leinster only to be displaced by Diarmait Mac Máel na mBó in 1042.

The Munstermen

In 1041 Donnchad, Brian Boru's son, king of Munster, together with Murchad Mac Dúnlainge, king of Leinster, invaded Uí Cheinnselaig, then ruled by Diarmait Mac Máel na mBó and burned his capital, Ferns. Donnchad's aim was to prevent the Osraige and the Eoganacht of Cashel from dominating Leinster. Unfortunately for himself he turned Diarmait into a bitter and revengeful enemy.

In 1072, when Diarmait Mac Máel na mBó had been killed at the battle of Uchbad, Turlough O'Briain, king of Munster, seized the opportunity to invade Leinster and Osraige. Uí Cheinnselaig was plundered. By 1077 Turlough Ó Briain was in effective control of Norse Dublin and Leinster. In that year he came with his army into Uí Cheinnselaig and reaffirmed his control over the territory and its ambitious ruler, Donnchad Mac Domnall Reamhair.

Twelfth-century raids

Due to its isolation in the southeast of the country and the difficulty of access because of mountains and forest, Uí Cheinnselaig may have suffered rather less than more exposed central parts such as Meath and north Leinster in this seemingly interminable warfare. But Diarmait Mac Murchada's ruthless hold on the kingship of Leinster and his feuding with the Osraige, Rory O'Connor and others, ensured that his home territory, despite its relative isolation, was not immune from attack. Most of these raids, those carried out by Mac Murchada as well as those against him, were mainly politically motivated. Submission and giving or taking of hostages was usually the end result as seen by the following accounts in Annals:

1128   A foray by Turlough O'Connor into Leinster until he reached Loch Garman. This was obviously designed to put the young king of Uí Cheinnselaig in his place (AU).

1133   Diarmait Mac Murchada exercised great tyranny and cruelties upon the Leinster nobility, killing Ó Faeláin, prince of Leinster and Murrough O'Toole; he put out the eyes of Mac Giollamacholmoge, which brought all Leinster under hand (these atrocities are given under 1141 in Ann. Tig. and Ann. Clon.

1135   Diarmait Mac Murchada attacked Kildare, forced the abbess out of her cloisters and compelled her to marry one of the said Diarmait's people. He installed one of his own family as abbess (Ann. Clon.).

1141   Turlough O'Connor attacked Uí Cheinnselaig as far as Loch Garman (AFM).

1142   Diarmait Mac Murchada made a predatory excursion into Laois (AFM).

1142   Turlough O Briain plundered Uí Cheinnselaig and carried off
        countless cattle (AFM).

1154   Osraige defeated Uí Cheinnselaig, many slain (AFM).

1156   Mac Murchada and his allies plundered east Meath 'and carried off
        many cows' (AFM).

1157   Murrough Mac Lochlainn led an army into Leinster. Mac
        Murchada gave him hostages (AFM).

1166   Rory O'Connor came into Uí Cheinnselaig and took hostages from
        Diarmait Mac Murchada (AFM).

There was also a secondary but important reason for such raids. Cattle raiding had been endemic in Ireland for centuries. In fact, to raid and come
home empty-handed was so unusual as to be noted in the Annals of
Tigerach for 1154 when Turlough O'Connor raided in Connacht 'but
returned without kine'.

What form this warfare took is not quite clear, but that cavalry was used
is shown by the Annals of the Four Masters for 1131 when there was a conflict between the cavalry of Connacht and the cavalry of Munster and for
1153 when Ua Lochlainn of Cenél Eoghan 'defeated the cavalry of Leinster'.
Since there were no standing armies of trained soldiers it was probably the
smaller chieftains and nobles who formed the cavalry, while the farmers and
perhaps some of their workers formed the foot soldiers.

4

Homesteads and settlement patterns

Most of our knowledge on the type of homesteads and their distribution pattern is gained from examining the location of ráths or ringforts and dúns in an area. These are circular or nearly circular enclosures surrounded by one or more earthen banks and ditches or fosses. In fact, the Irish word *ráth* means 'earthen rampart'. There are also examples of oval and D-shapes. A timber palisade would have been erected on the innermost bank. These enclosures contained the homesteads of the kings, nobles and freemen. Dating evidence shows that they were constructed mainly between the seventh and the ninth century (Stout, 1997, 24). Only one date has been determined for Co. Wexford. That was obtained from tree rings from a ráth at Robbinstown Great, near Old Ross, which proved that the timber was cut down in the middle of the eighth century (Moore, 1996, 42).

The publication of the *Archaeological inventory for Co. Wexford* (Moore, 1996) has enabled an examination of these earthworks under various headings such as size, shape, elevation and distribution pattern. From the study of aerial photographs, maps and remaining traces on the ground, Moore (1996, 28) has estimated that there were originally at least 600 examples in the county. By 1996 this number had been reduced to about 150.

Up to fairly recent times ráths were considered mysterious places, thought to be the dwellings of 'the fairy folk'. There was a strong belief that damage to them would offend the fairies and could result in terrible retribution, even death, on the perpetrator or members of his family. Such beliefs no doubt helped to preserve many ráths from destruction in the past.

Ráth sizes and buildings within enclosure

Of the original total number of ráths in the county 80% were circular or near circular, the remaining 20% being oval or D-shaped. Of the circular or near circular ringforts around 50% had internal diameters ranging between thirty-one and forty metres, 27% were between twenty and thirty metres,

22% were between forty-one and fifty metres, with the remaining 6% between fifty-one and sixty-two metres.

Reflecting the hierarchical structure of Early Christian society ráths varied in configuration depending on the status of the occupier. Those of highest status in Co. Wexford were trivallate, of which there were four in the county (Table 1).

Table 1: Location and diameter of trivallate ráths in Co. Wexford

Townland	*Civil parish*	*6" OS sheet no.*	*Internal diam. (m.)*
Bolinrush	Carnew	5	24
Clonleigh	Clonleigh	24	50
Donard	Clonleigh	24	35
Knockanduff	Templetown	49	35

Although of kingly status, the internal living spaces were relatively small, apart from Clonleigh. But this is not unusual for high status sites. Clonleigh (named *Rathnacrue* on the six-inch Ordnance Survey map) and Donard were located less than a kilometre apart and within a dense concentration of various-sized ráths. A number of much larger enclosures of unknown dates were also found in the county. Next in status, and occupied by kings or nobles, were the bivallates, of which there were fifty-two or nine percent of the total in the county. These varied from twenty-five to fifty-five metres in internal diameter.

Lastly, there was the huge number of single-banked sites which ranged in internal diameter from around twenty to sixty metres. These would have belonged mainly to the farming classes, although the very large ones may have been owned by the nobles.

The dwelling houses within these enclosures were mostly circular in shape and constructed of wattle and daub, with roofs of straw or reed thatch. Excavations have shown that houses were between 3.4 and 7.0 metres in diameter; the larger houses would have accommodated five to six people.

Ráths would have contained other houses, particularly in the case of farmers who would have needed a range of outhouses for small stock. In the brehon Laws these are listed as a sheep pen, a calf pen and a pig sty. There is no agreement on whether or not cattle were housed within ringforts; some, in fact, may have been used solely for that purpose.

That the strong farmer was a man of considerable means and could live quite comfortably is shown by the list of perquisites attributed to him in *Críth Gablach* (Byrne, 1967, 51-52):

All the furniture in his house is in its proper place:

a cauldron with its spit and handles;

a vat in which a measure of ale may be brewed;

a cauldron for everyday use;

small vessels; iron pots and kneading trough and wooden mugs, so
    that he has no need to borrow them;

a washing trough and a bath,

tubs, candlesticks, knives for cutting rushes; ropes, an adze, an auger,
    a pair of wooden shears, an axe;

the work tools for every season-every one unborrowed,

A whetstone, a bill-hook, a hatchet, spears for slaughtering livestock;

a fire always alive, a candle on the candlestick without fail.

a full ploughing outfit with all its equipment;

There are two vessels in his house always;

a vessel of milk and a vessel of ale.

He is a man of three snouts;

the snout of a rooting boar that cleaves dishonour in every season,

the snout of a flitch of bacon on the hook,

the snout of a plough under the ground;

so that he is capable of receiving a king or a bishop or a scholar or a bre-
    hon from the road, prepared for the arrival of any guest company.

He owns seven houses, a kiln, a barn, a mill (a share in it so that it
    grinds for him)

a house of twenty seven feet,

an outhouse of seventeen feet,

a pig-sty, a pen for calves, a sheep-pen.

He has twenty cows, two bulls, six oxen, twenty pigs, twenty sheep,
    four domestic boars, two sows, a saddle horse, an enamelled bri-
    dle, sixteen bushels of seed in the ground.

He has a bronze cauldron in which there is room for a boar.

He possesses a green in which there are always sheep without having
    to change pasture.

He and his wife have four suits of clothes.

Outside the ráth would have been the garden for growing vegetables and the
infield for other crops such as wheat, oats, barley or rye.

Dúns

The word *dún* normally has a military connotation. Thirteen place-names in
the county have *dún* as the first element but only seven *dún* sites can be
identified. The internal measurements of these are: Donard (trivallate, *c.*35
m.), Dunanore 1 (30 m.), Dunanore 2 (44 x 37 m.), Duncormick, later con-

verted into a motte by the Normans (*c.*21 m.), Dundrum (*c.*40 m.) and two at Dunmain (40 and 37 m.). This, of course, presupposes that these are the actual sites of the duns. Apart from the name there is nothing to distinguish them from other univallate sites.

Few firm dates are available for these sites. Two in Co. Wexford, Duncannon and Dundonnell (Ramstown), are promontory forts, perhaps indicating a date in the Iron Age.

The distribution pattern

The distribution pattern of ráths is shown on Map 7. It is immediately obvious that mountainous terrain such as on the Blackstairs and Forth mountains, the wet areas such as Oulartleigh and wooded areas such as the Duffrey (Dubhtire) west of Enniscorthy and the Slaney valley were not attractive to the ráth dwellers. But the most striking correlation is with well-drained soils on good slopes that have a southerly or southeasterly aspect (Map 8). This is clearly seen in the dense concentrations around Rathnure where the soils, being derived mainly from shale till, are naturally fertile. This fact was earlier noted by Bennett in her study of ringforts in the county (1989, 50-61). But concentrations are also found on the flattish landscape along the south coast from Carnsore to the Waterford estuary. It is very noticeable that the heavy clayey soils on the east coast stretching from north of Gorey down to Kilmuckridge and around the Rosslare harbour area, as well as the excessively drained sandy soils in the Screen–Curracloe area were avoided. The wet soils were not suitable for overwintering cattle and no winter fodder in the form of hay seems to have been made during this period, while the sandy soils make poor pasture for grazing animals.

Another feature of the distribution pattern is the preference for elevations ranging from 200 to 400 feet above sea level (Table 2).

Table 2: Number and percentage of ráths at varying elevations

Elevation (feet above sea-level)	*Number*	*Percentage*
800-900	1	–
700-800	4	–
600-700	5	–
500-600	6	–
400-500	19	13
300-400	35	23
200-300	33	22
100-200	28	20
50-100	18	11
0-50	2	–

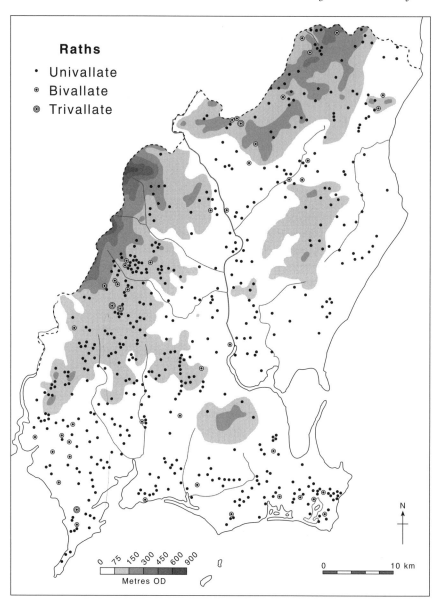

Map 7 Ráths once numbered around 600 in Co. Wexford, of which
some 150 remain. Most had a single ditch and bank; some (of higher
status) had two banks; while a few, belonging to the most powerful families, had three banks. Clusters of ráths occurred in certain areas.

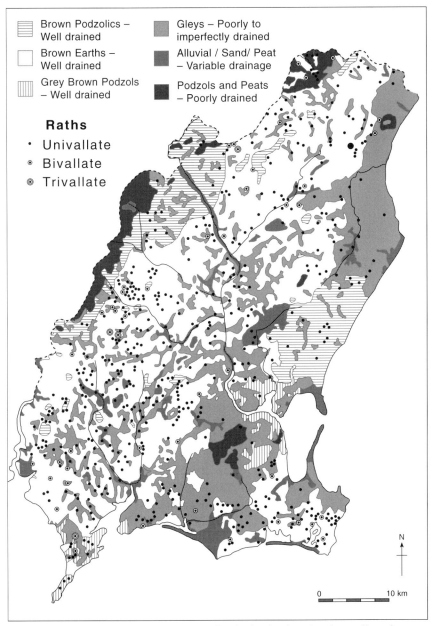

Map 8 The distribution pattern of ráths is clearly related to soil quality. The well-drained, fertile soils, on good slopes, in the west of the county, have the highest concentration. These could be grazed for most of the year in contrast to the poorly drained soils along the east coast which had a much shorter grazing season.

While Map 7 gives an indication of the ráth distribution, the pattern is more clearly seen on the large-scale maps in the archaeological inventory of the county where each site is numbered and described. Two distinct settlement types occur. One points to dispersed farmsteads occupying large areas mainly in the centre and east of the county. Some of this is undoubtedly due to the nature of the environment, that is, deep forest and rugged landscape in the centre and wet soils in the east. In contrast, the western and southern areas had a high density of ráths of various configurations.

These variations in ráth density must reflect the density in population, with comparatively low densities in central, northern and eastern parts compared to the rest of the county. Oddly, these are the areas occupied by the dominant Uí Cheinnselaig dynasties.

The location of the trivallate and bivallate ráths are also of great significance since they give us clues to the whereabouts of the homesteads of the kings and nobles. As already stated in Chapter 3, Co. Wexford was divided into eight or nine *tuatha*, each ruled by a king, with a substratum of noble families, from whom the kings were chosen. While it would be unwise to postulate as to which families occupied certain sites, it is interesting to compare the distribution of these ráths to the existing political situation. Was the trivallate fort at Bolinrush the home of the Síl nÉladaig and the one at Knockanduff that of the Síl Brain?. And what of the proximate sites at Donard and Clonleigh? Did the kingship rotate between two royal aspirants of the Benntraige? Or perhaps one family supplanted another and built their own high-status fort!

The fifty-two bivallate sites also pose intriguing questions. For example, some must have been occupied by kings of the *tuatha* since there were no trivallates in the territory of the Fotharta (Forth), the Uí Bairrche (Bargy), the Síl Máeluidir (Shelmalier), the Uí Felmeda (Ballaghkeen) and the Uí Dega (Gorey). However, in the case of Ballaghkeen the royal centre may have been at the dún of Dundrum, and for Bargy at Duncormick.

The presence of clusters of univallate ráths adjacent to a bivallate probably gives an indication of the number of client farmers held by a noble family living in the bivallate enclosure. Examples of such clusters were located in the following townlands: Money, Clologe, Grange, Haresmead, Sarshill, Ballyboher, Cotts, Ballynabarney and Kisha.

Not all bivallates had clusters; examples of relatively isolated sites occurred at Ballyandrew, Ballybeg, Kilcavan, Clonsharragh and Taghmon. The latter may have been the fort of the Fortharta chief, Dimma, who granted St Munnu the land on which to build his monastery (see p. 110, below).

Apart from showing areas of dense concentrations it is difficult to find a pattern in the distribution of univallate ráths. However, in a number of places, clusters of three or more can be detected as at Raheengurren, Rathfylane, Kinnagh, St Leonard's, Tullibards and Wilkinstown.

From this short survey of ráths and dúns it is obvious that a great deal could be learned from a more detailed study. Even this examination gives a good indication of the social and farming framework in Co. Wexford during the period from 600 to 900.

Around seventy-five percent of the total number of ráths which once dotted the landscape have been removed. This has occurred mainly in the south and southeast and has been attributed to the intensive farming methods of the Norman colonizers and their successors in these areas.

The later settlement pattern

The occupation of ráths apparently decreased from the eleventh century onwards, but some appear to have continued in use into the late medieval period. The type of homestead which replaced them is still a matter of debate among scholars. The nature of Early Christian society itself was changing. The increase in the numbers of the nobility resulted in them taking ownership of the land. The farmers were reduced to renting their holdings from them for which they paid in food rent (*biatach*) and other services. The territorial unit of the noble family was the *baile*, several in Co. Wexford still bear the family name, for example, Ballybrennan (Baile Bhraonáin), Ballycanew (Baile Mac Conmhai), Ballyregan (Baile Ó Riagáin). (For more examples see Chapter 15.)

Whether or not the noble families and their farmer clients remained in isolated homesteads within their defined land units is not clear. Neither is it known how the craftspeople and the unfree classes were housed. They may have lived in some type of village, perhaps close to a church, or in clusters of houses near their masters. Because the houses of the period were constructed of such perishable materials, we may never know the answers.

5

The origin, nature and progress of Christianity in Co. Wexford

Christianity originated within the Roman Empire. In Europe it spread quickly to Italy, France, Spain and Britain, but failed to reach Ireland, which remained outside the Empire. After several periods of persecution by the authorities Christianity became the official religion during the reign of Theodosius, AD 379-95). This early church was urban-based, sophisticated and literate and worlds apart from the largely unlettered, heroic, pagan, Celtic society of Ireland.

The first missionaries to Ireland

In 431, that is before the arrival of St Patrick, a bishop, Palladius, had been sent from Gaul, now France, *ad Scottos in Christus credentes*, 'to the Irish believers in Christ'. Since bishops were sent only at the request of groups of Christians, and then in a pastoral rather than a missionary capacity, the inference must be that a sizable number of converts existed in Ireland at that time.

Up to recently it was thought that Palladius spent only a short time in Ireland. It is now believed that, not alone did he spend several years here, but that he was joined by four other bishops from Gaul in 439. The four missionaries, Auxilius, Secondinus, Iserninus and Benignus appear to have concentrated their efforts in the Leinster region.

The confusion over Palladius and the others arose out of the claims in the Book of Armagh that Patrick converted the Irish. To substantiate this claim, the role of Palladius was reduced to the barest minimum and he was allotted only a short time in the country. Also, his companions were claimed to be not his, but Patrick's helpers.

In their efforts to prove the primacy of Armagh and to lay claim to the allegiance and therefore the incomes of all the churches in Ireland, the writers of the Book of Armagh, compiled after 807, had Patrick visit most parts of the country. A fragment in the book mentions how Patrick travelled from

Tara Hill near Gorey to Donaghmore (Keilin, Domnach Mor Maige Cria-thar) near Cahore. There he met Dubthach moccu Lugir, chief poet of the king of Leinster, and requested him to name a person from the province suitable to be a bishop. But according to modern historians Patrick spent his entire mission in the northern part of the country.

The Fragment in the Book of Armagh lists several places on the Wexford border in which Iserninus was active. These are in Idrone (Borris–St Mullins area), Larah (near Ballon), Rathvilly, Mount Leinster on the Carlow-Wexford border and Aghade (de Paor, 1993, 205-6). Secundinus died in 447, Auxilius in 459, Benignus in 467 and Iserninus in 468, accord-ing to the Annals.

An anonymous writer in *The Past* (1921, 100-12) quoted several sources which claimed that Palladius landed on the coast of Wicklow and that he established three churches in the south Wicklow-north Wexford area. These were Tigroney, Donard and Cell Fine. The latter he associated with Killa-vaney. However, this is more likely Killeencormac, Co. Kildare (de Paor, 1993, 45).

If one were to believe Shearman (1875, 382), Iserninus probably landed at the mouth of the Slaney and made his way to Carlow, where he convert-ed the people of Idrone. He was also said to have converted the seven sons of an important noble which incurred the wrath of Énna, king of Uí Cheinn-selaig, who expelled them. Eventually Énna's son, Crimthann, became king, was converted by St Patrick at Rathvilly around 458 and invited Iserninus and his converts back home. However, there is very little evidence to sub-stantiate any of these claims. St Patrick, for example, spent his entire mis-sionary period much further north.

Christianity spreads to Wexford

How then had Christianity filtered into the southeast corner of Ireland? There are various theories as to how and why this could have been brought about. Wexford harbour seems to have had extensive trading links with Britain, Gaul and the Mediterranean region in the Iron Age and again in the Early Christian period. At this time, too, the Irish were attacking parts of Britain for booty, and also for slaves. These slaves, like St Patrick, would have been mainly Christian, although it is debatable how much the religion of slaves would have influenced their masters in Ireland.

Proximity to a Christian milieu in Wales was obviously an important fac-tor. Wexford is a mere fifty-four miles across the Irish Sea from Fishguard where St David had his monastery. Contact between these two areas was easily established and migration to Wales followed. The most important group of migrants came from the Déisi who may have originated in Co. Meath where their name was preserved in the barony name of Deece.

Branches moved into south Leinster, Waterford and other parts of Munster (the Dál Cais were Déisi) in the pre-Christian period.

Thus, there were related kin or family groups in coastal areas on both sides of the Irish Sea, no doubt in constant contact. These contacts with Roman and post- Roman Britain would inevitably have an impact, not alone on the economic, but also on the cultural and religious ethos of the Irish, particularly along the east and south coasts.

Mytum (1992, 36 and 38) makes a cogent argument for the efficacy of these groups in introducing the new religion into Ireland, pointing out that many families would have contained both pagans and Christians. This would have given the Christians the opportunity to discuss their new religion and perhaps make converts in a familial social setting.

The biggest influence on the spread of Christianity in Wexford, without doubt, was the work of the early Irish saints. None of these came from Co. Wexford. In keeping with the mores of the time, which entailed depriving themselves of any status and taking on a life of poverty, they had forsaken their own areas to settle in distant parts. Despite restraints on the movement of ordinary people between *tuatha,* the evidence indicates that the clergy were free to travel wherever they wished. Thus Ibar, Abbán, Munnu and Aidán, after their formal education, made their way from Ulster to the southeast corner of Ireland. Here they travelled around the area preaching the Christian message, baptizing converts and founding churches. At their principal foundations at Beggerin, Adamstown, Taghmon and Ferns they established schools for the sons of the nobles, as shown in the Lives of Munnu and Cuán (see Chapters 10 and 11). The missionary method of approach was to try to convert the king of the *tuath* or an overking of higher status. The king's subjects would then follow suit.

Also, the early saints usually had a place to which they could retreat for prayer and contemplation. This was known as a 'disert' from the Latin *deserta*, meaning a wilderness or place apart. An example was Desert Munnu, later called Ishartmon, in Ballymore parish. There is evidence, that during the earliest period, churches were set up by hermits in isolated places such as Hook Head (St Dubhán) and Carnsore Point (St Vauk).

A major concern of the missionary movement must have been to give a Christian significance to places used for pagan ceremonies. Hence, we find a very early church at Carnsore Point, the Hieron Akron or 'Sacred Cape' of Celtic times. Springs were considered sacred by the Celts and were thought to have magical, or at least, curative powers. The early Christians, in order to exorcise pagan beliefs, dedicated these springs or wells to the saints. The curative powers were then attributed to the saints, some local such as Caomhán, Aidán and Munnu, some from further afield, for example, Brigid, Patrick and Columcille, and others from abroad such as Peter and Eusebius. These powers were thought capable of curing ailments such as blindness, deafness, in fertility and many others.

Valuable information on the holy wells in Co. Wexford is contained in John O'Donovan's Ordnance Survey Letters (1840), Flood (1916) and Ó Broin (1983-4, 27-35) who stated that, at the time of writing, at least one hundred and twenty were still traceable. Those marked on the 1920 Ordnance Survey maps have been listed by Culleton (1994, 40-53), many of them under their Irish name of *tobar*.

Up to the beginning of the nineteenth century many of the wells were resorted to by the public on the patron saint's feast day, known as the 'pattern day'. These were meant to be joyful, religious occasions but, because of the unedifying and irreverent, even violent, behaviour of some of those attending, they were gradually suppressed by the local clergy. The pattern at Kilcavan, Gorey, was prohibited about 1810 because a man had been killed at it (O'Donovan, 1840). Some sites have been carefully tended and are still visited, for example, St David's (Ballynaslaney), St Anne's (Killann), Tomhaggard and Ballinacoola (Bunclody).

Appeal and nature of the new religion

While Christianity differed fundamentally from Celtic paganism it had some things in common. Belief in the existence of another world, the prophetic powers of both the druid and the saint alike, and the performance of miracles and magic all helped to ease the path of conversion. But salvation now became a personal matter for each individual. The doctrine that wrongdoing was an offence against this new, all-powerful, all-knowing God which could result in eternal damnation if not forgiven, was not easy to accept. However, this was also a loving God who forgave those who truly repented, no matter how many or how serious their sins. The Christian faith did not overtly, exclude anyone from salvation; all people of whatever stratum of society could be saved.

The means to achieve salvation were clearly laid down by the Church. Baptism, adherence to Church teaching, prayer, fasting, abstinence from meat on certain days and attendance at Mass were required. The Mass was the central public act of Christian devotion. The earliest Mass rite practised in Ireland would have been a variant of the Latin form, with perhaps Gallican (French) and Mozarabic (Spanish and Byzantine) influences. The earliest extant Irish Mass rite is found in the Stowe Missal (Warner, 1915), which was compiled around 800 and is conserved in the Royal Irish Academy, Dublin. There is a Wexford connection with this famous book in that St Ibar is listed in the invocations in the Mass. As well as the Mass rite the Stowe Missal also contains prayers for Baptism and Extreme Unction, a treatise on the meaning of the Mass and three spells, one referring to St Ibar (see p. 83, below).

Communion was given under both species, that is, bread and wine, but appears to have been rarely received by the laity. Mass seems to have been infrequent at first. Later it began to be celebrated on Sundays and major feast days. Masses for the dead and other intentions also came into vogue.

Recitation of the psalms was one of the favourite forms of prayer. Other prayers included various litanies, including an 'Irish Litany of Pilgrim Saints' which refers to the Wexford missionaries Ibar, Abbán, Aidán and Munnu (Plummer, 1925).

Confession was an integral part of Christian life and involved not only a firm purpose of amendment but also very harsh penances. These were set out in very great detail in what were known as 'The Penitentials' where every conceivable transgression and its required penitential expiation was set out for the guidance of the confessor. Following St Augustine's strict views on the proper role of sex, sins of this nature figure prominently in 'The Penitentials', which cover every aspect of sexual behaviour even to the most deviant. In the very early church, for 'mortal', that is major sins, a penitent was obliged to confess on his knees and publicly. For very serious crimes, like incest, exile till death might be demanded. In the sixth century private confession and penance were introduced in the Irish Church. This was adopted in Canterbury in 668 and eventually in the entire western Church.

The principal features of penitential practice in the Early Christian period have been set out by Walsh and Bradley (1991, 113) as follows:

1   The penance was imposed by a private confessor of the penitent's choice
2   Most penances were of limited duration and so the sacrament could be resorted to repeatedly
3   Penances were graded according to the status of the sinner as well as to the nature of the sin
4   Sins of thought as well as deed were confessed and suitable penances enjoined
5   Long penances were often performed in monasteries to which lay penitents temporarily retired
6   The system of 'commutation' allowed for the conversion of a lengthy penance into a more moderate one or into one of greater severity but of shorter duration
7   Ordinary penances consisted of spells of fasting, often on bread and water, the recitation of psalms or corporal punishment, but alms-giving could be substituted for fasting in cases of infirmity or for other reasons.

The progress of the new religion
Christianity seems to have taken hold fairly quickly after its introduction, although it was resented by many at first. This is borne out by the words of St Patrick himself when he wrote in his *Confessio*:

At times I gave presents to chiefs, apart from the stipend I paid their sons who travelled with me. Nevertheless, once, they seized me with my companions, and on that occasion they were most eager to kill me. But the time had not come. They stole everything they found in our possession, and they put me in chains.

In Uí Cheinnselaig, Énna, the king, is alleged to have expelled the missionary, Iserninus, for converting some of his nobles to Christianity (de Paor, 1993, 107).

The druids, too, put up strong resistance. An old Irish poem, possibly as early as the sixth century, shows them mocking St Patrick:

Across the sea will come adze head
crazed in the head,
his cloak with hole for the head
his stick bent in the head.

He will chant impiety
from a table in front of his house
all his people will answer
'Be it thus. Be it thus.'   [Carney, 1967, 3]

According to Carney 'this poem is put in the mouth of a druidic opponent of St Patrick, and is a satirical picture of a bishop saying Mass'. Adze head refers to his headdress, the cloak means his cowl and the stick his crozier. When it was written memories of paganism were by no means dead, and there was probably some hankering after the old days.' In Adomnán's Life of Columcille (ed. Anderson and Anderson, 1961, 182), the story is told of how the saint drove the druids from a well and converted it to Christian use, whose waters then cured many diseases. Rules and admonitions against dealing with pagans were introduced by the Church as late as the seventh century (Bieler, 1963, 55 and 57). That the new religion eventually spread to every corner of the county is attested by the widespread distribution of ecclesiastical sites in the Early Christian period.

The early churches would have been constructed from timber planks, mostly of oak, then plentiful in Ireland. At Carnsore Point evidence for a timber church dating to the sixth or seventh century was found. Edwards (1990, 122) states that wooden churches were common up to the eleventh and twelfth centuries. Stone churches were unusual as shown by the fact that the Annals of the Four Masters considered the stone church at Ferns worth mentioning for the year 787.

Each church was dedicated to a saint. In Co. Wexford St Aidán was clearly the favourite choice with seven dedications – Ardamine, Clongeen, Clone,

Coolhull, Ferns, Fethard and Kilnahue; St Moling had five – Ballycanew, Kilnamanagh, Monamolin (2) and Toome; St Brigid had four – Kilbride (Ballylusk), Kilbrideglynn, Killilla and Rathaspick; St Munnu had two – Churchtown (Tacumshin) and Taghmon; and St Ibar had three – Beggerin, St Iberius-Wexford and St Ivor's (Broadway). See pp 156-7, below.

The church dedications also show the close connection with Wales; for example two, Killag and Killiane Little, were dedicated to St Degumen; two, Ballynaslaney and Churchtown-Kilmore; were dedicated to St David and churches on Hook Head were dedicated to St Dubhán and St Brecaun; a church at Rosslare was dedicated to St Brioc.

Surprisingly, perhaps, only four churches were dedicated to St Patrick (Wexford, Donaghmore, Kilmore and Kilpatrick) and two to Columcille (Ardcolm and Kilcomb). While no record survives of St Abbán's foundation at Adamstown the monasteries at Ferns, Taghmon, Beggerin and Templeshanbo appear to have flourished, at least until the eighth century, when they began to be taken over by lay people. This general monastic decline is reflected in the appearance of the movement known as the Céli Dé, literally 'the servants of God' who sought to reform the Church from within. That its followers were active in the Wexford area is shown by the dedication of churches at Screen, Ballinaleck and Ardcandrisk to St Maelruan of Tallaght, one of its chief promoters.

Church organization and the laity

Much still remains to be learned about church organization and its relationship to the laity from its origins in the fifth century up to the twelfth century. No doubt many changes took place over such a long period of time. Up to fairly recently it was thought that after a short phase of diocesan rule by bishops the monasteries took over the running of the Church and continued to do so until the reforms of the twelfth century.

A somewhat different story is now emerging, suggested initially by Corish (1972, 32-41) and elaborated on by scholars such as Hurley (1979, 329), Sharpe (1992, 81-109) and Etchingham (1994, 35-62). It is generally accepted that the very early church organization was based on the *tuath*, with a bishop over each *tuath*. As the eighth-century Rule of Patrick states (O'Keeffe, 1904, 216), 'Every *tuath* should have a chief bishop to ordain its clergy, to consecrate its churches, to give direction to its chiefs and nobles, and to sanctify and bless their children after baptism.' Given that for Co. Wexford the *tuatha* roughly corresponded to the later baronial divisions of Forth, Bargy, Shelburne, Bantry, Scarawalsh, Gorey, Ballaghkeen and Shelmalier, the county would have had eight bishops. The barony of Shelmalier East, created later, may have been a separate *tuath*, in which case there would have been nine bishops. Documentary evidence exists for only

Figure 1 Cross-carved stone,
Killell, Glynn, dated to the
sixth or seventh century

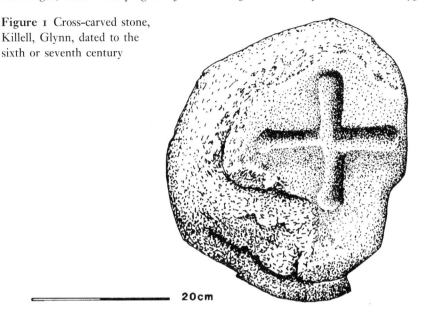

20cm

two locations, Ferns and Rathaspick. Within each *tuath* there were several kinds of churches including the mother church where the bishop was based and the small churches serving local communities. In addition there were private churches owned by a family and 'free' churches, whose relationship to the other churches is unclear. The Rule of Patrick shows that the community churches had to be maintained by the laity:

> Any church in which there is an ordained man of the tribe, apart from the great churches, he is entitled to the wage of his order, that is, house and enclosure and bed and clothing, and his ration that is sufficient for him, without exemption, without neglect of all that is in the power of the church, that is, a sack of its kitchen and a milch cow every quarter and the food of festivals.   [O'Keeffe, 1904, 216]

Participation of the laity in church services was probably limited, although it is difficult to estimate the size of the congregations, given that little or nothing is known about the scale of the wood churches in use in this period. Taking of communion seems to have been rare. Whatever about religious instruction or service to the laity, alms-giving to the poor seems to have been common if we can judge from the Lives of the saints.

The duties of the bishops as laid down in the Rule of the Céli Dé were to ordain men to Holy Orders (priesthood), to consecrate churches, to give spiritual direction to rulers, to those in authority, and to those in Holy

Orders. He is to bless and sanctify their families after baptism, he is to care for the infirm of every church, and to order the training of boys and girls in piety and learning. The priest's duties, apart from offering Mass on Sundays and major feast days, were the administration of baptism, the distribution of Holy Communion, and prayers for the living and the dead (Ó Maidín, 1996, 92-3).

The quality of church service provided to the laity depended, then as now, on several factors, not least the number and dedication of priests available to provide it. The literature contains several references to the scarcity of priests, caused to some extent, particularly in the early days, by the desire to lead the life of a contemplative monk instead.

There is little evidence to show that the monasteries became involved in the pastoral care of the laity. Rather they were centres for the contemplative religious life, filled mostly by monks, at least in the early period (see Chapter 12). However, they did provide a religious service for their clients, tenants and labourers who lived and worked on their farms and who also had their own churches.

There is even less information on how pastoral care was provided. Sharpe (1992, 108) proposes a model of tenth and eleventh century mother churches with a staff of several clergy and perhaps a few clerical students. In addition there were smaller churches with only one priest, if any. The size, number and distribution of ecclesiastical enclosures in Co. Wexford would appear to support this model, although lack of dating evidence precludes any definitive conclusion (see pp 147-62, below). Corish (1972, 38) makes the point that because of the bishop's power of ordination of priests, his role in pastoral ministry and in other spheres, his continued presence remained essential to the functioning of the church at all times.

The picture of church development in Co. Wexford then is one of early conversion to Christianity followed by the arrival of powerful missionaries in the persons of Ibar, Abbán, Aidán and Munnu. Gradually a network of churches was established throughout the county, many of whose sites can still be traced (see Chapter 13). As church discipline waned in the eighth century the Céli Dé reformers were active in the county as evidenced by church dedications to St Maelruan of Tallaght, one of its leading advocates. The range of church dedications shows a clergy which, while devoted to its own holy men and religious heritage, was also conversant with the names of saints of national and international significance. In common with those in the rest of the country the Wexford monasteries came under the control of laymen in the eighth and ninth centuries and the role of bishop was confined to purely episcopal functions. From the ninth century onwards the monasteries began to decline, although Ferns continued as a place of learning throughout the whole Early Christian period.

6

Introduction to the Lives of the saints

The cult of the saints first began to flourish in Europe in the late fourth and early fifth centuries when they were first thought of as being intermediaries between God and mankind. Veneration of holy people and martyrs goes back even beyond the beginnings of Christianity into late Judaism, and occurs in other cultures and religions.

In the Early Christian period men and women acquired the aura of saint-hood by virtue of their holiness and God-given powers. Also, according to Wilson (1983, 12) church founders might be granted the status of sainthood. The official declaration of sainthood, that is canonization, did not commence until much later. The support of the papacy was first sought merely to enhance the cult of a particular saint. Not until 1170 had papal authority to be obtained for venerating a local person as a saint. The first Irish person to be officially declared a saint was Laurence O'Toole in 1225. By 1587 the Vatican had established the Congregation of Rites to prepare for papal can-onization. In the next century Pope Urban VII, (1623-44) defined the offi-cial procedure for this practice, which holds to this day.

The title 'Island of Saints' (Insula Sanctorum) was first applied to Ireland in the Middle Ages. It was found, for example, in the late thirteenth-century Life of St Abbán, an early Leinster and Wexford missionary (Sharpe, 1991, 3).

The Lives of the saints
Information on the early Irish saints is found in various collections of their Lives. The earliest Lives were written in Latin between the mid-seventh and mid-ninth centuries. From the later ninth to the eleventh centuries versions were produced in Irish but no copies of these early Lives have survived, apart from a Life of Adomnán copied by Michael O'Clery which has been dated by language and content to 956-64 (Herbert and Ó Riain, 1988, 8). Latin and Irish versions of Irish saints Lives dating from the later medieval period are found mainly in three collections:

75

1. Marsh's Library and Trinity College, Dublin. This collection, in Latin, known as the *Liber Kilkenniensis* was probably compiled in Ferns by Bishop Ailbhe O'Mulloy or his assistant in the late twelfth and early thirteenth centuries (Sharpe, 1991, 348-67).

2. Bibliothèque Royale, Brussels. One collection in Latin is known as the *Codex Salmanticensis* from having been kept in Salamanca for a period. Another collection in Irish was mainly compiled by the Franciscan Friars at Louvain, Belgium, in the seventeenth century.

3. The Bodleian Library, Oxford. The Rawlinson Mss written in Latin in the fourteenth century.

The sources, dates, historical value, and comparisons of the various texts have been discussed by several scholars including Plummer (1922), Kenney (1929), Heist (1976), Ó Riain (1986), Doherty (1986, 1987) and Sharpe (1991). Incidental information on the Lives of the saints is found in the Martyrologies of Óengus, Tallaght, Gorman and Donegal and in various other medieval tracts.

Since they were written many hundreds of years after their deaths, the Lives tell us little about the actual lives of the saints. Paradoxically, such details were merely incidental to the real purpose of the biographers. Generally they were written to a common pattern depicting an unusual birth, an early life indicative of future greatness, a manhood founding churches, performing miracles, travelling to Rome and finally death in the bosom of their disciples. Historical accuracy was not important to these early writers. Even Brother Michael O'Clery, one of the Four Masters, expressed his scepticism about the material included in the Lives (Doherty, 1986, 363). The Lives are concerned mainly to bolster the sanctity of the saint so as to enhance the prestige of one or other of his foundations and hence of the ruling family in that area, and to establish or maintain claims to church property. In other words the cult of the saint was used for non-religious rather than religious purposes for hundreds of years after his lifetime.

This then led to additional material being added to their Lives to suit particular times and circumstances. For example, in the eleventh century when a writer from Bréifne in the north wished to write a Life of St Aidán as founder of the churches of Rossinver, Co. Leitrim, and Drumlane, Co. Cavan, he found that the existing Life referred only to events in Uí Cheinnselaigh. Nothing daunted, he proceeded to include many incidents from the northern kingdom in his new Life, thus enhancing the power and prestige of the ruling O'Rourke family (Doherty, 1986, 369). The Life of St Abbán was probably written by Ailbhe O'Mulloy, the Cistercian bishop of

Ferns from 1186 to 1223, to bolster his claims to the church property which was in danger of being appropriated by the newly-arrived Normans.

The saints and the people

The saints were usually from noble families; by the seventh century the saints and nobles had a high honour price, which determined their legal rights and privileges, as well as social position. Thus they were the social elite and as such carried immense status and authority. Added to that was their prowess as miracle workers, wrought by virtue of their holiness and sanctity through access to the power of God with whom they were thought to have a special relationship. Miracles, of course, were usually rewarded by gifts. That they were held in awe by the people is obvious. This in itself tells us something about how people thought in medieval times. A story in the Life of St Moling shows how even a king believed he could be denied access to heaven through disobeying a priestly command.

Other descriptions in the Lives show that some pagan beliefs had not been fully overcome. For example, the old Celtic veneration of trees revealed itself in the story of the famous yew tree at Leighlin, Co. Carlow, which was supposed to have the powers of an oracle, that is of revealing the will of the gods. When it fell, St Lazerian sent parts of it to all the saints of Ireland (Stokes, 1907, 27). Belief in magic was prevalent as shown in the use of mists to confuse the enemy.

The Lives give an insight into the Irish and European mind in the medieval period. The belief that saints were all-powerful is confirmed by a writer of the twelfth century, the cleric Gerald of Wales, who came to Ireland shortly after the arrival of the Normans. Before describing many stories which seem fabulous to the modern reader, and, fearing that he might be criticized, he wrote:

> I am aware that I shall describe some things that will seem to the reader either impossible or ridiculous. But I protest solemnly that I have put down nothing in this book the truth of which I have not found out either by the testimony of my own eyes, or that of reliable men found worthy of credence and coming from the districts where the events took place. And it should not seem surprising if wonderful things are written about Him who made whatever he wished for. For 'God is wonderful in his saints' and 'great in all his works'. And the psalmist is elsewhere made to say 'come and see the works of the Lord, the wonders he has worked on earth'. [O'Meara, 1951, 39-40]

The Lives of the saints became one of the most popular sources of reading material in the Middle Ages. It was inevitable, then, that such literature would become coloured by the historical perceptions and the literary and storytelling devices of each period in which they were rewritten. It appears that Rome was never enthusiastic about public access to the Lives, perhaps with good reason. In the early period public readings of the saints' Lives in France and Spain were celebrated with singing and dancing, perhaps not unlike the festivities associated with the 'pattern days' in eighteenth and nineteenth century Ireland before they were banned. As late as the seventeenth century the Jesuits found little support from Rome for their great project of making a systematic collection of the Lives of the saints. According to Dunn (1989, 75) it was felt that they would be laughed at by an educated French audience and would create scandal and not devotion.

Some common themes in the Lives of the saints
Apart from the standard Christ-like miracles, the Lives are characterized by certain themes common to most of the saints. The custom of travel far from home and family is evident in the Lives of Ibar, Munnu and Aidán. Ibar, originally from the Co. Down area settled on Beggerin island in Wexford Harbour, Aidán went from Bréifne to Wales before coming to Ferns. Munnu, as in most things, was even more extreme as shown by his shunning, not only his native place, but also his family:

> Afterwards the saint came to his own country (from Iona) and to the clan where he was born. However, he did not see the place, except only the road which he walked, for he did not wish to stay there or see the country, but it was necessary for him to pass through it. And he met (greeted) none of his relations, neither his mother, nor his brothers nor his sisters who were alive at the time. He directed his way towards the province of Munster and stayed in the district of Ely.
>
> [Plummer, 1910, ii, §ix]

Love of animals, particularly wolves, is evident in the Lives. The Life of Munnu describes how two wolves guarded Munnu's sheep while he studied. In the case of Aidán eight hungry wolves did obeisance before him for which he gave each one a sheep to eat but these were miraculously replaced in the flock. Moling's death was foretold by the arrival of a multitude of foxes at Ferns.

The legendary builder, the Gobán Saor, also makes his appearance in the Wexford Lives. When Abbán asked him to do some work he said it was impossible because he was blind. He had been blinded by other saints for charging too much for his work. However, Abbán restored his sight temporarily until the work was finished.

The following reference to the Gobán is found in the Life of Aidán:

> One day Máedóg was building a church and he could not find any
> wright to fashion it, so he blessed the hand of a man of his (monas-
> tic) family, named Gobán, and he erected the church with wondrous
> carvings, and brave ornaments, so that there was not the like of it
> (anywhere) and no one in his time surpassed this Gobán in wright's
> craft.   [Plummer, 1922, ii, 182]

Angels figure largely in the Lives, sometimes leading the saints to where
they should found their main monastery and from whence they would pass
to heaven when they died.

The role of the saints' relics
If the saints were important during their lifetime, they may have become of
even greater significance in death. The Life of Aidán tells us (Plummer,
1922, ii, 183) that 'Though Máedóg (Aidán) passed to heaven, he did not
cease from his miracles on earth. For by his earth (of his sepulchre), by his
clothing, and by his relics were healed blind and deaf and lame and all other
diseases.'

This cult of relics seems to have grown rapidly after about 800 in Europe
(Geary, 1994, 168). Apart from their religious efficacy, which centred mainly on the miraculous, such relics had a commercial value. In particular the
burial place of a saint usually became a place of pilgrimage and hence of
donations and gifts by the many visitors. Abbán's burial place was considered to be so important that competing monasteries tried to snatch his
corpse from the ox-cart on which it was being carried. The same story is
also found in the Lives of other saints.

Historical value of the Lives of the saints
Until fairly recent times the Lives of the saints were considered to have little historical merit, consisting as they do mainly of fabulous stories, common to many of the Lives. Recent studies, however, show that quite a lot
of information can be gleaned from detailed studies of these Lives, particularly about the times in which they were written, which was long after the
death of the saint.

Plummer (1910, i, pp cxxix-clxxviii) pointed out the core of pagan elements in many of the Lives, with particular reference to the Celtic gods of
water, sun and fire. Abbán is strongly associated with water, the very name
Áedh (Aidán) means 'fire'. Moling's face could become so bright that his
attendant could not look at him. More recently, Doherty (1986, 363-74) has
shown how the cult of St Aidán was used at various times to enhance the

importance of either the monastery of Ferns or the churches at Drumlane, Co. Cavan, and Rossinver, Co. Leitrim. In both these cases the real purpose was to show the importance of the ruling families of Mac Murchada of Uí Cheinnselaig, and O'Rourke and O'Reilly of Bréifne.

Abbán's Life, too, was rewritten to prove the importance of Ferns and possibly to establish the rights of the bishop to church properties which had been taken over by the Normans (Ó Riain, 1986, 165).

The Lives also throw some light on the conflict between the Uí Bairrche, who still ruled south Wexford at the beginning of the Early Christian period, and the ever-encroaching Uí Cheinnselaig. Thus, in Munnu's Life the territory of Uí Bairrche is raided by the Uí Cheinnselaig and in Abbán's Life his foundation at Camaross is attacked by Cormac Mac Diarmaita of the Uí Bairrche.

The earliest mention of many place-names in Co Wexford is found in the Lives of the saints. Some still retain their ancient title such as Ferns, Taghmon, Ross Mhic Treoin, Camaross, Templeshanbo, Clonmore, Loch Garman and Beggerin. Others, such as Adamstown, have been given English names, while many such as Ard Crema (Munnu), Magh na Taibhse (plain of the spectres, Abbán), Ath Daimh dha Ceilt (Abbán) and Acadh hUabhair (the ford of the yew, Abbán) cannot now be identified.

7

St Ibar of Beggerin

Ibar was one of the earliest saints to be associated with Wexford. Although the exact dates of his birth and death are not known for certain, there is little doubt that his active ministry must have been in the second half of the fifth century. He is usually referred to as Bishop Ibar, which places him among the first of the native bishops. His principal foundation was on Beggerin, then a small island in Wexford Bay (see pp 143-5, below).

A different Ibar had his foundation at Geashill, Co. Offaly. His genealogy (O'Brien, 1962, 90) shows that he belonged to the Loígis of Laois. He was one of the first bishops of the great monastery of St Brigid at Kildare, but had no connection with Wexford, contrary to Comerford's view (1883, i, 1), who confused him with Ibar of Beggerin.

Ibar's Lives
Two short Lives of Ibar exist (see pp 86-96). The earliest and shortest is found in the Book of Leinster and is reproduced in Grosjean, 1959. This merely gives his genealogy, some details of his birth and a reference to his teacher, Mochta, of Louth.

The longer version of Ibar's Life had a somewhat chequered history. It was known to James Ussher, Anglican archbishop of Armagh (1625-56), who included an extract from it in his history of the British Church (Ussher, 1639). It was also known to Henry FitzSimon (1566-1643), a Dublin Protestant who became a Catholic and a Jesuit. The Jesuits, early in the seventeenth century, accepted a proposal from one of their members, Heribert Rosweyde, to collect all available information on the saints. The main task was entrusted to Jean Bolland (1596-1665). For this reason his successors became known as the Bollandists and their publications as the *Acta* and *Analecta Bollandiana*. It was to the Bollandists at Antwerp that FitzSimon sent his copy of the Life of Ibar. These, however, considered the Life too fantastical to be published (Grosjean, 1959, 426). In the hope of getting more information on Ibar, the Bollandists, Henschen and Papebroch, referred it to

Thomas Sheeran, a Franciscan scholar at Louvain, whose reply is given on p. 90.

The Life then disappeared into the archives in Antwerp and eventually ended up in the *Collectanea Bollandiana* in the Bibliothèque Royale, Brussels (Identification no. 7773, fos. 550-1). Fortunately, another Bollandist scholar, Paul Grosjean S. J., discovered this copy of the Life three centuries later. Together with the fragment from the Book of Leinster he published it, with a commentary in French on each, in *Analecta Bollandiana* (Grosjean, 1959, 426-50). Because so little has been published on the life of Ibar it seemed useful to include an English translation of the two Lives, together with Grosjean's comments on them and a translation of Fr Thomas Sheeran's letter at the end of this chapter.

Genealogy and siblings
According to Ó Riain (1985, 16) Ibar belonged to the Uí Echach of Ulad who occupied east Co. Down. His descent is given as mac Lugna, mac Cuírc, mac Coirpre, mac Néill, mac Echach from whom the Uí Echach are descended.

In the Lives there are two different accounts of how the name Ibar was acquired. In the Book of Leinster it is said that he was so-called because he was the same colour as the yew tree (*iur* in Irish) at his birth. In FitzSimon's Life his mother, while pregnant with Ibar, turns red after eating a chive. When a messenger informs the king that 'a yew tree is not more red than her face' a soothsayer prophesied that 'the name of the son to whom she is about to give birth will be called Ybarus (Ibar)'.

Macalister (1920, 9) speculated that Beggerin may have been known as 'the island of the yew tree' before Ibar's time and that the name Ibar, meaning yew, became attached to the saint at the expense of his real name, which was eventually forgotten.

According to FitzSimon's Life Ibar had three brothers. MoBeooc is listed in the Martyrology of Óengus for 16 December 'the feast of my excellent Beooc, from lustrous Ard Cainross'. A note in the Martyrology of Gorman gives 'MoBeooc of Loch Garman or of Loch Gerg in the North'. Coeman, another brother, is given in the Martyrology of Gorman as Coeman of Ard Caemain, near Wexford. In the Martyrology of Donegal he is described as Caomhán of Ard Caomhán, by the side of Loch Garman, in Leinster. The Martyrology of Óengus gives 12 June as 'the feast of pious Caeman, who was named Sanct Lethan'. This would indicate that St Caomhán was, in fact, a brother of St Ibar.

The youngest brother was mac Lugna who became a bishop, according to the Book of Leinster. Thus it is possible, though not certain, that three brothers of the same family, Ibar, MoBeooc and Coeman or Caomhán, came to the Wexford area to spread the Christian message.

The Book of Leinster lists four sisters of Ibar as Cainech Apad, Mellit Manach, Brondfhind Breac and Corrtharach Cain. Cainech was reputed to have married the king of Leinster and to be the mother of Abbán, although the name usually given is Milla or Mella (Plummer, 1922, ii, 3) which seems closer to the second sister's name.

Education

Ibar was sent to St Mochta to be educated. Mochta, said to be British, founded a school at Louth, possibly in the time of St Patrick, of whom he called himself a disciple. Louth was an important monastery and was referred to in the Annals with respect.

Ibar's missionary work

Before coming to Wexford Ibar's main missionary work was in the kingdom of Meath, of which Brega was a part. Here, the Life says, he converted and baptized the king and an immense crowd of people before he departed for Beggerin. Ibar seems to have been very successful in his efforts, not only in Wexford, but also further afield. The Life of Abbán (Plummer, 1910, i, 7) tells how 'There were innumerable holy monks, clerics and nuns in different places throughout the whole of Ireland, at that time, under the mastership of Ibar.' However, apart from Beggerin, no other foundation has been attributed to him.

In Ibar's time Beggerin was a school rather than a monastery; the latter type of establishment only came into vogue a little later. (The first monastery in Ireland is attributed to St Enda of Aran, who died in 530.)

That Ibar was a bishop seems beyond doubt. The Irish Litany of Pilgrim Saints, composed around 800 (Hughes, 1959, 318) refers to him as follows: 'Three thousand anchorites who assembled with Mumu (from Munster) for one quest with bishop Ibar,' and also: 'Thrice fifty true monks under the yoke of bishop Ibar'. Similarly, all the martyrologies refer to him in this way as does a misplaced list from the Book of Armagh (de Paor, 1993, 198).

Ibar is also called a bishop in one of the three spells in the Stowe Missal which was compiled around 800 (Warner, 1915, 42). 'I honour bishop Ibar who heals … may the blessing of God and of Christ … heal thine eye … whole of thine eye.' The gaps in the writing are due to deterioration of the manuscript, which is now in the Royal Irish Academy. In the same missal Ibar is also one of the Irish saints invoked following the commemoration of the dead in the Mass.

The miracles

The few miracles attributed to Ibar fall into the usual pattern. Thus, he can control the sheep and lambs, order water to come forth from the earth, quench fire, cure disease, immobilize people who fail to keep a promise and tame a sea monster.

Was Ibar pre-Patrician?

The Life of Declán of Ardmore (de Paor, 1993, 251) declares that Ibar (along with Ailbhe of Emly, Ciarán of Seirkieran and Declán) was preaching Christianity in Ireland before Patrick arrived. Given that Patrick may have lived until around 490 and Ibar till around 500, this is not impossible. As Sharpe (1989, 376) states, 'no one has proved it false, or even historically improbable'. But what seems likely is that they all operated around the same time, that is, in the second half of the fifth century, but each independently, given that Patrick preached only in the northern half of the country. The recently discovered Life of Ibar included here indicates that the saint established a church in Mide (Meath) about the year 550 (Grosjean, 1959, 438).

The Life of Declán depicts Ibar as being reluctant to accept Patrick as head of the Irish Church. Building on this a note in the margin of the Martyrology of Óengus (Stokes, 1905, 119) describes him as follows:

> This is the bishop Ibar that had the conflict with Patrick, and 'tis he that left the roads full and the store rooms empty in Armagh. So Patrick is angered with him and said 'shalt not be in Erin'. To which Ibar replied 'Eire is the place I shall be and for this reason it shall be called Beg-Erin.'

However, this story, and the pre-Patrician claims for the saint, are more likely to be related to later church politics, when Armagh was seeking to assert its supremacy in the Irish Church, rather than to actual contemporary events.

Ibar and Monenna of Killevy, Co. Armagh

The Life of Monenna (Anon., 1980, 125) describes how she came to Ibar at Ard Conais (possibly a corruption of the present name of Ardcavan) in Wexford with many virgins and widows and lived under his direction. But trouble was fomented by a young nun 'who was inflamed by the fires of envy and persuaded by the devil'. Because of this, Monenna left Wexford and eventually founded a monastery at Killevy, Co. Armagh. That Monenna came to Wexford goes to prove the importance with which Ibar was perceived in his own time.

Ibar and Abbán

In the Life of Abbán (Plummer, 1922, ii, 3) his mother Mella is described as Ibar's sister. But in the Book of Leinster his mother is given as Cainech

Apad. Abbán was educated by Ibar at Beggerin. From there, according to the Life, he accompanied Ibar on a visit to Rome. Also in the Life of Abbán, Ibar is supposed to have gone sailing with him and St Patrick in Wexford harbour, but this is merely a way of associating Abbán with the famous saint, thus enhancing Abbán's stature.

Ibar remembered

The name Ibar (Latin, *Iberius*) has strong associations with the Wexford area. Ibar is still widely used as a Christian name; the Church of Ireland parish and church in Wexford town are named after him (St Iberius) as well as the local cemetery and a terrace of houses; the medieval parish of St Ivor's, now in Lady's Island parish, was dedicated to him. The memory of the saint has long been revered in the Wexford area. He was reputed by Giraldus Cambrensis, writing in the 1180s, to have expelled all the rats from the area for eating his books (O'Meara, 1951, 64).

Ibar and Beggerin

There are no accounts of Ibar's death in the Lives, but the Annals give the date as 23 April in various years between 499 and 504. This is also his feast day. Other records point up Beggerin as Ibar's most famous foundation and also as the place of his death and burial. The Martyrology of Óengus describes Ibar as follows:

> The light of bishop Ibar
> Who has smote every heresy's head
> A splendid flame over a sparkling wave
> In Becc-Eriu he departed.

The Latin Life of Abbán in an eulogy on Ibar describes Beggerin as his place of burial and in the usual fashion goes on to highlight the miracles and benefits to Wexford from this honour:

> In that monastery, indeed, the remains of the most blessed high-priest (master) Ibar lie, and they are revered with honour and the place itself is greatly honoured on account of the name of St Ibar because he himself was one outstanding dispenser of divine dogma by comparison with previous preachers whom God chose because of their relationship with the same race (Irish) to convert the Irish. And there, famous and very great miracles through him (i.e. Ibar) do not cease to be shown by God. He himself was sprung from the race of the Ulad (Ulster) which is a fifth part of Ireland. But God bestowed him on the Leinster men so that in the earth of their region his most

sacred body would lie, and in order that, both now and in the future, they would be defended by his voice. (Plummer, 1910, i, 7-8)

Ibar's grave is said to be under a large flat stone in the cemetery on Beggerin.

For further details on Beggerin see pp 143-5, below.

THE LIFE OF ST IBAR, FROM THE BOOK OF LEINSTER
translated from Latin of the Best et al. edition by John Dunleavy;
Fr Grosjean's comments have been made into footnotes.

§1. Bishop Ibar's life was of three years thirty and three twenties [that is ninety-three]. His father's name was Lugna and he was of the Ulti and specifically of the Artraige. The name of his mother was Bassar and she was of the Desi and (specifically) of Breg.[1]

§2. Lugna had four sons and four daughters, namely, Ibar the bishop, MoBeooc, Coeman Brecc, Mac Lugna. There were four daughters, namely Cainech Apad, Mellit Manach, Brondfhind Brecc, Corrtharach Cain.[2]

1　The age of three singles, plus three tens, plus three twenties, being 93, does not appear elsewhere, although the chronological difficulties would have led the medieval erudites to prolong, in various ways, the career of St Ibar.

　　The Artraige of the Ultoniens (Artraige Ulad), according to genealogists, take their name from Art, son of Mugdorn Dub, descendent of Colla Mend, and are placed with the Fir Breg. As one of St Ibar's disciples was named Sedna (*Vita Ibari* §8), it is not without interest to recall that another branch of the Artraige, those of Cliu farther to the south, in the middle of Munster, claim also a saint of this name, which came to him through the maternal line.

　　The mother of St Ibar would have belonged to another group of the Fir Breg, the Déisi, which name remains in the baronies of Upper Deece and Lower Deece, in Co. Meath. Bassar, that the *Vita Ibari* in the beginning calls *Paseria*, becomes *Paferia* in the manuscript and *Daferia*, due to a mistake in copying or reading, in Ussher, which, thankfully, the moderns have transcribed.

　　But a very different tradition existed, by which St Ibar's father was traced, not to the Artraige (from Art, son of Mughorn Dub) but to the Sortraige (from Sort, brother of Art), and not to the Ultoniens, but to the Crimihanna. This has a certain value because the *Vita Ibari*, from its earliest phase, shows the father and mother of the saint '*terra Crimtani*'. It was in a recension of this genealogical note that our author found mention of the greatness of St Ibar: cf. §4.

2　Without entering into details, one can tentatively try to identify the brothers of St Ibar, or at least those saints which the hagiography seems to have in mind in composing this list.

　　Mo-Beooc is most likely he who the martyrologies commemorate on 16 December and of who we know nothing except, thanks to a commentator of *Felire* of Óengus, that he was from Loch Garman, that is to say, from the town or the bay of Wexford.

　　Coeman Brecc ('*le Tachete*') should be recognizable: his name is not common and the epithet is a distinctive one. One hesitates, however, between a Coeman Brecc of Ross Ech, and another, nicknamed Sanct Lethan, whose church would have been in Ardne Coemain on the bank of the bay of Wexford. This last seems to command our attention in that, in

§3. Bishop Ibar had three names, Nennan was his name, that is to say Ninan (in modern Irish, *naoinean* meaning an infant) because of his child-like (innocence) Columcille declared that 'Nennan was the the noblest and chief bishop'.

§4. The name bestowed on him/nickname was Ecmacht, that is to say '*accu mo acht*', that is to say, many cubits, because he was 15 cubits high. The same man (Columcille) declares that he (Ibar) was an outstanding Catholic abbot, that is, the tallest/longest.[5]

the telling of the incident which gave him his nickname, the medievals introduce St Ibar, without indicating that Coeman recognized in him his brother. A third Coeman Brecc, perhaps identical to one of the two others, is mentioned in the *Vita Fechini*. As Fechin is saint of the church of Fore of which we have already noted that it is not so far from Rathkenny there is a certain link with the country of St Ibar. Coeman, brother of Ibar, is distinguished by *sacerdos* (priest: §11), then by *pontifex* (bishop: §13). This, in fact, is the clearest thing we know about him.

Mac Lunga became, undoubtedly, Mac Lugna, 'son of Lugna', because of the developments surrounding his name, which the tale tells of, and which appear known only to this text of the Book of Leinster with which we are concerned (§§2, 12-14) and §3 of the *Vita Ibari*, joined to the Treatise on the mothers of the Irish saints – unless one is to recognize him in the Mac Luga of the list of saints who were also priests.

The four girls are Cainech Apad, Mellit Manach, Brondfhind Brecc and Corrtharach Cain. Of two of these we have no information at all, but Cainech and Brondfhind appear in the Treatise on the mothers of Irish saints thus: the first as mother of Blat, alias Abbán, son of Laignech: the second as mother of Senach Garb of Cell Mor, of Miachu, of Toimtenach of Ros Glassi, and of Lithgen of Cluain Mor Lithgen. These genealogical compositions, with their ins and outs, are still waiting for a critical study, which should be undertaken as a whole, and of which we perceive only the first lineaments. In the seventeenth century, the final works of the old group, in forcing themselves to produce a definitive version of the genealogies of the saints, succeeded in marrying the two sisters successively to the same Laignech (alias Laigen).

3   Our source gathered information on the distinctions of the Roman *tria nomina*. On the other hand, he knew or thought he knew that his hero, apart from the name Ibar, had had two others. He proceeded, therefore, to the application of the doctrine, and the Latin word *nomen* undoubtedly figured in his original essay, in order to respond to *agnomen* and *cognomen* of the following paragraphs. No other source that we know of gives Nennan and Ecmacht as denominations of St Ibar. The Irish etymologies of these two names are fantastical. As for the Latin citation attributed to St Columcille, it is on a par with that alleged by the following paragraph and seems to come from the same piece of verse. Is it necessary to see in it at least two well-preserved heptasyllabes in order to respond? *Nennan nobilissimum et abbatem catholicum* would therefore be the first and third verses of a quatrain rhyming in *um*, and the two other verses would end in *episcopum* and *egregium*. No hymn containing this is known to us. If it really gave to one and the same person the double title of bishop and abbot, it would be from an ancient epoch.

4   The greatness of St Ibar is mentioned nowhere else, it seems. Perhaps the idea came from some commentator who translated badly the Latin word *egregius*.

5   Regarding §§5-9. The tale corresponds to 1 of the *Vita Ibari*. It adds to it an interesting development, the localization of the dún of king Colmán, son of Neman, at Rath Cennaig, that is to say, at the eastern extremity of that mountainous region called Sliab Breg. The *Vita Ibari* said: *in terra Crimiani*, and effectively, a group of the Uí Cremthainn did occupy the barony of Slane.

§5. His surname (epithet) on the other hand was Ibar, and so it was imposed on him. On one occasion Lugna was travelling in his chariot and his wife, namely Basser, was with him. They were travelling alongside Rath Cennaig. 'One chariot under one king alongside here at some distance,' said the druid from the interior of the house

§6. 'Go and see who is there,' said the king, namely Colmán, son of Neman (and Bishop Ibar baptized him later). And the messenger enquired and found out that it was Lugna who was in the chariot. And this is what the king said, 'The druid is a liar because the king is not in the chariot'

§7. But the druid said, 'Ask him (that is, Lugna) if his wife is sick' The messenger, carrying a stone hidden in his hand, went and said,' I have brought a cure for health for your wife, if she is in pain.'

§8. Lugna replied, 'What have you brought? And after the messenger (emptied) his hand of (the onion) ... And as he said, so was it, and it (the onion) had in it twelve shoot/sprouts. One of these changed colour ... (and grew) in size, and he (that is to say Lugna) gave that chive to his wife and she chewed it.

§9. And then she had heat in her whole body and her face was very red. And afterwards she gave birth to a son who had the same colour as that tree which is called a yew (*iur*=Irish for yew tree) and that infant was thus named Ibar.

§10. As to the second son MoBeooc, he was so named because his mother said, 'My son, lively and young.'[6]

One will note the expressions *aegra* and *in dolore*, both more decent than one would expect, used of a woman approaching her deliverance [*translator's note:* this could mean child-birth, death, freedom from captivity: the text is not more specific) but chiefly the word *cathedra*, in the sense of 'foot or seedling (of vegetation)'. By chance it reappears twice, without the slightest difficulty in reading for the first seven letters, and without there being any doubt that it consists of a theme in *a*. In vain, however, does one question the lexicographers: neither in antiquity nor the Middle Ages did the Greek word, Latinized as *cathedra*, take on any meaning which conforms with the circumstances of the tale, and, at the same time, is in accord with the recension of the *Vita Ibari* the Latin of which is far more knowledgeable, more complex and further removed from a direct translation of Celtic terms, than the half-Latin, half-Gaelic text of the Book of Leinster.

The author of this was well enough versed in etymology, in which he had a particular interest, to know that the Irish word *cathair* was no other than the Latin *cathedra*, and to replace one with the other. However, none of the meanings given by the dictionaries of the Gaelic *cathair*, in either the medieval or the modern periods, in Ireland, Scotland or the Isle of Man, are suitable here. One must turn to the Welsh, another branch of the Celtic family, who have adopted the Latin *cathedra* in the form of *cadair*. Outside of a series of meanings corresponding to those of the Gaelic languages, Welsh has one, specific to gardeners and botanists, known from the fourteenth century up until the seventeenth or eighteenth at least: 'tuft, especially of branches or trunks, which did spring from the same stock.' Our author, going back to the Latin word *cathedra*, indicates that the Irish *cathair* must have had the same meaning, from the twelfth century at the latest.

6   The mother imposing a name on her child is possibly just a biblical reminiscence. The etymology is worthless.

§11. The third son (called) Colmán, that is pleasant and splendid, and he was a priest.[7]

§12. The fourth son was a holy bishop, whom we now call Mac Lunge, as it were Mac Lugna. And he was so called because his father loved him greatly in preference to the rest.[8]

§13. When his disciples said to Mochta 'The sons of Lugna have not come' that is to say, Ibar the bishop, and Colmánus, the pontiff (or priest) and Mac Lugna. But Mochta said, 'Why (has) the third son (been called or not been called?) by the name of his own mother?'.

§14. The disciples answered 'Crinna (?) has his own name. He/she was unwilling (because of her love) that his/her be called otherwise ... since (because of love) of his son Lugna called.' And Mochta said, 'There will be mourning etc. ... and his site will be high, both now and in the future'.

VITA S. IBARI/LIFE OF ST IBAR
from Brussels codex 7773, fol. 551-550 as transcribed in Paul Grosjean, 'Deux textes inedits sur S. Ibar', *Analecta Bollandiana*, 77 (1959) 426-50, translated from Latin by John Dunleavy. The text is preceded by Fr Grosjean's preliminary remarks; and his comments are given in footnote form.

In gathering notes on the various sources of James Ussher's *Britannicarum ecclesiarum antiquitates,* and in studying the *Vita Commani,* believed lost until now, we elaborated somewhat – as do all those who have been interested in this question – on the, fairly important, fragments of a *Vita Ibari.* This seemed to have disappeared since the erudite archbishop of Armagh had consulted it, before 1640. It should, however, be sufficient, in order to trace it, to follow the activities of Fr Henry FitzSimon. His history is identical to that of the *Vita Commani* which is preserved within the *Collectanea Bollandiana,* now in the Belgian Royal Library (no. 7773. fos. 550-1), along with other documents carefully classified by our predecessors after the publication of the *Acta Sanctorum* of April, in which they deal briefly with St Ibar.

Rejected by them as fantastical, this piece is by the same, fairly negligent, scribe who transcribed the *Vita Commani* for Rosweyde. It carries many notes of all sorts in the handwriting of the first Bollandists along the margin. Bollandus marked the

---

7 Coeman refers assuredly to *coem*, 'pleasant, agreeable', but the second part is not a separate element, as the hagiography believes: it is a suffix, common among anthroponyms taken from an adjective.

8 §§12-14 deal with the name of St Mac-Lugna, youngest brother of St Ibar. The deterioration of the manuscript means it is not possible to precisely understand, at the end, the reason given to St Mochta by his disciples, but §12 gives an idea of it, the particular love of Lugna for this son. The last words attributed to Mochta are the beginning of a verse prophecy, work of several poets of an earlier age. We have not succeeded in identifying this piece.

date of the feast on the left of the heading '23 Apr.', and Papebroch added, on the right, 'Ex ms. P(ater) FitzSimon'. At the end (fo. 551), another note by Papebroch: '*Vide cetera in manuscripto FitzSimon*'. The *Vita,* clearly incomplete, closes on the account of a miracle. Nothing was said about the death of St Ibar. Papebroch became convinced that this was simply due to a mistake by Rosweyde and that the missing portion figured in a manuscript well known to our predecessors, by Fr Henry FitzSimon which contained the Latin Lives of the Irish saints. Meanwhile, unable to find what he looked for, he simply barred the reference as useless.

Thus, mutilated and carrying a minimum of historical details, the *Vita Ibari* appeared unworthy of the *Acta Sanctorum*. After recognizing these faults, and in the hope of remedying them, Papebroch resolved to write to Fr Thomas Sirinus (in Irish undoubtedly O'Sherin or O'Sheeran), a Franciscan of the Irish College in Louvain, inheritor of the papers of Christopher (Patrice) Fleming, Hugh Ward and John Colgan, and charged with continuing their work. Papebroch's letter has not been found, but P. Sirinus' answer survives in the same collection of the *Collectanea Bollandiana* (un-numbered page immediately after the *Vita Ibari*). Sirinus had received this too from Papebroch. This he expressly says, and, in the margin of this copy, his handwriting is recognizable in several notes – entirely devoid of interest, however. Here is the essence of the response, which alerts the Bollandist to a narrative document significantly older than the *Vita Ibari*:

> Reverend Father,
> I thank your Reverence for deeming me worthy to confer with on the incomplete Life of St Ibar which, attached, I return to you. It (that is, the Life) would be excellent if it were purged from the copyist blunders, as I hope it will be by your industry. I think that extrapolations from those Lives and from the Lives of other saints, which are kept by Ussher and Ware, are included here (i.e. have caused the errors). For my part I have never seen that mutilated/shortened Life of S. Ibar or any other, but only a few pieces from it which Ussher inserted in his own work about the churches of Britain, and even if they are interspersed with blunders it is possible to infer, whenever I have added in things from those and other lesser works towards the end of the Martyrology of Tamlact, the Appendix where it is legible, that these give this (i.e. the same) account. These things, Reverend Father, which I have discovered relating to your enquiry, apart from the many other things relating to the same S. Ibar which are extant in the Acts of the saints, Patrick, Brigid, Alba, Declán, Abbán, Saigir Kieran, Monenna etc are surely known to you. But if this (my information) helps you in regard to either this Life of Ibar or to another complete (Life) of the same man, it will take nothing away from the glory you gave me by conferring with me on this matter, and you will free me from weariness, and from some errors which will come consequent on my interpretation (conjecture). I wish for, Reverend Father,
> Henschen, for you Reverence and for your cooperation, everything that is best, with the joys of Easter.

> Leuven, 10 April 1671

> Your Reverence's unworthy servant
> Fr Thomas Sirinus

§1. At that time Lugna with his wife in his chariot had come to the court of Cemanus in the territory of Crimtanus, where Colmánus, son of Nemanus, is said to have reigned. There was a certain priest (soothsayer) staying with the aforementioned king, and hearing the sound of the chariot he said, 'This chariot which resounds is carrying a king' (literally resounds under a king). Then the king said, 'You inquire who is sitting in the chariot.' Then the king's messenger, advancing to the chariot, saw no one in it except Lugna and his wife, and returning, he told this to the king. Then the king declared that the soothsayer had spoken falsely; he said this because Lugna was not the king. Then the soothsayer asserted the same words and said, 'Let it be investigated to see if his wife is pregnant; and if she is about to give birth to a child, she will give birth to a king or a bishop of whose name Hibernia (Ireland) will be full.' Then the messenger, carrying a stone in his hand, inquired the same thing from Lugna. Then Lugna admitted the truth and said, 'And if she is ready to give birth, what did you bring with you for her?' Then the messenger, answering, said he had brought with him a stem/stalk of a real leek/chive. Lugna said to the messenger 'If you are bringing with you a chive, give it to her, don't hesitate.' The messenger, however, opening his hand and looking down at the leek made from a stone, and marvelling at the twelve heads of real chive growing from one head, immediately he handed them over to Paseria. She, greatly delighted, took the chive and ate it until her face, from the strength of the chive, had become more red than usual. The messenger, returning, told what he had seen to the soothsayer and the king. Then the soothsayer spoke and asked the messenger if the paleness of her face had turned red after she ate the chive? He said, 'A yew tree is not more red than hers (that is, her face).' Then the soothsayer prophesying said 'The name of the son whom she is about to give birth to will be called Ybarus.' Through this miracle which God wrought on Ibar himself while still in the womb, the name of God and of St Ibar, the bishop, was made great (extolled). This was the first miracle he performed.[1]

§2. Then, after the lapse of a moment the boy whose deeds we propose to write about was born. And when the king heard the boy had been born

---

1   The druid of king Colmán, son of Neman, during the course of a chariot ride with Lugna, father of Ibar, and his pregnant wife, declares that: *Hic currus sub rege sonat.* After some discussion the druid explained that his words were addressed to the child about to be born. A messenger brought a stone from the king to the expecting mother – a stone which metamorphosed into the foot of a leek with twelve shoots. Lugna made his wife eat it, whereupon her face took on the red hue of a yew tree. This is the origin of the name Ibar. You will note in this paragraph that some of the words are not medieval (*certificare*, and, twice, *explorare*). These indicate a hangover from the Renaissance.

through divine inspiration he said, 'He will baptize me.' And by this prophecy of the king he is reckoned to have been baptized by St Ibar.[2]

§3. Lugna had four sons, namely Ibar, the Long Son, Coemanus of the many colours, and Moloc. Ibar was the older, called Nemanus by small boys, just as St Columba called Nemanus the most noble and chief bishop. And Comactus was called by another name, that is, 'more increased/greater' because of his size, since he was eighteen feet in length.[3]

§4. On a certain day, St Ibar, having the care of the lambs and calves of his parents, marked out the ground between them and the mothers; and the thirsty young ones, although they were being held in a narrow space, did not advance beyond the set-out boundary to the line of ranks of their mothers who were dripping milk, nor did the mothers advance to their bleating and bellowing offspring. Seeing this they praised the Lord.[4]

§5. When St Ibar had come to the age of learning ecclesiastical behaviour and of cultivating himself in divine dogmas in order that, as is befitting, he himself should be (serve) under a master, he (that is, Ibar) who was predestined by God to become the master of many, and who, with the future help of the Holy Spirit, would lead many of the same stock from error to the Catholic faith, accompanied by his father came to Motta the master of the Lugnadensis state, and he waited with the bishop because he saw three angels ministering. And that day on which St Ibar had come to St Motta was Christmas day. And when they were sitting in the church St Motta began to recite the psalms to them. Ibar intent on the divine sermon, fell asleep secretly in front of the (his) master. Rising from his sleep, he had learned in his heart as if they were soliloquies, the bishop's sermons. Because he (Ibar) was reading the rules/canons with Motta, he became wise and very eloquent.[5]

2   The king predicts that the child will baptize him.
3   The names of the four sons of Lugna; the Book of Leinster, much more complete, cites rather four sisters of the saint. Two other names of Ibar are noted, together with an etymological essay after the fashion of Irish erudites of the Middle Ages: this too is further developed and clarified in the Book of Leinster.
4   As with most of the Irish saints, a childhood miracle is attributed to the pre-school days of the young Ibar, an invisible but unbreachable line separating the shepherds from their lambs, the cows from their calves. This particular miracle is to be met with elsewhere, occasionally enhanced by lively details.
5   At school age Ibar is entrusted to the care of St Mochta of Lugnad. The *Vita* spells it always as Motta but the identification is nevertheless clear: it is Mochta of Louth, commemorated in the Martyrologies on both 24 March and 19 August. Ussher presumed this hagiography to be referring to a different Mochta than Mochta of Lugmad, bishop and disciple of St Patrick. This indicates that he was not familiar with the *Vita Ibari* in its original form, only with Fr Henri FitzSimon's resume: the *Vita Ibari* is authenticated beyond all doubt by the testimony of the Book of Leinster. Here it must suffice to observe that both of these inedited texts place Ibar at a time far later than that of St Patrick.

§6. On another occasion St Ibar, setting out to visit his parents, came to the court of a certain queen, which had for its defence a rampart and overhanging towers, and, seeking to obtain hospitality from them, he was refused. Then Ibar in response to the queen said, 'I withdraw because these houses will be burnt by fire.' St Ibar left the court/villa and suddenly a funeral pyre began to burn the houses. A messenger was sent after St Ibar, and St Ibar returned to that same villa. When the queen surrendered totally to him her territory with its appurtenances, suddenly (swifter than the word) the fire vanished. Upon seeing this they hoped in God.[6]

§7. At another time St Ibar on his journey, wishing to baptize a child, and not being able to find water, ordered a sod of earth which he had uprooted and blessed to pour forth fountains, in which the baptism was performed. The boy having been baptized served God and St Ibar for ever.[7]

§8. At one time St Ibar visited his pupil Sethna. He, however complained bitterly about the lack of food for refreshing (feeding) his master (that is, St Ibar). Learning this, the saint said to him, 'Only proceed to your wine, and behold the king's manager (procter), bringing the food to his king, will come to you; and do not doubt but that he will hand it over to you. Because this night he will be freed from his king, and tomorrow he will merit admission to the heavenly kingdom.' And all these things according to the prophecy of

---

Ibar, during the offices of Christmas night, fell into a type of ecstatic fit. This episode is, however, very obscurely described. Ibar studied with St Mochta.

6 Ibar goes to visit his parents. Undoubtedly this took place early in his career. He was refused hospitality by a queen (or her people, the text is not clear on this point). As a punishment he predicted a fire in the royal residence, and then left. He was called back and miraculously put out the fire, but only after being given this territory (unspecified) by the queen. This incident is not unique among Lives of the Irish saints: any list of miracles punishing inhospitable people would be a long one. Chastisement by fire is, however, rare. The basis of this story may be quite old, but the reader will note that the terms used by the hagiographer would suggest the later Middle Ages, and are definitely later than the arrival in Ireland of a feudal vocabulary: *villa* for a Celtic *dún* and particularly the phrase *cum suis pertinentibus totaliter*. Neither is this popular Latin. The *Vita Ibari*, in general, resembles various other brief Lives of Irish saints – resumes of other pieces that are longer and richer in place- and personal-names. The only noticeable characteristic of the writer is a fondness for *ait* (rather than *dicit* or *inquit*). The expression *Concedo quod haec modo tecta comburentur igne* has a strongly Gaelic stamp to it. This would be, in a literal translation of the equivalent Irish, *I permit* or *It is permitted (by God and by me) that this house be burned* – in the sense of a prediction rather than a concession.

7 Ibar caused a fountain to spring up in order to baptize a child, whose name is not recorded, nor that of the place, although the original tale certainly aims to specify a place, the abridger clearly found such details of little importance. It was probably a water-source sacred to St Ibar. The child (and of course his descendants) became servants to the saint for all time. The way in which this perpetual service is expressed is noticeably more archaic than the previous paragraph, and more Celtic: *Sancto Ybaro per saecula serviebat.*

St Ibar concerning Sethna and the king's steward (treasure) were fulfilled by God.[8]

§9. On a certain occasion the king of Midie advancing with his army pitched his camp in the church of Faber. His soldiers with difficulty carried a wine cask to make a bath for the king. The king, however, having bathed in it could not get out of the cask because his limbs were securely stuck to its planks/boards. The king, realizing this, promised that he would make reparation to St Ibar, and the king was released from his bonds and got out of the cask safely.[9]

§10. At that time an intolerable disease, which in Irish is called *Budiconail*, (the yellow plague) and in Latin, *Fulva pestis*, was laying Ireland waste. To try for a cure of this, the nephews of Colmán, the Great King of Mide, came to St Ibar, and, St Ibar freeing them from this plague, they departed safe and well for their country.[10]

---

8 Ibar pays a visit to his disciple Sédna. Could this be the saint commemorated on 9 March in the Tallaght Martyrology: *Setna Chill Ané i Sleibh Bregh* (Sédnade Cell Ané in Sliab Breg)? Slieve Bray is the collection of hills which stretches towards the east from Clogher (Co. Louth) to Rathkenny (Co. Meath). The proximity of the plains of Mide and of Rath Cennaig would seem to confirm it is indeed this Sedna. Sedna appears to have received his master rather reluctantly, due to the cost of vitals. Ibar caused him to be given all that was necessary by a king's attendant (or the king himself) who happened to be passing. This version is but a clumsy abridgement. To judge from similar incidents in different Lives, the words *in vitem tuam perge,* spoken to Sédna, were a reference, in the original, to the public road, the highway, the royal way. The text would have explained too why the attendant was imprisoned by the king and then released, and finally the circumstance of his death the next day. The terms *procurator* and *dispensator,* applied to this attendant, seem not very ancient: before the year 1000 more or less, one would expect in the Latin of Ireland, various forms of the word *oeconomus*; perhaps the writer was not a royal civil servant, but a pretentious noble of inferior rank.

9 The king of Mide, with his army, struck camp in *Ecclesia Fabri*, one of the rare precise localities given by the *Vita Ibari* during this career of its hero from the end of his childhood till the moment when, abandoning his first monastery, he went to Leinster, to Beggerin (see §11 below). The identification of this *Ecclesia Fabri* would be precious, but it seems impossible. Supposing that, unable to discover this toponym in any other sources, one translated *Cell Gobán,*, 'Church of the Forge', and that this were an erroneous translation for some church named for a St Gobán or Gobán, *Cell Gob(b)áin,* very similar in pronunciation. This would be, for example, Kilgobbin, in the parish of the barony of Rathdown, Co Dublin – half-way between this town and Enniskerry. One St Gobán of Cell Gobáin figures in the genealogies, and his father is called Lugna, like that of St Ibar. To be thorough one must also recall Kilgowan, hamlet of the parish of Kilcullen in the barony of the same name, Co. Kildare, and the place called Tech Da Gabha or Tech Da Gobháin, anglicized as Teachgowe in 1406, as *tech* can also mean a church. In the author's opinion, a link surely exists between this *Ecclesia Fabri*, where it must be situated, and St Ibar. He intervened to chastise the king's people, who had captured a barrel and made a bath out of it. The king could not get out of his bath until he promised satisfaction to St Ibar.

10 The plague, called *Budiconaill* in Irish, in Latin *Fulva Pestis*, showed itself in Ireland – which dates us about 555. The *Nepotes Magni Colmáni regis Middiae*, that is, Clann

§11. After the king and an immense crowd of people of his race/stock had been baptized and converted, St Ibar with his followers entered the territories of the Laginenses (the Leinstermen) and came to an island which is called Beggerin, and in blessing it he said that neither would the living here be drowned, nor the dead be destroyed/annihilated for ever. And this was granted by God.[11]

§12. At another time a certain German hero named Tarlaeb, coming from Germany, arrived at the island of St Ibar the bishop, carried off with him to his own country the ring of the church. And when he arrived he gave the ring to an artisan/smith to cleanse it in the fire. But when the smith put it in the fire he lost his eyes. When he saw this miracle, the criminal tyrant, feeling that he himself deserved such (punishment) set out to return to the same island and he gave his offspring for ever to St Ibar the bishop.[12]

§13. On a certain sixth festive day guests came to St Ibar the bishop, at dinner/mealtime. St Ibar the bishop, thought it unworthy to offer such people food without fish. Rising suddenly St Ibar proceeded to the seashore and

> Colmáin Móir, later known as Uí Maelechlainn, the family of the Uí Néill of the South, rulers of Mide, came to St Ibar and begged protection from the danger. On the promise of his help they returned to their homes, *in suam patriam*. All we can conclude from this is that the author is representing St Ibar as established, either outside the kingdom of Mide or at least at some distance from the residence of the Uí Néill.
>
> 11 Ibar converts the king and a great people, undoubtedly that of Mide. He then emigrates to Leinster to occupy the Isle of Beggerin, which he blesses so that the inhabitants will drown no longer, and the dead will not perish- an obscure example of the one of the privileges which the Irish saints are frequently known to have granted those places where they fixed their abodes. The second part of the promise evokes a special and incongruous grace, also to be found elsewhere: those who are buried in the saint's cemetery will escape hell. Our abbreviator, if he understood something from the text under his eyes, did not reproduce it clearly.
>
> 12 This section includes the passage paraphrased by Ussher in his distinctive fashion. A *Germanicus heros,* named Torlaeb (perhaps Torlieb in the original), came from Germany to the isle of St Ibar and took the ring from the temple. Once home, he took this ring to his forge, which was struck by disaster. The tyrant returned to the saint's island, returned the ring to its place, and made a gift of all his descendants to St Ibar (that is to his church, to his monastery, to his successors): *suamque progeniem sancto Ybaro episcopo per saecula donavit.* It is difficult to see how a warrior living in Germany (or elsewhere on the Continent) would, in the Irish fashion, put his descendants at the service of a religious institution in the bay of Wexford. The hypothesis given below, from an inhabitant of the neighbouring city (Scandinavian since the tenth century at the latest), seems highly likely. The *annalus* of the temple would have the same origin: such an object does not form part, to the best of our knowledge, of the usual furnishings of a Celtic church, whereas the custom of swearing oaths on rings is well known amongst the Scandinavians. Very specific, localized genealogical research will enable us one day, maybe, to discover, in Wexford or nearby, traces of a family of Germanic, probably Scandinavian, origin, and the name of Torlaeb or Torlieb. Such a detail would confirm the tale, constructed in order to make sense of this anomaly: a Scandinavian family in the service of a Celtic church.

blessed the sea. When the sea had been blessed by the saint, a certain wild beast that was traversing the sea and carrying around three hundred and seventy fish was driven on to the shore. All seeing this miracle with wonder glorified God.[13]

13 St Ibar is receiving guests one Friday night. Before offering them fish, he blesses the sea. A sea monster reveals itself purposely in order to fulfil the obligatory role of a boat. We know of no parallels to this tale.

The text ends abruptly. It is silent on the final years of this saint whom other Lives represent as the founder of a school attended by people from near and far (at Beggerin).

It is permitted to agree, in concluding this critical analysis, with the opinion of Sirinus, who knew something of the matter. He was not entirely wrong in judging this Life '*incompletam, … sed egregiam si esset a librariis mendis expurgata*' – that which we are obliged to obtain. Thanks to this text, we can lift a corner of the veil which hid the first part of St Ibar's career, that which he spent in his native region and which had escaped even the most piercing eyes. It is easy, now, to see what others had missed: some of the details transmitted by Ussher should have located the first monastic foundation of St Ibar in the kingdom of Mide or thereabouts, at about the year 550. The name of this establishment has not come down to us. It is not impossible that the plague forced its abandonment and that it was never revived.

Some of the details briefly given in the *Vita Ibari* are confirmed by a more ancient and explicit text, the same one as that to which Sirinus directed Papebroch and which we print here. It is contained in the hagiographic file, created from many different bits and pieces – genealogies, lists, litanies, mnemonic poems, which are shown in the Book of Leinster after the Tallaght Martyrology. This vast collection, the composition of which is placed at about 1160, is most certainly later for the most part. The transcription of it was prolonged over many decades. M.R.I. Best, in his recent study, demonstrated that the scribe Áed Úa Crimthainn began it after 1151 and that he was still working on it in 1160, in 1189, in 1193 and in 1201. He laid down his pen, and possibly died, between this date and 1224.

The passage concerning St Ibar comes immediately before the (unedited) Treatise on the maternal ancestry of the Irish saints. His insertion at this point, which saved him from destruction, because there is no other witness to it, is undoubtedly explained by this. Effectively, a passage from the Treatise which follows it deals with St Ibar's mother.

8

St Abbán of Adamstown

The Lives of Abbán

There are five manuscript copies of the Life of Abbán in existence. A Latin copy in Marsh's Library, Dublin, has been published in Plummer (1910, i, 3-33). A similar copy, but with the final parts missing, is in Trinity College, Dublin. Another Latin version, considered to be a shortened version of those in Marsh's and Trinity College Libraries, is found in the Codex Salmanticensis. Now in the Bibliothèque Royale, Brussels, it has been edited by Heist (1965, 256-74). Two copies in Irish, one in the Stowe MS, written in 1627 by Domhnall O'Dinneen, now in the Royal Irish Academy, the other by Brother Michael O'Clery, in the Bibliothèque Royale, Brussels, have been collated and translated by Plummer (1922, ii, 3-10). Both Latin and Irish Lives may go back to a common source, but with many additions and omissions which obscure their relationship to one another.

The Lives of Abbán have been closely examined by scholars. Because of their complexity and the fact that he is listed for two dates in the martyrologies, 16 March and 27 October, the Bollandists suggested that there were two saints bearing the name Abbán. This, however, has been rejected by Plummer and Heist. Later scholars such as Ó Riain (1986, 159-70) and Sharpe (1991) ignore any such implication. Heist (1976, 84) tentatively suggested that the Latin Lives now in Dublin were written in the Wexford area, 'possibly Moyarney (Adamstown) where the saint is buried'. Ó Riain (1986, 163) disagrees with this, feeling that this monastery would not have been capable of producing such a Life. He believes that the Latin Life was compiled at Ferns by Bishop Ailbhe O'Mulloy and that one purpose of this undertaking was to establish his, the bishop's, right to certain church properties in Wexford, such as Templeshanbo and St Abbán's monastery, later dedicated to St Stephen, at Morrisseysland, New Ross, against the claims of the recently arrived Normans.

Genealogy and education

In the Lives Abbán is said to be the son of Cormac, son of Ailill, of the Dál Cormaic, who according to the Annals of the Four Masters died in 435. Abbán's pedigree is found in the Book of Leinster, Leabhar Breac and Rawlinson B 502, in Oxford. It is given in Ó Riain (1985, 46) as son of Laignech, son of Mac Cainnech, son of Cabraid, son of Cormaic, son of Cú Corb. His uncle was Ibar of the Uí Echach Ulad of Co. Down. Abbán's mother was Ibar's sister Milla who married Laignech of the Dál Cormaic, one of the principal families of Leinster. Abbán is said to have been raised by foster parents, as was the custom at the time, but at an early age he showed a love of the religious life. His parents wanted him as their heir, he refused saying, 'everything is nought save God'. A story in the Life describes how he was put in chains and placed in the hostages pit but by next morning he was miraculously freed, whereupon his parents no longer objected to his chosen path (Plummer, 1922, ii, 3-4). According to the Latin Life in Marsh's Library he was educated at Ibar's monastery on Beggerin Island, in Wexford Harbour.

When did Abbán live?

It is difficult, if not impossible, to know precisely when the saint lived since all the data on his Life is unreliable. If he was the son of Cormac of Ailill, who died in 435, he could belong to the fifth and early sixth centuries. He was nephew of St Ibar, who died around 500. Also, he is said to have baptized Finnian of Clonard, who died in 549. But Hughes (1954, 360) felt that this may have been a way of associating Finnian with a famous Leinster saint who was known as 'the apostle of Leinster'. Abbán's church at Camaross was attacked by Cormac Mac Diarmata, who was active in the second half of the sixth century. Plummer (1910, i, p. xxv) stated: 'It is probable that he belongs to the sixth and seventh centuries, and that his life has been prolonged backwards by local patriotism, the process being helped by silently dropping three or four links in his pedigree.' The year of his death is not recorded in the annals.

Abbán's missionary work

Judging by the account in his Life Abbán seems to have been a dedicated and tireless worker for the new religion. Foundations are attributed to him in Connacht before he journeyed into Munster, where he is said to have founded churches in Dingle, Co. Kerry, and Ballyvourney, Co. Cork. According to the Life he gave St Gobnat his church there.

On his arrival in Leinster, Abbán came into the territory of Slieve Margy, Co. Laois, where he founded the monastery of Killabban. Later he founded two monasteries in Co. Meath, one called Killabban, the other Ceall

Ailbhe or Sinche. This latter monastery was founded for St Segnich (Sinchea) and other holy virgins. Sinchea is said to have died in 597. According to Ó Riain, Ceall Ailbhe is probably the modern Clonalvy, near Duleek.

The claim that the monastery of Abingdon, near Oxford, was founded by Abbán is erroneous. The fiction was propounded in the Life of Abbán and was included in a revised version of the chronicle of that monastery, possibly at the instigation of Bishop Ailbhe O'Mulloy of Ferns. Abbán's supposed function there was to convert the king and his people. Ó Riain (1986, 165) thinks that Ailbhe, who was familiar with southern Britain, would have deliberately chosen this place 'because its Latin name, Abbendun, provided an ideal proof of the saint's dwelling there'. This was a subtle counter-attack by the bishop against English accusations of waywardness among the Irish clergy by inferring that Irish help was needed by the English church at that time.

Abbán's Wexford churches

The story of how Abbán was directed to Uí Cheinnselaig by an angel is in keeping with the Lives of other saints. He was directed to travel to Uí Cheinnselaig, from where he would go to heaven when he died. There, too, he would found monasteries and churches in the remaining time of his life.

Abbán's first foundation in Co. Wexford was at Magh Arnaidhe, meaning 'the plain of the berries'. The name was later changed to Adamstown after a Norman, Adam Devereux, whose family was granted land in the area. Magh Arnaidhe seems never to have developed into an important monastery, possibly because it was located in Uí Bairrche territory, which was taken over by the rising Uí Cheinnselaig, or because the family which supported it diminished in importance. This family may have lived in the large ringfort, now destroyed, at Coolnagree. The only references to Magh Arnaidhe are found in the saint's Lives, in his genealogy and in the Martyrology of Gorman. No abbots have been listed in the Annals and as Ó Riain states it is difficult to see the name of an important pre-Norman monastery being changed to Adamstown. Yet the presence of a cross, thought to date to the eighth century, points to continuity of religion and ritual on this spot.

Abbán is credited with founding a great monastery at New Ross (Plummer, 1910, i, 21), but it never became important. According to Abbán's Life, St Evin was associated with this monastery, but Gwynn and Hadcock (1970, 398) say that this is because the name of his monastery at Ros-glas (Monastereven) became confused with that of Ros Mhic Treoin (New Ross). The same authors suggest that Abbán's monastery may have been located at the present site of St Stephen's chapel and cemetery at Morrisseysland outside New Ross where there are two bullaun stones. But

Hore (i, 46 and 74) claims that his monastery was located near the later site
of the north gate of New Ross town.

Abbán's other churches were at Camaross and at Druim Cain Ceallaidh
(location unknown). The Life also claims that Templeshanbo (Seanboith
Ard) was given to Abbán, but this was probably to justify the bishop of
Ferns' title to the property when this version of the Life was being compiled early in the thirteenth century.

Abbán's miracles
The miracles attributed to the saint are standard for the time. There is a vivid
description in the Life of how Abbán, although old and decrepit, restored his
friend Conall of Templeshanbo to life, whereupon Conall offered his family,
servants and lands to Abbán's monastery for ever (see p. 145, below).

Abbán was reputed to have great power over the water, a myth which
led Plummer (1910, i, pp xxiv-xxv) to suggest that 'a cycle of stories connected with the Celtic Water-God has got attached to the saint; perhaps
through some vague idea that his name was connected with *abhann* the Irish
word for river'. This characteristic comes out, not merely in the incidents
related but in the special power over the waters which is expressly attributed to the saint. One incident relates how Abbán prevented a huge wave
from devastating the land, whereupon an angel informed him that God had
given him power over the sea such as he never gave to anyone before, and
that no one who goes to sea in a coracle or ship shall fail to return safe, if
he recited (this couplet) thrice in the name of the Trinity:

> The coracle of Abbán on the water,
> And the fair company of Abbán in it.   [Plummer, 1922, ii, 6]

Abbán also cured the sick, the dumb, the lame and the paralysed. The saint
is said to have visited Rome several times, at least once in the company of
his uncle, Ibar of Beggerin.

Historical value of the Lives of Abbán
The Lives of Abbán have several points of historical interest relating to Co.
Wexford. One incident relates how his church at Camaross was attacked; 'At
a certain time Cormac, son of Diarmait, king of Uí Cheinnselaig, plundered
Camross, the church of St Abbán, wishing to expel his household from it,
and to have the buildings under his own control' (Plummer, 1910, i, 23).
This Diarmait was of the Uí Bairrche. The Life of Comgall of Bangor
(Plummer, 1910, ii, 16) relates how he later became a monk at Bangor.

Several well known place-names in Co. Wexford are mentioned: Magh
Arnaidhe (now Adamstown), Camaross, Ros Mhic Treoin, (New Ross) and
Seanboith Ard (Templeshanbo).

In the Life, Abbán is stated to have had a special place in the woods called Dísert Cendubháin where he fasted and prayed. In the Charters of Earl Richard Marshal of the Forests of Ross and Taghmon (Orpen, 1934, 55) the place-name Kyldouan (Cill Dubháin) is listed in the vicinity of Colp, which Orpen identifies as Collop's Well, Newbawn.

Also listed is Find Magh, meaning 'the bright plain'. Here the saint immobilized those who attacked his church at Camaross but on relenting was rewarded with the Find Magh by the king.

Based on their dedications to a saint, Mac Ó Charmaig, two churches in Argyll in Scotland have been associated with Abbán. Plummer (1910, i, pp xxiii-xxivn) referred to Abbán's churches in Scotland and Mac Lean (1983, 49-65) identified them as being at Keills, Knapdale, and on Eilean Mór in the Sound of Jura. Ó Riain (1983, 21-4) has suggested that the dedications may be to St Columcille. There is no evidence that Abbán ever visited Scotland.

Abbán's death and burial

All the indications from the Lives are that Abbán spent the later years of his life in Uí Cheinnselaig from where the angel had told him he would go to heaven. Thus he probably died at Magh Arnaidhe. The day of his death is given in the martyrologies as 27 October but the year is uncertain. This is not surprising as the records for Leinster are poor until the eighth century.

A rather unedifying story about Abbán's funeral is found in the Codex Salmanticensis (Heist, 1965, 272-4). Because of the relic value of his body and its commercial significance for the monastery which possessed it, monks from two of his establishments, one in north Leinster, possibly Killabban, Co. Laois, the other in Uí Cheinnselaig, probably Adamstown, sought to have his corpse. While this was being secretly carried off by the north Leinster men the monks from his Uí Cheinnselaig monastery intercepted them. By a miracle his body was made to appear on two separate oxcarts. But the oxen going towards north Leinster rushed headlong into a stream and were never seen again. It is believed that Abbán's body was buried in his own monastery at Adamstown, although a grave reputed to be his, is located at Ballyvourney, Co. Cork, where it is marked by three ogham stones and a bullaun stone.

Abbán remembered

Churches in Adamstown and Whitechurch are dedicated to him and Abbán, pronounced Abban, is still commonly used as a Christian name in Co. Wexford.

9

St Aidán or Máedóg of Ferns

The Lives of St Aidán

The earliest Life of Aidán, or Máedóg as he is called in the Lives, in existence dates to around 1200 (Doherty, 1986, 364). It is a Latin version of an earlier Life in Irish which has never been found. Doherty (1987, 18-19) places the origin of this, now lost, Irish Life in the reign of Diarmait Mac Máel na mBó, who was king of Leinster from 1042 to 1072. The purpose of compiling it, no doubt, was to justify the premier position of Ferns at the expense of Clonmore, Co. Carlow, which belonged to a rival faction of Uí Cheinnselaig. This Irish Life was translated into Latin in the late eleventh and early twelfth century (Plummer, 1910, ii, 295-311). A copy now in the British Library is called the V (Vespasian) text.

Other copies of his Latin Lives are found in the Bibliothèque Royale, Brussels, (thirteenth century), in Marsh's Library, Dublin (fifteenth century) and in the Rawlinson Collection, Oxford. These versions of Aidán's Life deal mainly with the church of Ferns. Plummer (1922, ii, 177-83) has also translated into English a short Latin Life found in the Stowe MS.

According to Sharpe (1991, 362) the version in Marsh's Library, printed in Plummer (1910, ii, 141-63), was probably made at Ferns under the direction of Ailbhe O'Mulloy, bishop of Ferns (1186-1223) around 1218. The purpose, reflected in the association of an earlier powerful king, Brandubh (died 605) with Aidán was clearly designed to boost the importance of the monastery of Ferns.

A Life in Irish was copied by Brother Michael O'Clery, of the Four Masters, in 1629. This long Life, now in the Bibliothèque Royale, Brussels, was printed in English by Plummer (1922, i, 184-357). According to Doherty (1986, 366) this Life is basically a version of the Latin Life made in the eleventh century but with a large amount of additional material on churches in Bréifne, Aidán's native territory.

Plummer (1922, i, p. xxxvii) gives the following explanation for the diversity of material in this long Life:

A writer, who was probably connected with the monastery of Rossinver, wishing to compose a Life of his founder, took as the basis of his work the Latin Life of the M (Marsh's) recension, which he translated and expanded. But as this dealt mainly with Ferns, he interpolated it with various sections derived from northern sources, dealing with Drumlane and Rossinver, and the various families of Bréifne, Fermanagh and Oriel.

A complication in dealing with the Life of Aidán is that there was another saint Máedóg located at Clonmore, Co. Carlow, whose Life was conflated or mixed up with that of Aidán of Ferns. According to Doherty (1987, 10-22) this may have been done deliberately to play down, or even eliminate, the role of the Clonmore saint and to enhance the importance of Brandubh and of Ferns, and by association, the reigning Uí Cheinnselaig king, Diarmait Mac Máel na mBó.

The Lives of Aidán contain the standard incidents of the saints' Lives, most of them manifestly fanciful to modern minds. It was not until Doherty, in 1986, made a detailed study that the value of many of the references became intelligible, particularly as they relate to political developments in the kingdoms of Uí Cheinnselaig and Bréifne.

Genealogy and education

Aidán was born at a place now called Port Island, in the parish of Templeport, Co. Cavan. The exact year of his birth is unknown but it was probably before the middle of the sixth century. He was of noble birth like all the famous saints. His father's name was Setna of the tribe Uí Meic Uais, one of the tribes of the kingdom of Airgialla. His mother's name was Eithne of the Uí Amalgai tribe (Ó Riain, 1985, 11) Co. Mayo. Following the Gaelic custom of the time, Aidán would have been sent into fosterage at a young age.

In the Irish Lives Aidán is always referred to as Máedóg, now pronounced Mogue. This form of the name is derived from Áedh (Hugh) by the addition of the term of endearment *mo* meaning 'my' and the diminutive *óc* or *óg*, meaning young.

Aidán appears to have studied for some years at St David's foundation at Menevia (now St David's), in Pembrokeshire, South Wales, where he was probably ordained a priest. This area was then under the control of the Déisi from the Waterford region.

Aidán's missionary work

Aidán left Menevia and crossed the Irish Sea to Uí Cheinnselaig, landing at a place called Ard Ladrann, which is thought to be around Ardamine in north Co. Wexford. There he built his first church on land given to him by the local chief, Dimma, son of Fintan (Plummer, 1922, ii, 205). Over the following years Aidán is reputed to have founded churches in Uí Cheinnselaig at Clonmore, Clone and Clongeen (Flood, 1916). In Co. Waterford churches attributed to Aidán were at Fennor, Kilmoyemore and Dysert, Ardmore. These were in Déisi territory, as were David's foundations in Wales. Churches are also attributed to him in his native Bréifne at Drumlane, Co. Cavan, and Rossinver, Co. Leitrim.

Ferns founded

It was at Ferns that Aidán established his most important foundation. The likely sequence of events seems to be that land there was first given to Aidán by a local landowner named Becc, a cousin of Brandubh, king of Uí Cheinnselaig and Leinster. Later more land may have been given to Aidán at Ferns by Brandubh himself in thanksgiving for curing him of a terrible sickness. For this cure Brandubh was also said to have made Aidán the first bishop of Uí Cheinnselaig, (which was later to become the diocese of Ferns), and also archbishop of Leinster, although no such position existed in the seventh century Irish church. The chronological sequence in the Life is hopelessly confused, a matter criticised by O'Clery as early as 1629 (Doherty, 1986, 366).

In a late version of the Boruma story Aidán was reputed to have helped Brandubh defeat the high king, Áedh Mac Ainmire, at Dunbolg, Co. Wicklow (Stokes, 1892). But earlier versions of the Boruma story attribute the victory to the intervention of St Moling and Máedóg of Clonmore.

The close relationship between Aidán and Brandubh, the powerful Uí Cheinnselaig king of Leinster (killed 605), was promoted to enhance the prestige of Ferns by a writer from Ferns, or at least of Uí Cheinnselaig stock.

Monastic life and manual work

Since Aidán was educated at St David's monastery in Wales it is likely that the regime of work and prayer practised there would have been followed in Ferns. Unlike Taghmon, it was not regarded as particularly harsh, though to a modern view it was extremely austere. In Wales, as described by Ryan (1931, 161), each monk toiled at daily labour, they 'dig the ground with mattocks and spades, carry in their holy hands hoes and saws for cutting, provide with their own industry all the necessities of the community. The rest of their time is spent in prayer and chanting of the psalms'.

At Ferns, apart from his religious duties, Aidán seems to have been involved in the farming activities on the monastic lands. Thus, he is credited with possession of two cows and a calf at Ard Ladrann (Ardamine).

There are references to him sowing barley, reaping corn with one hundred and fifty other monks at Ferns and grinding wheat in the mill. He is mentioned as sowing cherries, apples and alders, as well as having a fruit garden. He also had sheep at Ferns.

St Aidán's miracles

In common with all the other saints various miracles are attributed to St Aidán. He raised two children to life, who had been drowned in Lough Erne. In Wales he cured the blind, deaf and lame son of the king of the Britons. At Ferns, when the monastery was being built, his disciples complained that there was no water near the place. Aidán ordered them to cut down a large tree, whereupon a spring gushed forth which was named after the saint. Some of the miracles have an agricultural basis. For example, one describes how Aidán, looking from Ard Ladrann, saw a ploughman fall between the share and the coulter at Ferns (a distance of twelve miles). Aidán raised his hand and the ploughteam of oxen stopped, so saving the man.

Not all the miracles were of the benign kind. It was well known and greatly feared that saints could call down mighty curses and inflict great suffering on those who offended them. Aidán was no exception as the following extract from the Life shows:

> Another day Máedóg was grinding wheat in the mill, the brothers being all engaged on other business. An Ossory man came in, and took some of the meal from him by force. The same man came again afterwards, having changed his look and appearance by deliberately closing one of his eyes, and asked for some of the meal as a gift. Máedóg looked at him, and asked him what made him look like that, though he knew very well. And he added: 'Thou shalt have some meal to take with thee; nevertheless, thou shalt be permanently blind of one eye, and thy seed after thee shall never be without some one-eyed man among them'. And this was fulfilled.
>
> [Plummer, 1922, ii, 208].

The cult of St Aidán

St Aidán has been revered in Ferns probably since his death in 624. The Life written in Ferns points up his friendship with Brandubh, king of Uí Cheinnselaig and Leinster, who made him bishop over his kingdom. In this case the Life of Aidán is being used in the twelfth century to enhance the prestige of the monastery of Ferns.

His Life is used even more explicitly by the O'Rourke's of Bréifne. As Doherty (1986, 368) explains, Drumlane, the chief church in Bréifne, was claiming headship of Aidán's establishment, including Ferns, in the eleventh century. Conaing Ua Fairchellaig, who died in 1059, was coarb of Drumlane and Ferns (AFM). This reflected the growing power of the O'Rourke dynasty. Later Rossinver became important in the struggle between the O'Rourkes and the O'Reillys. Aidán's death and subsequent burial at Rossinver would have conferred considerable prestige on that establishment. More likely, however, Aidán died at Ferns and was buried there, although the site of his grave is unknown.

The inter-family struggles for the kingship of Uí Cheinnselaig are also reflected in the Lives according to Doherty (1987, 10-22). The main branch of the family residing at Ferns was being challenged by another branch from Clonmore, Co. Carlow, in the late tenth century. The person who led the revolt, Áed Mac Echtighern, was killed at Ferns in 1003. In 1040 Diarmait Máel na mBó plundered Clonmore. Later the Life of its saint, also named Máedóg, was suppressed. It was probably around this time that the Lives of the two Máedógs were conflated. Various churches within Co. Wexford, such as Ferns and Enniscorthy cathedrals, Ardamine, Clone, Clongeen, Coolhull and Kilnahue are dedicated to St Aidán. The medieval parish of Shemoge (St Mogue), now part of Bannow, is also called after him. The name Mogue, derived from Máedóg, was popular in Co. Wexford up to recent times.

Death and burial

The year of Aidán's death is not known for certain. The Annals of the Four Masters record it at 624 and the Annals of Tigernach at 625 and 656. The erroneous 656 date is repeated in the Chronicum Scotorum (Hennessy, 1866), but this obviously refers to Máedóg of Clonmore, Co. Carlow.

The significance of a saint's place of burial is clearly shown by the last passage in Aidán's Life:

> And though Máedóg passed to heaven, he did not cease from his miracles on earth. For by the earth (of his sepulchre), by his clothing, and by his relics were healed blind and deaf and lame and all other diseases. And though we have related some of the miracles of Máedóg, we have not related the whole of them. On the second day of the month of February Máedóg joined the company of angels and archangels in the Unity of the Blessed Trinity, Father, Son, and Holy Spirit, Amen.   [Plummer, 1922, ii, 183]

The Breac Máedóg

It is as well to mention this tomb-shaped shrine here, if only to clear up the confusion surrounding its date of origin. Traditionally the Breac was supposed to have been given to Máedóg by St Molaise of Devenish and to have contained a relic brought from Rome. However, art experts such as Francoise Henry (1970), date the shrine to the eleventh or twelfth century. A leather satchel, also used to carry it, is in the National Museum along with the shrine itself.

According to the Life (Plummer, 1922, ii, 258) the Breac was given to Rossinver by Máedóg. It was a reliquary containing 'relics of Stephen, Lawrence, Clement, the ankle of Martin and some hair of the Virgin Mary and many other relics of saints and holy virgins'. This unlikely collection of material gave rise to the name *breac*, meaning speckled. The Breac was kept at Drumlane, where solemn oaths were sworn on it. In the last century it was loaned for this purpose by the parish priest for a security of one guinea. The borrower, however, sold it, but fortunately it was acquired by George Petrie and eventually passed to the National Museum.

A detailed description of the Breac Máedóg can be found in Mahr, 1941, 152-4.

10

St Munnu or Fintan of Taghmon

The Lives of Munnu

Of the many accounts of saints Lives which have come down to us few are more informative than that of Munnu of Taghmon. No saint's Life was written during their lifetime, most of those surviving date to the eleventh and twelfth centuries. However, the earliest Life of Munnu is thought by scholars such as Sharpe (1991, 338) to date to around 800. This dating is based mainly on linguistic evidence but also on some historical references in the Life.

There are four versions of Munnu's Life, all in Latin. The earliest and fullest text is found in the Codex Salmanticensis, in the Bibliothèque Royale, Brussels. Other versions derived from this are in Marsh's Library and Trinity College Library, Dublin, and in the Rawlinson B Mss, Oxford. A copy of the Brussels text was printed in Heist (1965, 198-209). A shorter version derived from this is printed in Plummer (1910, ii, 226-38). Plummer's text has been translated into English by John Hunt, MA. A copy is included at the end of this chapter. Unless otherwise referenced, the following account of the saint's life is based on this version.

Munnu's genealogy and education

Munnu belonged to the Cinél Conaill of the northern Uí Néill whose territory at this time covered most of Donegal and whose stronghold was at Grianán Ailech. His father's name was Tulchán, whose genealogy is well documented (Ó Riain, 1985, 26). According to the Martyrology of Óengus he was a druid; in fact, Munnu himself was accused of being a druid in his youth (cf. Manus O'Donnell's *Betha Colaim Cille*, edited by O'Kelleher and Schoepperle, 1918, 161). Munnu's mother, Fidelma, was also of Northern Uí Néill lineage.

The year of the saint's birth is not known for certain but must have been around the middle of the sixth century. He was named Finn or Fionn, or Mo-Fhionn-u, which was easily elided into Munnu, the name by which he became known. He was also known as Fintan, the name by which he is called locally. The names Finn and Fionn are synonomous, both meaning 'fair'.

Columcille, who had obviously known him, gave a colourful description of the physical appearance of Munnu: 'After my death there will come to you from Eire a certain youth, holy in character, renowned in intellect, fair in person, curly of head, and rosy cheeked, whose name is Munnu and whom I often saw on earth.'

He was highly educated, having studied under Comgall of Bangor, and also at the monastery and school at Kilmore, Co. Roscommon, founded by Columcille, and at Cleenish, an island in Lough Erne, under Silell Mac Mianaig.

Munnu's missionary work

Following his education, Munnu journeyed to Iona in 597 (Reeves, 1857, 372), wishing to become a monk there. He was refused admission by the abbot on the orders of Columcille, who had died in January 597, Columcille having foretold that Munnu would found his own monastery in South Leinster. This story was told to Adomnán by Ossíne, an abbot of Taghmon who died in 687, who had got it from Munnu himself (Anderson and Anderson, 1961, 212-15).

Munnu reputedly returned to Ireland, founding several churches in Scotland on the way home. The Life mentions two of these, neither of which can be traced. In his notes on Adomnán's Life of Columba (Reeves, 1857, 22) states that his principal church there was at Kilmun, in Cowal, to which the Breviary of Aberdeen assigns his burial place, and where local tradition even marks the supposed site of his tomb by the name of Sith-Mon, despite the clear evidence in Adomnán's Life of Columba that he returned to Ireland. There was also a church called after him on the island of Eilean Mor in Loch Leven. According to Watson (1926, 307) churches were also dedicated to him at Kilmun on Loch Avich and at Kilmun near Inveraray. All these churches were in Argyll.

In Ireland he travelled to Ely O'Carroll territory before coming into Leinster, where he is associated with the monasteries of Tihelly, Durrow, Co. Offaly and Taughmon, Co. Westmeath. He eventually reached Uí Cheinnselaig, whence it appears he made his way into south Wexford, which was then still under the control of the Uí Bairrche, a non-Uí Cheinnselaig sept, which at one time ruled most of south Leinster. According to Byrne (1973, 146) the monastery of Bangor had been granted extensive lands in Leinster by an Uí Bairrche king who was a disciple of St Comgall. This may explain why Munnu was given control of an establishment run by monks of St Comgall since Munnu, too, had been a disciple of Comgall and monks from Bangor were active all over the island. After twelve years in this place, named Ard Crema, Munnu was asked to leave, which he did, but not before calling down a curse on the spot.

In the Martyrology of Óengus (63) Munnu is referred to as:

> A splendid flame with the father's fervour
> Fintan, true gold proven
> Tulchán's son, brave, abstinent
> A battle soldier, trustful, crucified.

'Crucified' refers to Munnu's affliction with leprosy.

Munnu founds monastery at Taghmon

Next Munnu came to a place called Acadh Liathdrom, meaning 'the grey field or ridge', where the chief, Dimma Mac Áedh, gave him land on which to build his monastery. This Munnu did, possibly towards the end of 597, after the death of Columcille, and the place became known as Teach Munnu, which was later anglicized to Taghmon. The site was marked out by four crosses made of timber; the broken stone cross now on the site of the monastery is of a later dates, see Chapter 12.

Munnu must have laboured for over thirty years in Taghmon. He was twenty- four years there when he contracted leprosy. This disease was relatively common in Ireland in the medieval period: there was a leper hospital in Maudlintown, outside Wexford town (Hore, v, 228-9).

Munnu's personality

Munnu has been generally regarded as a harsh and strict taskmaster and this seems to be borne out in some of the stories in the Life. The rules in many of the early Irish monasteries were particularly severe, and Sinell's school on Cleenish, in Lough Erne, where Munnu spent many years, had such a reputation. Thus, Munnu, not unused to these, became a strict disciplinarian as the following stories show:

> After a sojourn in Scotland he did not visit his own people.
> He threatened to leave Ireland if his relations came near him again.
> He was less than pleasant to the virgins who asked for his blessing.
> He put a curse on Ard Crema when the monks asked him to leave the place.
> An angel warned him that he treated his monks too harshly.
> Another story found in Manus O'Donnell's Betha Colaim Cille (O'Kelleher and Schoepperle, 1918, 161) tells how Munnu was called in as 'the hard man' to support St Patrick's demand to Christ, that he, Patrick, should be the judge of the Irish on the Last Day.

Munnu's obduracy was shown on one of the few occasions that the Irish Church disagreed with Rome. The controversy surrounded the dating of Easter, a question still debated. In 525 Rome adopted a new system based on a more accurate lunar cycle of nineteen years in comparison with an older system brought to Ireland by St Patrick. In the famous convention held at Old Leighlin in 630 to discuss the matter, Munnu vigorously led the opposition to the new system. Although his side was defeated in the debate the old dating system persisted in parts of Ireland for many years afterwards.

Plummer (1910, ii, p. xxxv) saw Munnu in a different light 'a man of somewhat harsh and hasty temper, but placable and conciliatory when the momentary irritation was over'. In the Martyrology of Donegal Munnu is credited with the patience of Job for the way in which he endured his leprosy.

In an 'Irish Litany of Pilgrim Saints compiled around 800' (Hughes, 1959, 305-1) the following reference to Munnu is found: 'Thrice fifty martyrs under the yoke of Munnu, son of Tulchán, on whom no man may be found buried until doom'. Thrice fifty martyrs is the standard number of monks attributed to the saints and has no basis in fact. The word 'martyr' in this case refers to what the Irish called 'white martyrdom' indicating a harsh, ascetic life, rather than the 'red martyrdom' of death by violent means.

Munnu remembered

Munnu, undoubtedly, was a man of importance in his lifetime. His monastery at Taghmon, which boasted around 230 monks (Mart. Donegal, Mart. Tallaght) became famous and lasted until 1060, when it is recorded in the Annals of Inisfallen that Domhnall Deisech died there.

St Munnu's well, recently restored, is located in a secluded, picturesque area known as Brownscastle, in Mulmontry townland, Taghmon. A smooth piece of shale bedrock nearby is called St Munnu's bed. There is also a well named Tober Munnu located down a lane almost directly opposite the Catholic church in Taghmon. This is still in working order and is regularly cleaned-up by parishioners.

Apart from Taghmon, several places in south Wexford are named after the saint. Ishartmon, Ballymore parish, was probably the place where he had his *disert*, that is, his chapel or hermitage, where he could retreat from worldly cares. St Mun's Well was situated in the townland of Ballyboher, Ballymore.

In the late 1600s a church at Churchtown, Tacumshin, was dedicated to St Munnu, who was also known as Fintan (Hore, 1862, 68). A small promontory near Churchtown, Carne, called Cross Fintan Point, may be named after the saint, although the name Fintan goes back to pagan times. There was also a church dedicated to St Fintan at Carne in 1680 (Hore, 1862, 60).

A holy well dedicated to St Fintan is situated in Churchland, Mayglass, but the 'pattern' date of 17 February shows that this was St Fintan of Clonenagh, Co. Laois, and not the saint from Taghmon.

Gorteenminoge, Murrintown, may refer to the saint, 'mun' having been changed to min, the original wording possibly being Goirtín-mo-Fhionn-óg, meaning Munnu's field. Munnu is also commemorated in the townland name of Aughermon, near Rack's Cross. According to Williams (pers. comm.), ancient pathways from Taghmon can be traced to there. There was also a monastery at Taughmon, Co. Westmeath, founded by Munnu (Gwynn and Hadcock, 1970, 406).

Up to recent times Mun was not uncommon as a Christian or first name in south Wexford.

Munnu's miracles and extraordinary powers

In contrast to the Lives of other saints Munnu's contains a minimum of fabulous episodes. However, in keeping with the custom of the time, it was essential to attach extraordinary, superhuman powers to every saint to show that he was no common mortal, but that he had a close affinity with God and access to his almighty power. This was done by having the saint perform Christ-like miracles such as raising the dead to life. Munnu is credited with two such miracles; on one occasion he raised his sister Conchinne from the grave; another time he brought a dead man back to life.

He also had prophetic powers: he predicted the death of Guaire Mac Eoghain for disobeying him, he foretold the contrasting futures of Dimma's two sons – one to be a murderer, the other to be a bishop, and the imminent death of one of his monks.

He was believed to know the thoughts of his monks, a good strategy, no doubt, for keeping them in check. Munnu also had magical powers. Once he saved Dimma's Life by making him invisible to his enemies by wearing his, Munnu's, tunic.

Historical value of Munnu's Life

Unlike many saints' Lives which simply recount miracles, extraordinary powers and fabulous exploits, the Life of Munnu provides real historical information. Thus, the names of most of the people mentioned can be verified from other sources, and the places named give a genuine topographical background for the events described.

The genealogy of his father, Tulchán, is recorded in the literature. While the place where he was under Comgall's rule is not listed, the other two places where he studied are well documented. Kilmore, Co. Roscommon, was founded as a monastery and school by St Columcille, and Cleenish on Lough Erne, Co. Fermanagh, was founded by Sinell Mac Mianaig.

The Fothart territory seems to have extended as far as Taghmon at one stage. Dimma Mac Áedh Chamchos is given as a chief of the Fothart (O'Brien, 1962, 85) with his fortress in Taghmon. The Life of Abbán also gives Camaross as being in Fothart showing that the Fothart lands once extended further west than previously thought.

Munnu reputedly came into south Wexford. This area would seem to have been under attack from the Uí Cheinnselaig further north around the end of the sixth century. Munnu's Life describes how one of them, Guaire Mac Eoghain, seeking the kingship of Uí Cheinnselaig, plundered the people and drove off their flocks and herds, only to be slain by his enemies.

A number of place-names in Uí Cheinnselaig are mentioned in Munnu's Life but few of them can be identified with certainty. Thus, when Munnu enters the area, his first stay is at Ard Crema alongside the sea, among the Uí Bairrche. This place was obviously in an elevated (ard) position beside the sea but its location has not been established. Artramont may be a possibility as the Uí Bairrche probably still controlled south Leinster at that time. The place in which Munnu located himself was Achadh Liathdrom meaning 'the grey field on the ridge'. This is undoubtedly Taghmon (*in regionibus Fothar*, Heist, 1965, 15) where his monastery was established. Though not in Plummer's Life, Airbriu is listed in other versions of the saint's Life as 'the place of Cuán, the anchorite' (Heist, 1965, 18). This is very likely the present site at Kilcowan, Rathangan parish. The Martyrology of Gorman lists Cuán Airbre, in Uí Cheinnselaig, and the Martyrology of Donegal gives Cuán of Airbre for 10 July. More problematic is the location of the island of Barry (*insula Tobairri,*), although Bannow Island seems the most likely place. The island of Liachán *(insula Liac Ilain)* is also unknown. The fact that boats were used to reach it points to either one of the Saltee Islands or the Keeraghs.

Several anecdotes in Munnu's Life throw a little light on the mores of the time. For example, to be shaved in front of someone was considered insolent; beheading was the favourite way of killing an enemy. On one occasion Columcille seems to be acting like the charismatics, chanting 'of those things which the Holy Spirit dictated'.

The monasteries were obviously schools for the sons of nobles. For example, Dimma sent one of his sons to Taghmon to be educated and another to St Cuán at Kilcowan. The monasteries were also open to people from abroad as shown by the description of the monk who came to Taghmon from Britain and who 'was learned in the craft of wood and who used to make wagons and other appliances for the brethern'.

Munnu's death and burial
Munnu's death is recorded in the Life as follows:

And one day the saint, knowing that the day of his reward was come, directed his people should be summoned to him and blessing them he committed to them all the divine commands. Afterwards, having received the Body and Blood of Christ in the presence of his disciples, on the twenty first day of October, he happily sent forth his spirit among the choirs of angels into the presence of Jesus Christ, who with God the father and the Holy Ghost lives and reigns for ever and ever. Amen.   [Plummer, 1910, ii, 9]

According to the Annals of the Four Masters Munnu died on the twenty first October 634, and his feast is celebrated on that date. It seems certain that the saint would have been buried in his own monastery at Taghmon.

THE LIFE OF MUNNU
from C. Plummer, *Vitae sanctorum Hibernae*, 1910, ii, 226-38;
translated from the Latin by John Hunt

§1. There was a man of venerable life, Munnu by name, of a renowned family of Ireland, namely the O Neills. His father was called Tulchán, who was descended of the line of Conal, son of Niall. Moreover, the mother of St Munnu was called Fidelma and she was born of the same clan, that is, of the descendants of the son of Diva son of Niall. St Munnu indeed was born above a stone, which was venerated with great honour by the people of that district on account of the grace of the holy infant who was born over it. For miracles are performed upon that very stone; from that day until the present snow does not lie on that stone.

§2. One day when St Columba came to where the holy boy Munnu was, he said to his followers: 'Go thither and bring to me the beautiful boy whom you will find there. And they brought him to St Columba. Columba, the man of God, asked whose son he was, and he was told that he was the son of Tulchán. Then St Columba, filled both by the [atmosphere of] piety that surrounded Munnu and by love for him, took him to himself and said: 'Tulchán will find grace with God and men because of his son. He himself will be a famous man in the future because of his son.' To the son he said: 'Thou are full of the Holy Spirit, blessed son, and you will be reckoned among the great saints of Ireland.' And he diligently blessed the holy boy, and going on his way he gave great testimony of him.

§3. At one time the blessed boy Munnu in his boyhood years used to mind his father's flocks by himself in the woods. Nearby was Cruimter Grellain living in a cell called Achad Bidam. And the holy boy Munnu used to leave his flocks in the lonely places and go to the aforesaid holy man to study and to learn the ways of the church from him. The holy abbot used to receive him, rejoicing in his heart, for he knew that he was full of the Holy Spirit. The father of the blessed Munnu, Tulchán, knowing of this, rebuked him saying: 'Why do you go to read and leave the flocks unattended to the wolves in the wilderness?' But his mother gently excused him and defended him, saying quietly: 'Nothing has been lost so far.' Then the blessed boy said to his father: 'Don't be afraid: for as long as you are in this world nothing of your flocks shall perish by the wolves, if you leave me to study with the servants of God.' On the following day, however, knowing that his son had gone to study, Tulchán went out to view his flocks, and on coming to where the flocks were he saw two wolves guarding his flocks like ordinary dogs, and then he knew it to be true what his holy little son had said, that is, 'Nothing of your flocks shall perish by the wolves.' From that day, therefore, as long as Tulchán was a lay man, the wolves guarded his flocks. For he himself became a *peregrinus*, and, having been approved, was made a monk in the end of his life. And the holy boy Munnu, with the permission of his parents, was sent to study.

§4. At one time the holy abbot Comgall came near to where the pious boy Munnu was; and wishing from his boyhood years to be under the direction of great men, Munnu came to him, and the holy father Comgall received him gladly. One day when they had been walking on their way, they were celebrating Terce [around nine in the morning] near the ford of the Fianna, and the holy boy Munnu asked for a draught of water to drink; for the heat of the sun was excessive. St Comgall told him: 'Hold out, my son, until midday.' And when they had celebrated Sext [around noon] near the streams of Assail, the boy again asked for a cup of water. And the holy father said: 'Wait a little until Nones.' When they were fulfilling the Nones [3.00 p.m.] near Coman Glas St Comgall directed blessed Munnu to wait until the evening without a drink. On that day, moreover, St Comgall with his boy had nothing in the way of food, and no one invited them to a meal. But as the evening was coming on, they found in their way a great dinner prepared for them by the angels of God, along with excellent drink. Then St Comgall said: 'What we did today, that is, to discipline Christ's athlete in thirst, is only beneficial, because in return for that thirst this excellent dinner, after our great hunger, has been sent to us by Christ.' And he said [to his followers]: 'Fill the cup from which I drink, and give it to the boy, that he may first taste the meal sent to him by God; for by his grace, He has provided this meal for us in our hunger.' Thereupon, giving thanks to God, they took that dinner and ate. And for several months blessed Munnu remained with St Comgall, studying under him and learning his rule.

§5. Thereafter, having obtained permission from St Comgall, blessed Munnu came to the school of St Columba, who at the time was master in a place called in the Irish language Ceall Mor Dhithraimh, which is the 'large secluded church', and there holy Munnu studied with the sage Columba. On a certain day, in accordance with usual occurrence, St Columba was filled with the grace of the Holy Spirit, and for a great part of the day he chanted of those things which the Holy Spirit directed. And after the grace ceased, Columba said: 'Who was nearer to me at the time I was chanting the words of the Holy Spirit?' Blessed Baithenus answered him, saying: 'Blessed Munnu sitting at your right hand was nearer to you.' Then St Columba said: 'I say to you that he will be imbued with the Holy Spirit and will be the spiritual master of many and a pre-eminent doctor of this whole school.' And blessed Munnu remained at that time with St Columba, living quite devoutly.

§6. And having received the blessing and the prayer of St Columba, Munnu the servant of God, went out to a holy man who was the wisest of all in Ireland and Britain; he was called Silell Mac Miannaidh and he was the abbot in the monastery of Devenish which is in Lough Erne in the northern part of Ireland. And the saint abode with the aforesaid man, studying industriously before him. And there were nine other very pious youths with him under a very severe rule; and they were in a cell apart. And the harshness of their life can be seen from this: they did not allow their flour to be sifted; instead, complete with its chaff, it was mixed together with water in a basin, and so cooked on stones that had been heated in the fire. And so blessed Munnu lived for eighteen years with Silell only.

§7. After this St Munnu proceeded to the island of Iona that he might become a monk there in the house of St Columba. But St Columba had gone on his way to heaven before his arrival. And before his death he prophesied concerning St Munnu, saying these or similar words to Blessed Baithenus: 'After my death there will come to you from Ireland a certain youth, holy in character, renowned in intellect, fair in person, curly of head, and rosy cheeked, whose name is Munnu, and whom I often saw on earth, but have seen more often [in spirit] in heaven among the angels of God. He will come hither with this purpose, to become a monk here. But do not receive him, however much it displease him, but you [apparently to Baithenus] will tell him "Go back, son, to Ireland, because there you will be the head of a great people," and let him go to the southern region of Leinster which is called Ui Cheinnselaig, for there shall be his honour and resurrection. And although my parish is greater on earth than his, yet my love and my influence with God are not greater than his.' And all this came to pass.

§8. St Munnu now went back from that island to Ireland, grieving in his heart that he was not accepted there [at Iona]; and he came to the island of Coirmrighi and established a place there which is called Ath Caoin, that is, the Gentle Ford. One day the holy man left his followers and went out alone onto a lofty mountain of that island to pray to God. And while praying there he heard the noise of men shouting about the punishments of hell. On that very day indeed was fought the great battle of Slane. Then St Munnu quitted that island, saying: 'I will not live longer in a place where I have heard shouting from hell.' God did this on purpose to bring his servant to the place of his resurrection. When he was travelling along the road he met a rich man by the name of Eran, whose flocks had the plague. And being besought by this man, the man of God blessed a certain ford there, and the flocks of that rich man were cured by that water. And to this day, through the operation of divine mercy, by the grace of the man of God, men and beasts are cured of diseases by the water of the same ford. The rich man offered that field to St Munnu in honour of God, and the saintly man established a chapel there, named Achad Leicce and he left there seven brothers, followers of his.

§9. Afterwards the saint came to his own country and to the clan where he was born. However, he did not see the place, except only the road which he walked. For he did not wish to stay there or see the country, but it was necessary for him to pass through it. And he met (or greeted) none of his relations, neither his mother, nor his brothers nor his sisters who were alive at the time. He directed his way towards the province of Munster, and stayed in the district of Hely. And he built there a monastery called Teach Telli; and he was there for five years.

§10. On one occasion his mother sent a deputation to St Munnu when he was staying in the same place, asking him to giver her permission to come to meet him. He sent back to her saying: 'Come to the place called Lughmadh, and approach no nearer here; and I will come to you there.' So his mother came, and her three daughters, two married, one a maiden, and others with them. While the lady was waiting the arrival of her holy son in the town of Lughmadh, the unmarried daughter, smitten by a pain, died and was buried. On the following day St Munnu arrived at the appointed place. And when he was first going to the church to pray, he saw the fresh grave and, filled with the spirit of prophecy, he said to his brothers: 'That grave is the grave of Conchinne my sister.' Then his sorrowing mother came to him saying: 'I beseech you, my son, in the name of the Lord, whose service you have kept since your birth, to rcvivc my daughter who came here on your account.' The saint said: 'Leave me a while, and tomorrow come to me, that you may see the power of God.' On the approach of night the man of God sent everyone away from him, and all night long he prayed alone to God for her beside her grave. And by the divine power the grave was opened before the man of God and the girl arose from it in health and returned safe with her mother. And the saint told them: 'Take care not to come to me again; for if you do otherwise [than I say] I will leave Ireland entirely and sail off into distant lands.' And giving them salutary admonitions he let them go in peace and went back with his followers.

§11. And when Munnu arrived at a certain chapel, the inhabitants of the place cunningly said to him: 'O saint of God, behold a man he is at home sick and gives us no response. Come, then, that you may bless him in the name of the Lord.' But the man was dead, and they concealed his death. Then the man of God went out with his followers to the man, not knowing that he was dead. And in all simplicity and with a pure heart he blessed him in the name of Jesus Christ with the sign of the Holy Cross. And immediately he arose in health, blessing God, and giving testimony that he had been dead. Afterwards the servant of God, bidding them farewell as they gave thanks to God, went on his way.

§12. When Blessed Munnu had lived for five years in the district of Hely, there came to him a virgin, Emher by name, with five other virgins. The servant of the hospice went to greet her and to receive her into the hospice. The handmaid of God said to him: 'Go to your senior servant of God, and tell him to give to me a place where I can serve God with my daughters.' On hearing this the man of God said to his followers: 'Our resurrection is not here; so, let us leave this place of ours and our work to the maidens of God. And you will bring nothing with you but the essentials for the journey and the books of the services and the holy oils, and your everyday clothes, and of the animals only two oxen for the wagon.' When the handmaid of God asked a blessing from him, he replied to her: 'A blessing be upon your place, and it will be hallowed in the sight of God and man; but yet your place will not be named in your name.' She said: 'In whose name then will it be named?' St Munnu said: 'That man who today gave three shouts in the fields of Midhluacra, he will possess this place. He is Telli Mac Segeni, who will come eventually to this place; and it will be named after him.'

§13. Afterwards St Munnu departed to the confines of Leinster, and one night he stayed near the crosses of the plain of Methe; and that same night there came to that place a chief of Fothard, by the name Dimma, with sixty soldiers. And the man of God constrained them to dine with him, and he ordered one of his oxen to be made ready for them. And they, being unable to resist him, dined. Dimma, the chief, then offered that place to God and St Munnu, and there is now a monastery there in his honour. On the following day, the one ox was courageously pulling the wagon on its own; and a certain man met them on the road with wild oxen and he said: 'Catch one ox and place him under the wagon'; and immediately one became tame and was put under the yoke.

§14. Afterwards St Munnu, in accordance with the prophecy of St Columba, departed to the country of Uí Cheinnselaig and dwelt in a place which is called Ard Chrema among the descendants of Barradh: that place was alongside the sea. There was a chapel in which were monks of St Comgall; and St Comgall's pupil, Aedh Gobbain, was master of that settlement. He respectfully called St Munnu to him and handed over his position to him, he himself going on a *peregrinatio*. St Munnu was twelve years in that place. And God gave to him the fruits of the sea and of the soil in abundance, such as was never in that place either before or since.

§15. And one day there came Guaire Mac Eoghain seeking the kingship of Cheinnselaigh, and he plundered the people of the Uí Bairrche and drove off their flocks and herds. Then the women and children of the people came to St Munnu and wept before him. And the man of God, seeing their misery, said to his monks: 'Go, salute prince Guaire: and ask him from me, in the name of God to give back the loot belonging to these poor people. And if he listens to your prayers, tell him that he shall be king until old age, and shall never get his throat cut; and his descendants shall hold the throne of Ui Cheinnselaig till the end of time. But still, I know he is a hard man and will not listen to you and will give you back neither; and he will insolently be shaved in front of you. And you shall tell him: "If you do not, for the honour of God, deliver to us what you have plundered, you will never be shaved again; but before your beard grows, you shall be murdered and your head shall be struck off." ' They therefore went out and did as their holy superior directed. Guaire indeed scorned them and their words; and on the fifth day, as holy Munnu predicted, the tyrant was slain by his enemies and beheaded.

§16. After the death of St Comgall, a certain brother of his community came, wishing to expel St Munnu from his position. The saint told them: 'I will do this if blessed Aodh comes, who entrusted this position to me twelve years ago.' They said: 'Go and look for him.' Then the man of God with five monks arose and went away. And when they had travelled a short while, they met Aodh coming back from his travels after twelve years. And kissing and greeting each other, they returned together to the chapel. Then the man of God said to them: 'I will go from here; but after my departure, your place shall go down, and shall have no area of ecclesiastical authority; and the sea will not yield its fruits.'

§17. Then an angel of the Lord came to St Munnu and said to him: 'Arise and go to the place which is called Achadh Liathdrum, for their is your [place of] resurrection.' And the saint proceeded at once to that place and halted there. And one day when the saint was alone in the wood there, working with his hands, he saw three men in white garments coming towards him. And forthwith he asked a blessing of them. And they said to him: 'Come with us awhile.' And when they had walked [some way] they said to him: 'In this place will be your town.' And they marked out in his presence four places wherein afterwards would be the chief buildings of the town. And the man of God erected four crosses in those very places.

§18. One night the chief, Dimma MacAodh, was in triumphant mood in his fortress which was near to St Munnu. And they were rejoicing because they had beheaded their enemy that day. But the chief was stricken with remorse and said to his soldiers: 'Our rejoicing is different from that of St Munnu with his monks; our joy is in accord with the will of the devil, but their joy is according to the will of God.' And when morning was come, the chief came to St Munnu and offered him the land on which his town now stands. And the chief said: 'What shall be given me in return for this present?' The man of God replied: 'The kingdom of heaven shall be given you.' The chief said: 'Along with this I want length of this life, and that I shall not be slain, and that I shall be buried here among your monks.' The man of God said to him: 'All this shall be granted you; where you now are, there you shall be buried.' and the chief went back [to his *dún*] rejoicing. There the saint of God built his monastery, as the angels of God had decreed to him. And a town was built around it, which is called by the same name as the monastery, that is, Teach Munnu, which is rendered in the Latin language Domus Munna.

§19. Then the saint made these petitions of God, and God granted them through his angels: namely, that in his monastery a younger man should not die before an elder; that no one of his race should be alive seven years before the Day of Judgment; that whosoever should be buried in the cemetery which he defined with his own hand, should have eternal life; and whoever should be buried within the limits to which is heard the sound of his cymbal (which was always in his community and was never struck except on the passing of a soul), that over him hell should not close after Judgment Day.

§20. There was a certain man doing penance in St Munnu's town, named Becanus, and, he being an invalid, the man of God blessed his cup, and from that day for seven years there was, by the grace of God, milk in that cup, although water was filled into it.

§21. The chief of the Fotharta gave one son of his, who was called Ceallach, to the monastery of St Cuán, and the other, Cillene by name, to St Munnu. One day that chief came with his nobles to visit his sons. And they saw the son who was with Cuán [treated] with all honour and grandeur, and that greatly pleased those grandees and they said: 'This son of yours is well looked after.' Then they came to St Munnu's monastery; and they saw there Cillene in servile array, pulling a wagon along with the rest of the monks. And this greatly displeased the chief's retinue, and they said: 'There is no respect for you in his place, for your son is badly treated here.' Then the chief told them: 'You speak ill; for surely St Munnu by the power of God can hear this in his cell.' Then the man of God, summoning the master of the guest-house, told him: 'Go, receive the chief with his followers, and give them good care; and say to them, "That son who is being brought up ceremoniously at Cuán's house shall possess neither heaven nor earth, and the people of Leinster will cut his throat. But the son who is brought up here like a slave shall be wise, a scribe, an anchorite, a church authority and a bishop; and he shall possess the kingdom of God." ' And so it was accomplished. This prophecy both pleased and displeased them.

§22. After this the chief himself requested some little gift from St Munnu, and the saint gave him his tunic which he himself had worn for one night, and he told the chief: 'Mind this tunic carefully, for the day will come when it will be essential for you, and it will rescue you from great peril.' Later on Ceallach, the chief's son, became a layman and it was he who murdered Aedh Sláne, the son of Criomthan, king of Ui Cheinnselaig and Leinster. Criomthan indeed raised a great army and beset the aforesaid chief with his son and his soldiers on the island of Barri [Bannow] in Lough Eachtach. But the chief escaped from the island on his horse, having St Munnu's tunic around him. And so he came out through the army and nobody saw him, because the grace of God [operating] through the tunic of the man of God, concealed him. But his army was destroyed and eighty of his nobles were made prisoner. And his son Ceallach, as the man of God had predicted, was slain; and two of them [the captives] were put to death every day. And the chief [Dimma] himself was made prisoner while pursuing the king's army. Then St Munnu said to his brethren: 'We ought to go to the king, because the chief who donated this ground to us is held in bondage by him; and the king intends to put him to death tomorrow.' And taking twelve monks with him, the man of God came to the king's camp. The king, learning of this, said to his soldiers: 'Take the chief secretly outside the camp and slay him quickly before Munnu comes to us.' Then the saint arrived before the king, and said to him: 'Deliver unto us the chief, because he is our friend' The king told them: 'He has been slain.' The man of God said: 'That is impossible because he shall never be slain.' Indeed, those men who had been sent to kill him were unable to lift their hands, and their swords and spears were unable to wound him. And the king, hearing this, presented himself with all his [followers] to St Munnu. And the man of God made peace between them, and blessing [them] he returned to his own place.

§23. A certain soldier, Maolmurrogh by name, was with Ceallach the son of the aforementioned chief when slaying Aedh Sláne, the son of King Criomthan. He was caught by the king, and the kind determined to put him to death; and he was a friend of St Munnu. The king at the time was on the island of Liachan. The man of God said to his brethren: 'Go forth to free our friend who is put in danger. Five monks, going out, came to a halt in the harbour of the island. The king, knowing this, said to his soldiers: 'Bring the man bound on a ship and slay him on the waters in front of the monks.' When they had moved off some distance, the ship stopped in one place, and could not be moved this way or that. And the hands of the soldiers dried up around their weapons; and so they stayed for half the day. Then the king, calling the monks, did penance and released unto them the soldier unharmed.

§24. A certain woman, suffering a long time from an issue of blood, was brought to St Munnu's monastery to be cured. The master of the hospice told this to the man of God, requesting that water should be blessed by him for the woman. The man of God said to him: 'Do you want to make me an exorcist for [all] the women of Leinster?' And the saint got up forthwith, fearing to be defiled by the crowd of people. Then the master of the hospice privately took his cap with him, and placed it on the woman; and immediately the bleeding ceased and she was cured by the grace of the man of God, and she went back home with her friends in good health.

§25. An angel of the Lord always came to St Munnu on two days of the week, that is, Sundays and Thursdays. It happened, however, that on a certain Thursday the angel did not come to him until the following Sunday. St Munnu said to him: 'Tell me, if it is through my fault that you did not come to me on the usual day?' The angel replied: 'It is not through your fault or my negligence that I did not come to you; but in these days a very dear friend has entered heaven; on his arrival all the angels were occupied [all] this week in united exultation and joy, and did not come to salute the saints of Ireland.' The saint asked: 'Who was he?' The angel said: 'He is Molugha Mac Cocha of Clonfert.' The saint said: 'It appears plainly that he alone before any of us more truthfully fulfilled the commandments of God. Go therefore and come back to me with a reply, that I may know for what reason it was better to rejoice more [than usual] at Molugha's arrival than to come to me in the accustomed way.' And the angel came to him a second time, saying: 'Hear your question resolved. The whole court of heaven was fully taken up with rejoicing over the arrival of St Molugha because he never caused the face of any man to blush, and his monks are numerous, as are yours, and he treated them as servants of God, respectfully and wisely, as a prudent father would his sons. But you chide your monks too harshly and [put them to] shame. The servants of God should not be treated thus.' Then St Munnu said: 'I know what I will do; I will go off alone on a pilgrimage [*peregrinatio*], and I will not exercise any more my zeal for correcting or assembling the monks.' The angel said to him: 'It shall not be so; but on Tuesday your body will be touched (that is, afflicted) and you will suffer in patience. And as there was joy in heaven at the arrival of St Molugha, so shall it be on the day of your death.' On that very night indeed Munnu, the man of God, was suddenly stricken by a most painful leprosy, and so he remained for twenty-four years. From that day, so the learned men report, the man of God neither shaved himself nor took a bath, except once a year in honour of Easter.

§26. At one time there was a great convention of the peoples of Ireland in the plain of Ailbe in which there was great contention over the ordering of Easter. For Laserian, abbot of the monastery of Leighlin, under whom there were one thousand and five hundred monks, defended the new order, which had recently come from Rome; but the others were defending the old order. But St Munnu did not arrive immediately at the council, and they were all waiting for him; he was already defending the old order. Then Sweeny Mac Donald [or O'Donnell], chief of the country of Hy mBarchi [or Uí Bairrche, etc.] said: 'Why are you waiting so long for that leper?' The abbot Laserian said to him: 'O chief, don't use such a word of holy Munnu; for although he is absent in the flesh, he is nevertheless present in spirit. And certainly what you are saying here, wherever he is, he is hearing and God will avenge on you this insult to his servant. Now on that day before evening St Munnu came to the meeting, and the saints came together to meet him. When St Laserian and St Munnu had greeted each other, the aforesaid chief Sweeny presented himself, asking a blessing from St Munnu. The man of God said to him: 'Why do you ask a blessing from a leprous fellow? Truly I say to you that when you spoke ill of me, Christ, on the right hand of his Father, blushed. Now I am a true member of Christ, and He is my head; and whatever hurts the member, by it the head is pained. And so before this month is over, your own kin shall slay you and cut off your head and your head shall be thrown into the river Barrow and never be seen again.' And so it was fulfilled. For that very month his brother's son killed him near the Blathach steam, and his head was thrown into the river Barrow in accordance with the prophecy of the man of God.

§27. After that St Munnu, in the presence of all the peoples, said to Abbot Laserian: 'It is now time this council was ended that each one may go back to his own place. And as they were disputing about the ordering of Easter, St Munnu said: 'Let us cut short the wrangling and in the name of God let us make a decision.' Three options are offered to you, Laserian: one is that the two books, the book of the old order and that of the new, be put into the fire so that we may see which of them is saved from the fire. Or that two monks, one mine and one yours, be shut up in the same house and the house burned down; and we shall see which of them comes out unscathed by the fire. Or let us go to the grave of a just monk who is dead and revive him that he may show us by what order we should celebrate Easter this year.' St Laserian said to him: 'We are not going by your judgment, because we know that on account of the greatness of your work and sanctity, if you were to say that the Margy Mountain should be changed into the place of the Plain of Ailbe, and that the Plain of Ailbe to the place of Slieve Margy, God would immediately do it for your sake. For they were at the time in the Plain of Ailbe over which rises Slieve Margy. After that the peoples, agreeing with the saints, went back to their own places.

§28. A certain monk of the nation of the Britons was at St Munnu's [monastery], and he had a cell apart and was like a hermit. And he was learned in the craft of wood[working] and he used to make wagons and other appliances for the brethren. And on a certain day, St Munnu came to his cell at daybreak; and he was at the time in the kiln, drying out the timber for a wagon. And the monk bent the knee before the saint and said: 'Sit down for a while, father, on the chair beside the fire, to warm your feet.' To which the man of God assented. And as he sat beside the fire, the monk took his sandals, and discovered in them wet sand. And removing it he tied it up in his handkerchief. And he said to the man of God: 'I ask you, father, in God's name tell me, what is that wet sand?' And the saint said to him: 'Promise me on your faith, that you won't tell anyone in my lifetime.' And he promising, the saint told him: 'Really, I've only just got back from the Land of Promise. St Columba was with me and St Brendan, and St Canice. And it was the power of God which brought us there and brought us back again. And I brought back with me this sand for my grave.' After the death of the man of God, that monk related this story, and showed the sand, which was put into the grave as the saint had directed when alive.

§29. A certain monk in St Munnu's monastery, who was called Finan, asked the man of God to let him go to his own country to visit his friends. And the man of God said to him: 'Go in peace, for I know it is from God. But take care not to drink anything but water until we greet each other [again].' And the man of God blessed the cup of that brother on his setting forth. But after he had departed, St Munnu went to heaven. The brother, hearing of the death of his abbot, determined to drink nothing but water until he should depart from this world. And he lived for thirty years drinking nothing but water. One day Abbot Mocreomóg absentmindedly tasted of his cup and he found the taste of excellent wine in the water [which was] in it. And this he related to the brother. And the brother said to him: 'Father, give me the divine Viaticum. For on the third day I shall go to heaven. For the sanctity of St Munnu and the kindness of God provided the taste of wine and its efficacy in the water this long-time past. And it was made plain to me by God that in whatever hour another person should know this, I should go to heaven on the third day afterward. And so it happened as they gave thanks to God.

§30. To a certain brother in good health St Munnu said one day: 'See, the time has come for you to go to heaven.' And that brother on the third day went to heaven. And then the man of God said to another brother who had been very ill for a long time: 'Get up, and do the tasks of the man who has died.' And forthwith he arose strong and well and went to work with the brethren. St Munnu had this gift from God, that he knew the thoughts of all his monks; and he pointed out to them whatever was in their hearts; and every word which the brethren spoke in his absence, he knew; wherefore he praised them or rebuked them, as if he had been present with them. And in blessing the hearts of the wicked, he by the grace of God cast out all evil from them. Every word and action of St Munnu was full of divine grace. And one day the saint, knowing that the day of his reward was come, directed that his people should be summoned to him, and blessing them he committed to them all the divine commandments. Afterwards, having received the body and blood of Christ, in the presence of his disciples, on the twenty-first day of October, he happily sent forth his spirit among the choirs of angels into the presence of Jesus Christ, who with God the Father and the Holy Ghost lives and reigns for ever and ever. Amen.

[Here] Endeth the Life of St Munnu, Abbot.

11

Other saints associated with Co. Wexford

St Caomhán of Ardcavan

This holy man, of whom little is known, is associated with the island of Dairinis, meaning Oak Island, in Wexford Harbour, and also with Ardcavan, which is named after him. The exact location of Dairinis, or Inis Beg, as it is named in the Annals of Ulster, is not known. Along with Beggerin, it was plundered by the Norse in 821, according to the Annals of the Four Masters. In the *Tripartite Life of St Patrick* (Stokes, 1887, 192-3) it is distinguished from Beggerin or Inis Fáil as being the lesser island, and with having a church and two monks, named Erdit and Augustin.

In the Martyrology of Donegal the saint is described as 'Caomhán, of Ard Caomhán, by the side of Loch Garman, in Leinster: and this is Caomhán, or St Lethan ...' In the Martyrology of Óengus his feast day is given as 12 June, 'the feast of pious Caeman, who was named St Lethan'. The appellation Sanct Lethan is explained in the Martyrology as follows:

> Sanct Lethan was queen of a king in Leinster. With her Coeman was in bondage when he was a little lad, and Bishop Ibar took him from her through a great contest: and Sanct Lethan gave her word to him (Ibar) that the lad should bear her name, and that he would carry off Bishop Ibar's monks from him, though he was greatly entreating for them: and this was fulfilled.

He is also listed in the Martyrology of Tallaght as being in Airdne in Santletan. According to the Life of Ibar (Grosjean, 1959, 442) Caomhán was his brother. This would mean that he belonged to the Uí Echach of Co. Down and that he was also Abbán's uncle.

That Caomhán was held in high esteem by his contemporaries is evidenced by the fact that Finnian of Clonard is reputed to have visited him on Dairinis (Colgan, 1645, 191).

Apart from Ardcavan, Caomhán has given his name to Kilcavan

(Bannow), and to Kilcavan (Killinierin). Drinagh church, Piercestown, was also dedicated to him.

St Moling of St Mullins

This founder of the important monastery at St Mullins was closely associated with and later revered in Co. Wexford. The Life of Moling (Stokes, 1907) describes a meeting between himself and St Aidán at Clongeen. He became bishop of Ferns sometime after St Aidán but later returned to St Mullins where he died in 696. That he was held in high honour is shown by the fact that five churches in the county were dedicated to him. These were at Ballycanew, Monamolin (Rathnure), Monamolin (Kilmuckridge), Kilnamanagh and Toome.

St Cuán of Kilcowan

This would appear to be the saint listed in the Martyrology of Óengus as 'Cuán of Airbre, in Uí Cheinnselaig, and he is identical with Maethail Broccan in the Déisi of Munster'. In the life of Munnu, Airbriu is mentioned as a place where St Cuán had a school for young men (Plummer, 1910, ii, §xxi). A monastery was founded at Maethail Broccan, now Mothel, Co. Waterford, in the sixth century, by St Brogan, who was succeeded by St Cuán (Gwynn and Hadcock, 1970, 188). Cuán's feast day is given for 10 July in the Martyrologies of Óengus and Gorman. A St Cuán, feast day 3 February, was venerated at Kilcowanmore (Ballybrennan).

St Colmán of Templeshanbo

The Martyrology of Óengus gives Colmán of Ua Fiachrach at Seanbotha Fola (Templeshanbo) in Hy Kinsellagh and his feast day as 27 October. He is also venerated on the same day at Inismurray, an important early monastery off the coast of Sligo. The Ua Fiachrach were important chiefs, with lands in the present counties of Mayo, Galway and Tyrone.

St Senán of Enniscorthy

This famous sixth-century saint founded a church at Templeshannon (Teampeall Senáin), Enniscorthy, and his name is perpetuated in several places around the town. These include St Senán's Church, St Senán's Mental Hospital, as well as the parish of St Senán's on the left bank of the Slaney. The Book of Lismore (Stokes, 1890, 208) describes how 'Senán set up in Enniscorthy, beside the Slaney, in the province of Uí Cheinnselaig. Then he and Máedóg (Aidán) of Ferns made a union. Máedóg bequeaths his place and his crozier after him to Senán and Senán takes the abbacy of Ferns after Máedóg. Senán goes from his abbacy to Rome'. However, it is highly unlikely that such an event ever took place.

Senán's most famous foundation was on Scattery Island at the mouth of the Shannon. It is not known for certain when he lived, Colgan states that he flourished around 540 (Gwynn and Hadcock, 1970, 96).

St MoBeooc

In the Life of Ibar (Grosjean, 1959, 442) MoBeooc is listed as his brother. The Martyrology of Óengus gives 16 December as 'the feast of my excellent Beooc, from lustrous Ard Cainross'. Stokes (1895, 240) suggested that Ard Cainross is a variant of Ard Camross. A note on the margin by an unknown hand in the Martyrology of Gorman reads 'From Ard Camrois, on the brink of Loch Garman, in Huí Cennsalaig'. The location of Ard Camross is problematic. If the name is taken as Camross, it must refer to Abbán's foundation at Camaross, which may itself have been situated on Camaross Hill. But Camaross is some twelve miles inland from Loch Garman. If Cainross is accepted, the most likely location is Ardcandrisk, in the parish of Glynn, which is close to Wexford Harbour.

St Vauk of Carne

The name of this saint survives in the dedication of a small church and holy well near Carnsore Point, in the southeast corner of Co. Wexford. No reliable information exists on the saint, although several theories have been put forward as to his identity. One of these suggests that he was an Irishman who went to Brittany, where he was known as St Vouga. Several churches are dedicated to him there. His feast day was 15 June. O'Hanlon (1875, vi, 668) suggested that his name and fame were propagated by the Normans.

Several saints bear a name closely resembling Vauk, for example, Beoc, MoBeoc and Dabheoc. This led Margaret Stokes (1893, 382) to conclude that Vauk and Beoc were the same person. Whatever the name of the person who came to live in this beautiful, but isolated area, he must have been an ascetic, seeking solitude for prayer and contemplation. He may also have deliberately chosen this place to combat paganism. The area had a reputation as a pagan centre, being called Hieron Akron on Ptolemy's second-century map (Byrne, 1984, 98), meaning 'The Sacred Cape', no doubt a reference to a druidical ritual or educational establishment.

St Ellóc

According to the early Martyrologies, Ellóc was an Irish saint with a feast day on 25 June. He is reputed to have built a church at Kilcloggan, Templetown. In fact, the townland name, Kilcloggan, pronounced locally as Killoggan, may be a corruption of the Irish name Cill Allócáin (the church of Allóc). He was patron of Templetown parish where a holy well was dedicated to him. This is now called Toberluke, a corruption of the Irish Tober Allóc.

1 Celtic hillfort, Courthoyle New

2 Ogham stone, Cotts, Broadway, showing notches representing letters

3 Rath at Monanarrig, Ballyvaldon, showing contrast between ancient and modern farmsteads

4 Crop marks, Haresmead, Horetown. The location of many ráth sites can be identified only from the air.

5 Diarmait Mac Murchada is said to be buried beneath this ninth-century decorated shaft of a high cross, Ferns.

6 Latin cross, possibly ninth-century, Adamstown, marking the site of St Abban's monastery

7 St David's well, Ballynaslaney

8a

8b

8a and 8b:
Heads of high
crosses, Ferns

9a

9a and b: Carved stone slabs from Beggerin: a) head of ringed cross with interlacing showing Viking artistic influence; b) three badly worn figures above a man astride a pony (Photo: Brian Lynch, Bord Fáilte)

9b

10a

10a and 10b: The smallest high cross in Ireland (?) measuring only 56cms in height. Kilmokea: a) south-west face with Latin cross within incised circle; b) north-east face with incised Latin cross

10b

11 Worn-through bullaun stone, Clone

12 Bullaun stone, Kilnahue

13 Inscribed stone crosses, Kildoran, Kiltealy

14 High cross, Rossminoge

15 Inscribed stone cross from Killannduff, Ballygarret

16 Sundial, Clone

17 Ferns abbey, founded *c.*1160 by Diarmait Mac Murchada

A church at Kerlogue (originally Killilloge), near Wexford town, was also dedicated to him. The Martyrology of Donegal and Ó Riain (1985, 179) give him as Welsh and list him as Ellóc, Cilli Moellóc ic Loch Garman, that is, 'Ellóc of Cill Moellóc in Wexford'.

The Welsh connections
The early movements of groups of people from southern and southeastern Ireland into South Wales are dealt with in Chapter 5. But there were also contacts in the opposite direction. Several Early Christian church or holy well sites in Co. Wexford are dedicated to saints of Welsh/Irish parentage. A twelfth-century document *De Situ Brecheniauc* (Bowen, 1969, 59) tells how Marchell (Marcella) daughter of a Welsh king, Teuderic, travelled to Ireland, where she met and married the king, Anlac, or Amlach. By Thomas' calculations (1994, 160) this would have taken place around 485-90. From this union was born a son, Brecaun, or in Welsh, Brychan, after whom Breconshire is called. Brecaun was reputed to have had a large number of children, but the term 'children of Brychan' probably applied to his followers rather than his actual family.

Thomas gives a list of his children, but this bears no relation to that of Ó Riain (1985, 178-9), who names his wife as Dina, daughter of an Anglo-Saxon king. Among the offspring of this union with church or holy well dedications in Co. Wexford are Dubhán, Ellóc or Allóc, Cairín and Mochonóc. There was also a church dedicated to Brecaun himself on Hook Head.

A St Breccán is commemorated in the martyrologies on several different dates for churches at Moville, Co. Down, Ardbraccan, Co. Meath and other places. He belonged to the Dál Fiathach, a branch of the Ulaid (Mac Giolla Easpaig, 1996-7, 82).

St Dubhán of Hook Head
According to the Martyrology of Donegal, Dubhán was a pilgrim priest at Rinn Dubháin, the ancient name for Hook Head. Dubhán is also the Irish name for a fishing hook, and in the sixteenth century Rinn (Head) and Dubhán were anglicized to Hook Head (Colfer, 1978, 11).

Dubhán established a church or cell at Churchtown on this isolated promontory. The dedication was changed from St Dubhán's to St Saviour's by the Normans. However, as Colfer stated (1978, 11), 'Dubhán's name was not completely forgotten. There is a well on the seashore near the church which is still known as Duffin's well. In all probability Dubhán was associated in some way with this well and his name has been connected with it, in a corrupt form, over the centuries.'

Dubhán's feast day is given as 11 February in the Martyrologies of Óengus and Donegal.

St Cairín

This saint also reputedly made her way to Wexford. Ó Riain (1985, 314) places her in Carne (Chill Chairinni). The Latin Life of Finnian of Clonard (Hughes, 1954, 366) describes how the saint 'landed at Kylle Caireni, near Carnsore Point'. Similarly, the 'Life' in the Codex Salmanticensis (Colgan, 1947, 195) has Finnian landing '*portum Kylle Caireni*'. Chapel Carron in Glynn parish may also have been associated with Cairín.

St Degumen

Churches dedicated to this saint were at Ballyconnick, Killag and Killiane Little. His feast day was 27 August. Doble (1971, 50) associated Degumen with 'a group of Brecon saints who founded monasteries in south Wales ... and from which missions to Somerset and Cornwall were sent out. He may have been associated with the great saints of Cardigan and Pembroke, namely Carantoc, Petroc and Brioc'. His name was sometimes changed to St Tenen.

St Brioc

A holy well at the Burrow, Rosslare, is dedicated to St Brioc. According to Doble (1971, 9) he lived between 440 and 530. His feast day is 1 May. He is reputed to have been educated by St German of Auxerre and to have spent most of his life in France, where he is buried in the cathedral of St Brieuc, in Brittany. His cult spread to Wales, Scotland and Ireland. A Latin life of the saint was published in *Analecta Bollandiana*, 2 (1883), 161-90.

St David of Menevia

He was founder of the famous monastery of Menevia, at St David's, in Dyfed, where many Irish students, including St Aidán of Ferns, were trained for the priesthood. There is a holy well dedicated to him at Ballynaslaney, near Oylegate, where a 'pattern' is held every year on 1 March. A church at Mulrankin, Kilmore, was also dedicated to him. He died in 601.

St David was venerated by the Normans. The *Song of Dermot and the Earl* describes how they invoked his help before doing battle with the Irish (Orpen, 1892, 57).

12

The Wexford monasteries and convents

Monasticism originated in Egypt and spread quickly across Europe. Its ideals of seclusion and devotion seem to have appealed greatly to the Irish temperament, and monastic settlements were quickly established throughout the island. During the seventh, eighth and early ninth centuries, Ireland entered a golden age of scholarship and craftsmanship. The Book of Kells and the Ardagh and Derrynaflan chalices were produced during this period when Ireland was known as 'the island of saints and scholars'. As the ninth century advanced, the monasteries began to decline as they came more and more under the control of laymen. Attacks on them by the Irish and the Vikings and bloody dynastic struggles for power also contributed to the decline.

Religious life in the monastery

The basic aim of those joining a monastery was to lead an ascetic life of prayer which would enable them to attain the reward of eternal happiness in the presence of God. All thoughts and actions were to be directed to this end. Such a life, particularly the pleasing of God and contemplation of his many attributes, could also bring joy to his faithful servants on earth.

The ascetic life then consisted firstly of prayer, both in private and in community. Physical work was also essential, not only to serve the needs of the monastery, but also as a means of curbing the desires of the flesh. As no set rules existed in the church, the regimen in each monastery differed depending on the approach of the founder and his successors. For example, Munnu of Taghmon was reputed to be harsh, and Aidán, following the rule of David in Menevia, where he was educated, may not have been very different.

Much of our information on monastic rules comes from the eighth century through a reform movement known as the Céli Dé, meaning the 'servants of God'. Generally the monks attended community worship at certain times of the day and night. Fasting and abstinence from meat were also practised. The practice of mortification of the flesh through flagellation was also carried out, as we can see from references in the literature. The Rule of

Tallaght (Ó Maidín, 1996, 123) states that 'Maelruain ruled that the flagellation to be given on Sunday evening be done on Saturday out of respect for the day of the Lord.' Multiple genuflection as a form of godly respect was also enjoined on the monks. The Rule of Comgall (Ó Maidín, 1996, 31) states that the monk should make one hundred genuflections while chanting morning and evening. The Rule of Tallaght (Ó Maidín, 1996, 129) tells how a monk became crippled from making seven hundred genuflections each day.

Apart from monks, the monastery had priests and in some cases a bishop. The monasteries also functioned as centres of education to which the noble families sent their sons. As shown in the Life of Munnu the monasteries of Taghmon and Kilcowan accepted two sons of the king of Fothart into their schools.

Sons were also given to monasteries to be trained as monks. For this instruction a set scale of payments was laid down in the Rule of the *Céli Dé* (Ó Maidín, 1996, 95). This type of training would only have been carried out at the larger monasteries such as Ferns.

The monastic economy

Over the Early Christian period and throughout Ireland, monasteries varied hugely in size and status, the latter in particular being related to the fame of the founding saint. As evidenced by the size of their enclosure some, such as Ardcolm, were quite small. Others like Ferns, Taghmon, Clongeen, Templeshanbo and Killegney grew large over time from donations of land and other forms of wealth.

As well as being a religious centre, the monasteries were also economic units or estates which required a whole host of skills, both administrative and manual. As Corish (1972, 44) states:

> The successful monastery was now in fact an ecclesiastical territorial state, its centre the monastic city. Around this lay its wide possessions, held by lay tenants who made up the community (*muintir*) of the monastery equally with its monks and ecclesiastics; every citizen of the monastic jurisdiction was legally a monk (*manach*).

This monastic community was made up of a diverse range of people, differing in ecclesiastical and social status, function and relationship to the monastery. Some had taken vows, others were tenants of monastic farms or labourers. However, all were in a special relationship with their monastery, which catered for both their physical and spiritual welfare in return for their services.

Administration was in the hands of the abbot and erenagh or steward. Below these were the *manaig* with a range of skills such as woodworking, leatherworking and cooking. Farming the monastic lands also involved skills such as animal care, and sowing, harvesting and milling the grain.

By the eighth century the monasteries were becoming wealthy from endowments. According to Doherty (1982, 308), 'Actual grants to churches consisted of chattels, animals, people, churches or dwellings, land, fishing rights, water mills, etc. Wealth consisted of gold and silver or articles made from them'.

Tithes were also a valuable source of income. These consisted of one tenth of the produce of the land, including animals and grain. Other sources of income came from officiating at baptisms and funerals, from school fees and from fosterage of the children of nobles.

Farm surplus became available from exchange and in time markets sprang up around the monasteries. These in turn attracted more people, travelling craftsmen, for example, who eventually settled there to form a town. Doherty (1982, 308) dates the beginning of this development to the tenth century.

The monastic enclosures varied widely in extent, but in the fashion of the time they were surrounded by a wall or earthen bank and ditch. This could be circular, oval, D-shaped or even rectangular. Within the enclosure could be found at least one church, monks' cells, a guesthouse and various workshops.

Decline of the monasteries

During the ninth century the monasteries began to decline. This was not peculiar to Ireland, having started on Continental Europe in the eighth century. A central factor in this decline was the increasing hold of lay people on the monastery. Married abbots and clergy, too, passed on their offices and property to their children or other relations. Thus the wealth which should have benefited the monasteries had the opposite effect, leading to a loss of discipline and ultimately to a decline in the religious life.

Because of their wealth, monasteries had become subject to attack long before the arrival of the Vikings towards the end of the eighth century. Their political power also ensured that the monasteries became involved in dynastic disputes, even between families of the same dynasty, as witnessed by the battles between different branches of the Uí Cheinnselaig for control of Ferns.

The numbers of priests and monks seems to have decreased dramatically following the early enthusiasm for the monastic Life. A twelfth-century charter of Kells seems to indicate that only one priest then remained there (Kenney, 1929, 754).

MONASTIC CENTRES IN COUNTY WEXFORD

As shown in the previous section, Co. Wexford contained many ecclesiastical sites. Some of these were large and were obviously more than just church
sites, for example, Clongeen, Killegney and Kilmokea. However, in the
absence of written records it is not feasible to ascribe monastic status to
them. On that basis only four sites are definitely described as monasteries.
These are Ferns, Taghmon, Beggerin and Templeshanbo.

FERNS

St Aidán is reputed to have landed at Ard Ladrann, which is probably
Ardamine, near Courtown. Sometime towards the end of the sixth century,
he was given land at Ferns by a nobleman named Becc on which he probably built a small wooden church. The Life of Aidán describes how
Brandubh, the Uí Cheinnselaig king of Leinster, gave great offerings to
Máedóg and land on which to erect a monastery at Ferns (Plummer, 1910,
ii, 141-63).

O'Donovan (1840, i, 54) quotes the following from an Appendix to the
Life of Aidán in the Codex Kilkenniensis in Marsh's Library: 'At length he
returned to Ireland ... and some years after was by command of Brandubh,
king of Leinster, who gave him the city of Ferns, consecrated bishop (or archbishop) about the year 598.' Ussher (1639) quoted in O'Donovan's note in the
Annals of the Four Masters (i, 221), stated that after the fall of Áedh I, son
of Ainmire, king of Ireland, in the battle of Dunbolg in 598. Brandubh, king
of Leinster, had bestowed his seat at Ferns upon Aidán, and also made it the
metropolis of all Leinster. The king himself resided at Baltinglass.

The story, probably fanciful, is told (Mac Niocaill, 1972, 81) that the son
of Áed, the Uí Néill high king, when visiting Brandubh, demanded the
ancient right to sleep with his wife. This was refused, and the king's son
was slain. Inevitably the high king invaded Leinster. Acting on advice from
Máedóg, Brandubh fought and defeated Áed at the battle of Dúnbolg. In
appreciation of his good advice Brandubh not alone bestowed lands around
Ferns on Máedóg but also made him bishop over his kingdom. But
Brandubh was slain by his own people in 605 following a defeat by the Uí
Néill. Sharpe (1991, 356) has questioned the supposed role of Brandubh in
the foundation of the monastery. He suggests that the close relationship
between Aidán and Brandubh was concocted centuries later to boost the
importance of the Uí Cheinnselaig and the monastery of Ferns. However, it
is not unlikely that he, Brandubh, being king, was at least required to confirm the grant of his kinsman Becc to the saint.

Ferns, then, with Aidán as abbot, and under the patronage of Brandubh, became the ecclesiastical centre of Uí Cheinnselaig. As the appointment of bishops was largely controlled by the rulers of the time, Brandubh would undoubtedly have been pleased to elevate a famous man such as Aidán as bishop of his kingdom. This was supposedly in gratitude for Aidán's help in curing him of a terrible sickness (Plummer, 1922, ii, 210-11).

The Uí Cheinnselaig territory at that time roughly corresponded to Co. Wexford with some adjoining parts of Wicklow and Carlow. The part of north Wexford controlled by the Uí Enechglaiss, a non-Uí Cheinnselaig sept, (the later parishes of Castletown and Coolgreany) was outside their territory. The churches of Kilgorman and Kilbegnet in this area may have been attached to the monastery of Glendalough and later became part of that diocese, which was incorporated into the Dublin diocese early in the thirteenth century.

The question arises as to why Ferns was chosen as a monastic site. Unlike many others it was not located on a major river crossing or important land route. It seems likely that Aidán's landing at Ardamine and subsequent settling at nearby Ferns was a calculated move. A branch of the Uí Cheinnselaig was already settled in this area, and Aidán, seeking to associate his mission to a powerful family made his way there. Ferns then became the principal church of south Leinster and can still claim that honour.

The successors of Saint Aidán

An outline of the history of Ferns during the Early Christian period can be traced by following the long line of Aidán's successors there.

Table 3 Abbots of the monastery of Ferns, 598-1183
(source: Byrne, 1984, 254)

Name	Status	Died
Áed mac Sétnai (St Aidán)	bishop	624/25
Da Chua Luachrae – Cronán	abbot	654
Ernóc mac Finntain	abbot	663
Commán	bishop	678
Máel Dogair	bishop	678
Díraith	bishop	693
Mo Ling Luachair	bishop	696/97
Cilléne	bishop/abbot	715
Airechtach mac Cuanach	abbot	742
Bressal Mac Colgan	abbot	749
Reóthaide	abbot	763
Dub Indrecht mac Fergusso	abbot	781
Cronán mac Fernae	?	791

Name	Status	Died
Fiannachtach	abbot	799
Cilléne	abbot	814
Findchellach	abbot	862
Diarmait	abbot	870
Lachtnán mac Mochtigirn (also bishop of Kildare)	abbot	875
Fergil abbot	883	
Lachtnán	abbot	905
Laidcnén (also abbot of Tallaght)	coarb	939
Flathghus	abbot	946
Fínnechta mac Lachtnán (of Síl Máeluidir)	erenagh	958
Cairbre mac Laidcnán (also abbot of St Mullins)	abbot	967
Conaing mac Catháin	abbot	977
Conn Ua Laidcnán	abbot	997
Conchobar Ua Laidcnán (also abbot of St Mullins)	erenagh	1043
Diarmait Ua Rodacháin	bishop	1050
Conaing Ua Fairchellaigh (also abbot of Drumlane)	?	1059
Murchad Ua Laidcnán	erenagh	1062
Úgaire Ua Laidcnán	erenagh	1085
Cairpre Ua Cethernaig	bishop/abbot (Colgan)	1095
Cellach Ua Colmáin	bishop	1117
Máel Eoin Ua Dunacáin	bishop	1125
Brigtán Ua Catháin	bishop	1172
Joseph Ó hAodha (made bishop in 1160 or 1161)	bishop	1183

The pope was called the coarb of Peter, that is his spiritual heir, and bishop of Rome. Thus, the coarb was the successor of the founding saint of a particular monastery or church. The erenagh was one in charge of a dependent church but could also be coarb in his own right as standing in for a particular local saint.

Aidán died in 624 or 625. St Moling, founder of St Mullins, is quoted both in his own Life and that of Máedóg as succeeding him in Ferns. The year is given as 632, but this seems much too early, given that Moling lived until 696. He seems to have resigned early and returned to his beloved St Mullins, as the death of his successor, Da Chua Luachrae, is given for 654. This man, otherwise known as Cronán, is listed in the Martyrology of Óengus as 'the mighty Cronán of Ferns'. His feast day is listed in the Martyrologies as 22 June. A holy well dedicated to the saint, located at Killagowan, Oulart, was called Tober Mhic Lura. The 'pattern' which was held there on 22 June was abolished in 1810. Cronán and his successor, Ernóc who died in 663, were both abbots, not bishops. But bishops were in charge from sometime before 678 until 715.

From 713 until the death of Diarmait Ó Rodacháin in 1050 no bishop is recorded for Ferns. This does not mean that no bishop resided there, bishops were essential for the ordination of priests and other reserved functions. Ferns, then, was ruled by abbots for around 300 years. This is in line with what was happening elsewhere as the monasteries came under the control of particular families. Although somewhat later it can be seen that the Ó Laidcnán family virtually monopolized control of Ferns from 937 to 1085.

Abbots were sometimes married; for example, the Annals show that the abbot Lachtnán died in 905 and his son Fínnechta, erenagh of Ferns, died in 958.

From sometime before 1050, coinciding with the rise to power of Diarmait Mac Máel na mBó, Ferns had a bishop, Diarmait Ó Rodacháin, but he appears to have been followed by erenaghs up to 1095. This would fit in with the spiritual headship, the coarbship, passing to Drumlane, Co. Cavan.

A prosperous monastery

The foregoing list of the rulers of Ferns shows that the monastery functioned for centuries after its foundation. One indication of its importance is the presence of high stone crosses. Ferns has the heads of three large granite crosses. These have raised mouldings at the edges of the crosses and ringed heads, without perforations. The bases have survived but new shafts had to be fitted. These crosses are over 1. 0 metre in height and 1. 20 metres across the arms. There is a small cross to the east of the cathedral. These crosses are probably ninth century in date and may mark the boundary of the monastery at that time. A decorated cross shaft south of the cathedral is said to mark the grave of Diarmait Mac Murchada. Harbison (1992, 89) has described it as follows:

> A decorated shaft fragment stands in an unusually large flat granite base 1.40 m by 1.17 m, with raised mouldings on the edges and surrounding the bottom of the shaft. The granite shaft itself is 95 cm high, 57 cm wide and 34 cm thick. There are broad raised flattened mouldings at the edges. It has a meander pattern on the south side and fret patterns on the north side, as well as on the two faces.

According to Harbison the shaft is probably of ninth-century date.

The earliest churches on a monastic site would have been made of timber. But there may have been a stone church at Ferns in 789 (AFM).

Another indication of the wealth of Ferns is shown by its attraction to
the Vikings, who attacked it first in 835 and again in 921. With the rise to
power of Diarmait Mac Máel na mBó in the eleventh century the town of
Ferns assumed even greater importance, becoming the effective capital of
Leinster, and remaining so until the demise of his great-grandson, Diarmait
Mac Murchada, in 1171.

Trouble with Taghmon

Another indication of the importance and wealth of Ferns is found in its disputes, and even battles, with the monastery of Taghmon. The background
to the problem has been explained by Doherty (1987, 16). By the eighth century Taghmon lay in the control of the Síl Máeluidir, a branch of the Uí
Cheinnselaig. In the 730s the Síl Chormaic, another branch of the Uí
Cheinnselaig, were in control of central Wexford, including Ferns. But the
Síl Máeluidir coveted the kingship, including its powerhouse of the
monastery. In 769 (AU) they attacked Ferns. In 783 a 'war' took place
between the abbot, one of the Síl Chormaic, and the Síl Máeluidir steward.
Eventually, in 809 the Síl Máeluidir gained the kingship, but their territory
(approx. the barony of Shelmalier) did not include Ferns. Given the power,
prestige and wealth of Ferns this situation had to be remedied. In 817 a
major battle was fought between the forces of the monastery of Taghmon,
led by Cathal Mac Dúnlainge, and Ferns, in which 400 people were killed
(Ann. Clon.). The result seems to have favoured Taghmon; when Cathal
died two years later he was king of Uí Cheinnselaig and vice-abbot of Ferns
(AU). But Viking incursions into south Wexford soon gave the Síl Máeluidir
problems in their own territory.

Decline of the monastery

As the record of the rulers shows, Ferns did not escape secularization and
ultimate decline. However, it appears to have remained a seat of learning. In
1117 the Annals of the Four Masters record the birth of Áedh Mac
Crimthainn, described as Ferleighinn or lector at Ferns. He was to become
a friend to the young Diarmait Mac Murchada and later coarb of the
monastery of Terryglass, Co. Tipperary, and compiler of the Book of
Leinster. The Annals of the Four Masters also record the death of Mac
Muirgheasa, professor of Ferns in 1129. According to Ó Riain (1986, 163)
the Life of St Abbán may have been written at Ferns by Ailbhe O'Mulloy,
the last Gaelic bishop of Ferns, who died in 1183. There is also the possibility that St Aidán's Life was compiled there under Ailbhe's direction
(Sharpe, 1991, 362).

There seems to have been little trace of a monastery when Diarmait
granted a charter for the foundation of the abbey for the canons regular of

St Augustine around 1160. The only building mentioned for Ferns is 'the cell of Finach,' which is obviously a small structure. Could it be that Sharpe (1992, 102) is correct when he suggests that as far back as the late eighth century a regular monastic or contemplative ideal was no longer in vogue and that the monasteries had become simply communities of priests and monks?

The Augustinian canons regular arrive in Ferns

As part of the church reforms twelfth-century religious orders from Continental Europe were brought into Ireland. The canons regular of St Augustine were introduced by Malachy of Armagh around 1127. Their religious code was based on the rule of St Augustine of Hippo in eastern Algeria, or Numidia, as it was then called. They became important in restoring religious life and church discipline in the twelfth century and later. Canons regular were intermediate between monks and secular (not in religious order) priests; they should not be confused with the Augustinian friars who also followed the rule of St Augustine and who came to Ireland in the wake of the Normans.

Around 1160 Diarmait Mac Murchada granted a charter to the Augustinian canons for St Mary's abbey (more correctly called a priory) in Ferns, adjacent to the old monastic site. A Latin copy of this charter was printed in Dugdale (1673). The following translation was published in Hore (vi, 180-1):

> To all the sons of Holy Mother Church, archbishops, bishops, abbots, earls, barons, and all others, as well as clergy and laity, Dermot, by the will of God, king of Leinster (sends) greeting. Be it known that I, by the counsel and advice of the principal men (of my Council), have given and granted and by this charter have confirmed to God and the blessed Virgin Mary (for the monastery) which I have founded at Ferns and to the canons there serving God the following lands, namely Balisifin, Balilacussa, for one village; Borin and Roshena and Kilbride for two villages; the lands of Ballifislan in Forth near Wexford, the village called Munemethe in Ferneghenan and a certain cell at Thaghmoling being the chapel of St Mary with all belongings with the land of Balligery with all the fisheries and my chapel with all the tithes and first fruits of the Lordship of Uí Ceinnseallach, and a certain measure called Scaith out of every measure called a lagen or gallon in the brewing of beer made in the town of Ferns; to be held of me and my heirs by the said canons in pure and perpetual alms for the health of my soul and my ancestors and successors.
>
> As also the cell of Finach in Ferns with Baliculum and Balinafusin and three acres close to the same cell.

I also will and firmly ordain that the said house and canons there serving God shall have hold and possess the said lands in the aforesaid alms from me my heirs and successors completely in peace fully and wholly without paying any rent or (rendering) any secular service neither to bishop, king, earl nor any other man, in wood, in plain, in meadows, in pastures, and in fisheries which belong to me and to my heirs, in waters, in mills, in roads and paths, in moors and marshes, and in all other liberties and free customs which I and my heirs are able to grant and warrant to the said canons and their successors. I and my heirs are bound to warrant the same house in the aforesaid lands and possessions to the same canons and their successors against all men and women. I have also conceded to them that in any elections or removals of abbots of the same house no heir of mine ought to meddle but that he who is to be ordained should be freely constituted according to the rule of St Augustine by the consent of this convent or the major part of them and after the election of the same, before he be created abbot by the archbishop or bishop he shall be presented to me or my heirs or their seneschals by reason of the lordship that through us he may be blessed by the bishop.

Given this 21 February at Ferns, these being witnesses: Christian, bishop of Lismore and (apostolic) legate of all Ireland (1150-70); Dermot, bishop of Leighlin (1168-85); Joseph, bishop of Ferns (1155-85); Donald, bishop of Ossory (1152-78); Malachy, bishop of Kildare (1158-76); Celestine, bishop of Glendalough; Laurence, abbot of Glendalough; Florence, the king's chancellor; Mark, the chaplain; Lorcán, the son of Dufgill; Gillapatrick ó Murchada and many others.

The Romanesque-style priory has been described in detail by O'Keeffe (forthcoming) who suggests that it dates to the 1140s or at the latest the early 1150s. A brick stair was inserted in the turret in the nineteenth century.

Diarmait Mac Murchada died at Ferns in 1171 (AFM). A decorated cross shaft in the cemetery is said to mark his grave.

TAGHMON

The foundation of the monastery
The Life of Munnu describes how the saint came to a place called Achadh Liathdrum meaning 'the field of the grey ridge'. The local chief, Dimma or Diarmait, a nobleman of the Fothart, gave him land on which to found his

monastery. This he marked out with four crosses. The monastery and the town which grew up around it were later called Taghmon, or Teach Munnu. In Early Christian times *teach* had an additional specialized meaning, apart from house, of 'a (monastic) church'.

The monastery appears to have functioned as a school and to have flourished from the start. In the Martyrology of Tallaght, Munnu is credited with having two hundred and thirty monks under him there. At least one of these came from Britain. He is described in the Life (§xxviii) as being learned in woodworking and to have made wagons and other appliances for the brethern. Another indication that Munnu and his monastery were held in high esteem is shown by the fact that St Aidán paid a visit there. Three members of the Taghmon community Commán (died 678), Díraith (died 693) and Cilléne (died 715) became bishop/abbots of Ferns.

Munnu's Life describes how the chief of Fothart gave his son Cillene to Taghmon to be educated. On a visit to the monastery the chief was not pleased to find his son 'in servile array, pulling a wagon with the rest of the monks' (Plummer, 1910, ii, p. xxi).

The monastery flourishes
It is clear that the monastery continued to flourish for centuries after the death of St Munnu in 636. Apart from a hiatus between the death of Munnu and that of Ciarán, who died in 777, a complete list of abbots up to 953 has been documented.

The following dates of death of the abbots are taken from the Annals of the Four Masters, apart from Ossíne, who is mentioned in the Life of Adomnán (Anderson and Anderson, 1961, 101-2):

Munnu	636	Dúnghal (vice-abbot)	885
Ossíne	687	Diarmaid	886
Ciarán	777	Cochlán	889
Crundmáel	817	Soichleachán	925
Laisren	854	Dúnlang Mac Donnagáin	
Fiachra	859	(also abbot of Inis-Doimhle)	953

The suggestion put forward by Dalton (1921, 24), based on a paragraph in Colgan (1947, 135), that St Munnu desired St Fechin of Fore to succeed him at Taghmon has little historical merit. The reference, if it has any validity, may be to Taughmon, Co. Westmeath, an early foundation of the saint.

The decorated high cross also points to a prosperous monastery in the ninth century. This cross, of which Crawford reported (1905, 269) that the

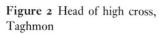

Figure 2 Head of high cross, Taghmon

shaft was missing, and one arm broken, has a head with flat bosses or roundels, with hollows in the centre. The base has a large cross in relief.

The Annals of Ulster record that in 828, Cairpre, son of Cathal, king of Uí Cheinnselaig, and the men of Taghmon, defeated the Norse, or Gentiles, as the monks who recorded such attacks named them. Undeterred, they plundered the monastery in 835 and again in 921.

War with Ferns
During the eighth and ninth centuries two powerful segments of the Uí Cheinnselaig contested the kingship, the Síl Máeluidir and the Síl Chormaic. However, kingship without control of Ferns meant little, or rather meant war. The ensuing conflicts are detailed under Ferns.

The decline of the monastery
In common with the other monasteries of the Early Christian period Taghmon probably began to decline in the ninth century. That it remained in existence until at least the eleventh century is shown in the Annals of

Inisfallen. These relate how Domhnall Deisech, 'chief of the Gaedil in piety and charity, chief soul friend of Ireland, who had travelled where Christ travelled on earth, died in Taghmon in 1060'.

BEGGERIN

The monastery on Beggerin island was established in the latter half of the sixth century by St Ibar, who died around 500. It must have been one of the earliest such foundations in the country. At that time Beggerin was just one of the small islands of glacial drift protruding above the mudflats in Wexford Harbour. Given that the island was only seven acres in extent, it is doubtful if it could have supported many people, unless provisions were brought by boat from the mainland. So why did Ibar chose such an isolated spot?

He already had a considerable reputation in the country so there was no chance, even if he wished, of leading an eremetical life there. The most likely explanation seems to be that he wanted to set up a school where he could isolate his followers from the worldly temptations of the mainland. Or he may have been protecting them from the pagan influence of the majority population around Wexford. The more mundane explanation may be that he was given the island or that he took it because it was a fairly safe location. The fanciful story is told in the Life of St Declán of Ardmore (de Paor, 1993, 251) that Ibar came to an island in Wexford Harbour, which he named Beggerin, rather than accept the jurisdiction of St Patrick on the mainland (see p. 84, above).

Later history of Beggerin
Although references to the monastery are few, they show that it survived throughout the Early Christian period. The Annals of the Four Masters note that in 821 it, and Dairinis, were ravaged by the Vikings. In 884 Diarmait, abbot of Beggerin, died. In 964 Crundmáel, the abbot was drowned. He was also bishop and lector of St Maelruan's monastery in Tallaght, which indicates a strong connection between both foundations and also the influence of the reform movement known as the *Céli Dé* in the Wexford area. In the late ninth-century Tripartite Life of St Patrick (Stokes, 1887, 192-3), it was claimed that Crimthann, king of Leinster, gave the church of Beggerin or Inis Fáil, as it was sometimes called, to Patrick, thus making it subject to Armagh. The names of two monks, Mo Chon-óc and Mo Chat-óc are listed.

Flood (1916, 154) stated that the monastery was closed in 1160, but no evidence has been found to substantiate this claim. In 1171, the Norman leader, Robert Fitzstephen, was imprisoned on Beggerin by the inhabitants of Wexford town.

In 1181 the Anglo-Flemish family of Roche, to whom the area had been given after the Norman conquest, presented the island to the Benedictine monks of St Nicholas, Exeter. The remains of the church which they constructed in the thirteenth century can still be seen. In 1400 it passed to the Augustinian canons of Selskar Abbey, but there is no evidence that they established a church there.

In 1682 Solomon Richards, a Cromwellian officer, stated that there was on the island a little wooden chapel with 'a wooden idol in the shape of an old man called St Iberion' (Hore, vol. v, 364). This statue was an object of veneration, and, like many ancient relics, was used for taking oaths.

An account by the geologist, Kinahan (1872, 436), mentions two islands southeast of Beggerin and two more to the northwest. A causeway linking the islands to the southeast to Beggerin, discovered during the reclamation of the North Slob in the 1840s, consisted of two rows of oak piles, one foot six inches by nine inches in section; the rows were four feet apart, with about five feet between each pair.

Kinahan also states that the lower part of a large saddle quern stone and a possible grinder for this were found on the island at that time.

The stone slabs of Beggerin

Two unusual stone slabs were found at Beggerin. The art work on these stones, one now in the County Museum, Enniscorthy, the other in the National Museum, has always posed something of an enigma for scholars. The most recent opinions point to a strong influence from the Isle of Man, Scotland and Cornwall.

The stone in the County Museum has been discussed by Harbison (1988, 59-66). One face shows a cross in high relief whose closest affinities are found, not in Ireland, but in Cornwall. The upper part of the other face has been badly worn, but, according to Harbison, may have shown an encircled Maltese cross. Below this are three robed figures, badly worn. The lowest, and perhaps best known figure, is of a man astride a pony, apparently without reins or saddle. Carved comparisons to this figure are found in Scotland and the Isle of Man and a ninth-century date has been suggested for them.

The stone in the National Museum has been discussed by Nessa O'Connor (1983, 142-43). One face of this stone is undecorated, the other shows the head of a ringed cross. Some interlacing on this face shows the Viking influence and O'Connor has suggested that the best comparisons are again found in Scotland, Wales and the Isle of Man. She dates this stone to the tenth century. It seems likely that some Vikings had joined the monastery as happened in monasteries in other parts of Ireland (Ó Floinn, 1998, 164).

As Harbison states, the art work on these two stones could suggest that in the ninth and tenth centuries the southeast of Ireland was at least as culturally attuned to the artistic developments on the far side of the Irish Sea as the rest of Ireland. It would also suggest, perhaps, strong links between Viking Wexford and Viking centres in Britain.

TEMPLESHANBO

The church at Templeshanbo was dedicated to St Colmán, of the Tyrone branch of the Ua Fiachra, the founder of Kilmacduagh, Co. Galway, whose feast day is on 27 October. In the Martyrologies his church and well are stated to be at the foot of Mount Leinster. In the Martyrology of Donegal it is stated that he was abbot of the monastery of Templeshanbo, in Uí Cheinnselaig, where he was interred. The grave of such an important saint would have considerably enhanced the prestige of the monastery. The Martyrology of Óengus tells how the ducks at St Colmán's Well cannot be injured, 'and in his church are the ducks, and they are not touched, for though by mistake at night they are put into water on a fire, and all the woods of the world are burnt under the cauldron, the water does not get hot until they are taken out and put into the same pool in which they were before'.

The Life of Aidán (Plummer, 1922, ii) contains two references to Templeshanbo, one that Aidán paid a visit there (209), and another that Saran, called the squinting, who was erenagh of Templeshanbo, killed Brandubh, king of Leinster, in 601 (224). This is also recorded in the Annals of the Four Masters for 601.

Moore (1996, 117) lists the ruins as part of a Romanesque church, with a bullaun stone in the doorway, within an oval-shaped graveyard. Another bullaun stone, now missing, was located at St Colmán's well, 150 metres to the southeast.

An aerial colour photo of the site (Moore, 1996) revealed a large double-ditched enclosure, with a maximum diameter of about 250 metres. This would indicate that Templeshanbo was an important Early Christian foundation. The Life of St Abbán (Plummer, 1910, i, 29) describes how the saint raised his friend, Conall, of Templeshanbo, from the dead. He immediately bestowed all his lands on Abbán and his seed and territory to the monastery of St Abbán. Since the Life of Abbán was written in the twelfth century, possibly by the bishop of Ferns, Ailbhe O' Mulloy, this probably reflects the bishop's objective of laying claim to the church property at Templeshanbo. That he succeeded is shown by the fact that his successor, John St John, held a manor there and was granted a weekly market by the king (Hore, vi, 185).

Convents

There are only two references to nuns in Co. Wexford in the Early Christian period. The Life of St Ibar tells how St Monenna, with her nuns, came from the north to live under the rule of the saint in Wexford. She may have been attracted by the fact that Ibar himself had also come from the north. There is no record of where they established their convent; it may have been on Beggerin island itself. After a young nun created discord Monenna moved to Killevy, Co. Armagh, where she died in 517 or 519.

According to Flood (1916, 183) there may have been a nunnery in Taghmon before the arrival of the Normans. This was taken over by nuns of the Arroasian rule of St Augustine at the end of the twelfth century, but it became derelict about 1330 and its lands were assigned to the prior of St John's, Wexford.

13

The Early Christian ecclesiastical sites

The sites of many churches can still be found on the landscape (Map 9). The problem is to identify those belonging to the Early Christian period. Even then, it is not always possible to say during which part of the Early Christian period they functioned as religious centres. Not all would have been in operation for the whole period. Some would have prospered or failed depending on the fortunes of their owners; the survival of others may have depended on factors such as the availability of priests, a perennial problem, apparently. Ó Corráin points out (1981, 339) that some churches 'lost their right to ecclesiastical privilege – the church which has become a den of thieves or a place of sin, the church ruled by a layman or by a backslider who has failed to honour his vow of chastity, the church from which the bell and psalm have departed and the derelict church'. Depletion of the population through plagues and famine also led to the closure of churches at various times.

It should be noted that churches founded as part of the twelfth-century reforms are not include in this survey.

Criteria for identification
Several studies have been carried out on the identification of Early Christian ecclesiastical sites using a number of criteria (Hurley, 1982, 297-330: Swan, 1988, 274: O'Brien, 1988, 504-24). Only two of those suggested by them, the presence of burials and graveyards and where a section of the enclosure forms part of a townland boundary, do not seem to have general application in Co. Wexford. Taking the evidence of the other criteria and using the additional information of references in Irish and early Norman literary sources, a list of criteria has been drawn up to help verify the authenticity of the sites designated as Early Christian in Co. Wexford. In this way it was hoped to eliminate any subjectivity or wishful thinking from the survey. Not all the criteria are of equal importance. Some may be conclusive on their own. Ardcolm, for example, is mentioned in the Annals of the Four Masters

for the year 890. Others have high crosses and cross slabs which can be dated with some certainty.

Only in cases where at least two of the criteria listed below have been fulfilled are the sites assigned to the Early Christian period:

* Large circular, subcircular, oval or D- shaped enclosure
* Smaller circular, subcircular, oval or D-shaped enclosure
* Ecclesiastical element in place-name
* Church and adjacent holy well dedication and 'pattern' date
* Stone crosses, cross slabs and ogham stone
* Architectural feature
* Mention in Irish and early Norman sources
* Bullaun stone

Although not all these criteria are of equal importance in the evaluation it was not feasible to give a precise priority rating or weighting to each site. Despite such rigorous criteria and critical scrutiny, inevitably some sites will have been omitted and other post-Early Christian sites included in the survey.

Based on the criteria outlined it was found that of the ninety sites classified as Early Christian (apart from Wexford town) only two featured five criteria, ten (10%) had four, twenty-eight (30%) had three and fifty-four (60%) had two. Though not included in the definitive list an additional twenty-nine sites contained one of the criteria.

Sourcing the information

The principal source of information on Early Christian church sites was Michael Moore's *Archaeological inventory of Co. Wexford* published in 1996, which provided the location and physical description of most of the sites. Other valuable sources were An tAthair Seamas de Val's 'Origin and meaning of townland names in Co. Wexford' (1994), *The history of the diocese of Ferns* (Flood, 1916), the Martyrologies of Óengus, Tallaght, Gorman and Donegal, O'Donovan's 1840 Ordnance Survey letters as well as the Ordnance Survey six-inch maps of 1840 and the Lives of the saints. Including these references for each individual site would have made the text very cumbersome. For this reason they are omitted in most cases, but occasional references are given in the usual manner.

Some early Norman documents such as the foundation charter of Tintern abbey, and those pertaining to the bishop of Ferns claims to certain lands and churches in the county are also useful in establishing an Early Christian date for some sites.

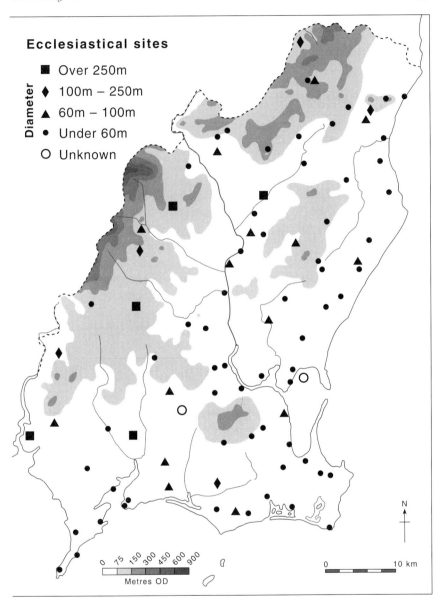

Ecclesiastical sites

Diameter

■ Over 250m
♦ 100m – 250m
▲ 60m – 100m
• Under 60m
○ Unknown

0 75 150 300 450 600 900
Metres OD

N

0   10 km

Map 9 Ecclesiastical sites which can definitely be assigned to the Early Christian period vary greatly in size, from a maximum of around 450 metres diameter to as little as thirty metres. No doubt this reflected the importance and wealth of each site.

Large circular, subcircular and oval enclosures

From early in the period the ecclesiastical sites were surrounded by a circular, near circular or oval bank of earth or stone similar to the ráths. The area within the enclosure contained the church, and in the case of large enclosures, other churches and buildings. Access to certain areas was forbidden except to the priests and monks and those seeking sanctuary, perhaps from an enemy. Of the large Early Christian sites of these shapes in the county twenty eight are sixty metres or more in diameter, many being much larger. The following table shows the range of sizes within this category:

Table 4: Location, shape and dimensions of circular, subcircular, oval and D-shaped Early Christian enclosures over 60 metres in diameter

Location	Shape	Dimensions (m.)
Ferns	oval	450 x 300
Kilmokea	oval	330 x 260
Clongeen	circular	300 approx.
Beggerin	an island	−
Taghmon	not traceable	−
Killegney	circular	250 approx.
Templeshanbo	circular	250 approx.
Morrisseysland	subcircular	155 x 140
Kilcashel	oval	137
Kilcowan	circular	136
Killann	circular	120
Kilmurry	circular	100
Ballybrazil	subcircular	94 x 86
Grange-Kilmore	circular	90
Kilmakilloge	D-shape	82 x 60
Killabeg	circular	83
Kilcavan	subcircular	80 x 72
Kilbride	oval	80 x 62
Kilmuckridge	D-shape	80 x 50
Kildoran	circular	70
Kilmallock	circular	70
Coolhull	subcircular	70 x 60
Kilrush	subcircular	65
Kerloge	oval	64 x 30
Kilcormick	subcircular	61 x 55
Kilgarvan	circular	60
Templeshannon	D-shape	60 x 60

The lower limit of sixty metres diameter for the larger sites is somewhat arbitrary, although it does approximate to the upper size limit of ráths in

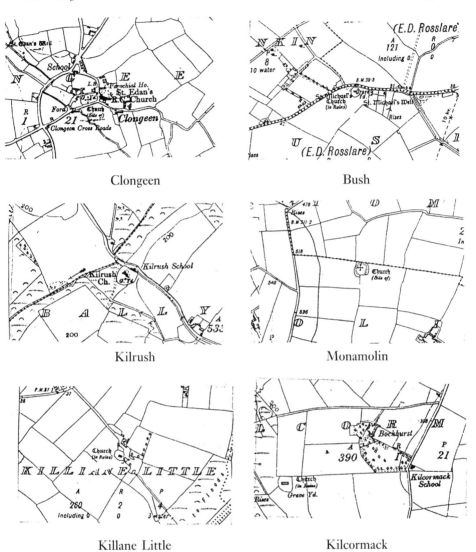

Figure 3 Many Early Christian ecclesiastical sites were surrounded by a circular or nearly-circular earthen enclosure; note how parts have been removed at Clongeen, Kilcormack and Kilrush. This figure is an extract from Ordnance Survey six-inch Map C 1924 © Government of Ireland Permit No. MP001499.

the county as derived from Moore (1996). Most, however (seventy five percent), are in the range thirty to forty metres in diameter. Interestingly, the average diameter of circular ecclesiastical sites as found by Swan (1988, 274) is between 90 and 120 metres, with a significant proportion ranging between 140 and over 400 metres.

It is obvious that, apart from Taghmon whose size is unknown but can be presumed to have been extensive, the largest sites were the well-documented monasteries of Ferns and Beggerin Island. Some slightly smaller sites get a brief mention in the literature, for example, Clongeen and Templeshanbo. But, as in the case of many large ecclesiastical centres in Ireland, many such sites in Co. Wexford such as Kilmokea and Killegney are shrouded in mystery. Also totally lost to posterity are any records of the slightly smaller sites, apart from the name of the saint to whom the church or holy well is dedicated. References in the Lives of the saints show that several, at least, were probably in operation by the seventh, if not the sixth, century.

The size of these sites raises questions as to their function or functions. The Life of St Munnu shows that some operated as schools for the children of the nobility, although most of the nobility were thought to be illiterate. But were they more than this? Doherty (1982) has pointed out that the larger monasteries and major churches also functioned as market centres and towns from, at least, the tenth century. Perhaps the other large sites fulfilled a similar role. Kilmokea was obviously a thriving centre, with its own water-powered corn grinding mill.

Some may have started off as small churches but with endowments, dues and gifts from the laity may have become enlarged as the church grew richer.

Smaller subcircular, oval and D-shaped enclosures

Not all ecclesiastical sites in the county are large. Some twenty-one are less than sixty metres in diameter. In these cases it must be stressed that their identification is not based on this single factor; usually several other factors give conclusive proof of the Early Christian and ecclesiastical origin of these sites.

Undoubtedly the circular enclosure or a variant of it, such as oval or D-shaped, was the most common shape of earthworks in Early Christian times. This is evident in the shape of the large number of ráths or ringforts in the country.

The D-shape may be a remnant of a circular enclosure or at least it shows the predisposition towards circularity in this period. Alternatively, it may have been as a result of topographic or economic constraints.

As in the case of the larger enclosures, the smaller sites are usually surrounded by an earthen bank, with stone revetment in some cases. Originally, they would have had a fosse or ditch on the outside similar to the ringforts but only traces now remain at Doonooney, Killell and St Dubhán's.

Many of the well-proven Early Christian sites such as Clone, Donagh-more, Kilcowanmore (Ballybrennan td), Killincooley, Kilmacree, Kil-mannon, Rathaspick and Toome (Ballinclare td) are, in fact, rectangular. Whether they still retain their original shape or became altered over the centuries is now impossible to tell. But it does indicate that shape alone cannot be used as a defining factor in ascribing an Early Christian origin to a particular site. Of course, D-shaped or rectangular enclosures may represent later attempts to define parts of the old enclosure still in use for burial. Obviously a variety of shapes was constructed, perhaps influenced by local factors such as existing boundaries or inhibiting topographical features.

Table 5 Location, shape and dimensions of circular, subcircular, oval and D-shaped Early Christian ecclesiastical sites less than 60 metres in diameter

Location	Shape	Dimensions (m.)
Ardcavan	oval	53 x 18-30
Ardcolm	circular	46 x 42
Ballycanew	subcircular	44 x 30
Ballyvalloo	oval	35 x 23
Bush	circular	30
Kayle	subcircular	46 x 44
Kilbrideglynn	oval	50 x 34
Kildavin	circular	47
Kildenis	circular	40
Killell	circular	40
Killiane Little	circular	40
Killilla	oval	52 x 40
Killinick	circular	45
Killisk	circular	42 x 39
Kilnahue	oval	50 x 44
Kilpatrick	D-shape	46 x 46
Kiltennel	D-shape	52 x 46
Kiltilly	subcircular	35 x 33
Kilturk	circular	42
Monamolin (Rathnure)	circular	46 x 44
St Vauk's	subcircular	48 x 42

Ecclesiastical element in place-name

A common criterion of Early Christian ecclesiastical sites is the inclusion of the element 'kill' in the place-name. Kill is the anglicized form of the Irish word *cill*, meaning church. As Thomas points out (1995, 57) the Old Irish word cell is a direct loan from the Latin *cella*. In Ireland cell originally referred to 'the establishment of a Christian solitary', that is, a hermit or anchorite. By the sixth or seventh century the word meant an enlarged oratory or main church. The Royal Irish Academy Dictionary defines cell as 'usually church – monastic settlement or foundation, collection of ecclesiastical buildings'. Care must be taken not to confuse it with 'kill' which also may denote 'a wood'. In this case it is derived from the Irish word *coill*. Usually, it is possible to differentiate between the two meanings from other evidence such as a saint's dedication, for example, Kilbride-the church of Brigid.

As Flanagan (1984, 32) pointed out the word 'kill' is not confined to this period:

> While the majority of Irish *cell* (kill) names (as entered in Hogan's *Onomasticon Goedelicum*) belong to the native Irish period of monasticism, there is evidence that cell continued to be used, although apparently less frequently, in place-name coinage of the post-twelfth century period with reference to the churches and occasionally monastic houses … The indications are that the appellative cell in the sense of 'church' (or monastery) went out of use in the course of the later medieval period, and, it is assumed, out of use in place-name coinage, although retained in its transferred sense of 'graveyard' … The name may postdate the establishment of the unit itself, irrespective of how reliable the attested historical associations are seen to be.

Over fifty Early Christian sites with the element 'kill' meaning church have been recognized in Co. Wexford. Of these, some are dedicated to identifiable saints such as Aidán. Others such as Killag, Killincooley Beg, Killisk and Kilrush are associated with topographical features. Several contain the names of people who cannot be identified, for example, Kildenis and Kilscoran. Two sites may have been churches of family estates, Kildoran which possibly belonged to the Ó Doráin (Doran) family who were hereditary lawyers to the Uí Cheinnselaig, (there is a St Durán in the Irish calendar of saints: Ó Riain, 1985, 134) and Killynann, which probably belonged to the powerful Ó Laighnán family, which was associated with the monastery of Ferns. That the church at Kilnamanagh once belonged to the monastery of St Mullins is indicated by its dedication to St Moling. Killagowan, which was obviously a very important ecclesiastical centre, means 'the church of the smith'.

The location of several church sites which are undoubtedly of Early Christian date cannot now be traced on the ground. These are Kilbegnet, dedicated to St Begnet, Kilmacoe, dedicated to St Cronán, feast day 22 June (see Killagowan), Kilmichael, probably a Norse foundation, dedicated to St Michael, the archangel and Kiltealy, dedicated to a St Teile, about whom nothing is known.

Place-names with the word 'donagh' from domnach meaning church in Old Irish, also denote an Early Christian origin. Donaghmore is the only example in the county.

The word 'temple' was not in use in Early Christian times, but some sites in Co. Wexford with the word are shown by other criteria to date from this period. These are Templeudigan, Templeshanbo and Templeshannon. It seems that the original Irish words were changed after the Early Christian period.

Church and adjacent holy well dedications and 'pattern' dates

Of the ninety ecclesiastical sites identified in Co. Wexford (apart from Wexford town) seventy percent were dedicated to early Irish saints. The rest included St Patrick, several saints with Welsh connections, and some early foreign saints such as Peter, Eusebius, John the Baptist, Martin, Stephen, and the heavenly St Michael the Archangel.

The main saints to whom churches were dedicated are as follows (number of churches in brackets):

St Aidán or Máedóg (7): Ardamine, Clone, Clongeen, Coolhull, Ferns, Fethard, Kilnahue,

St Moling (5): Ballycanew, Kilnamanagh, Monamolin (2) Toome

St Caomhán (4): Ardcavan, Kilcavan (Bannow), Kilcavan (Gorey), Kilmacree

St Brigid (4): Kilbride (Ballylusk), Kilbrideglynn, Killilla, Rathaspick

St Cuán (3): Kilcowan, Kilcowanmore, Kilturk

St Degumen (2): Killag, Killiane Little

St Patrick (4): Donaghmore, Kilmore, Saunderscourt, St Patrick's in Wexford

Enóc or Innick or Enán? (3): Killinick, Kilscoran, Rossminoge

St Ibar (2): Beggerin, St Iberius-Wexford

St Munnu (2): Tacumshin, Taghmon

St Columcille (2): Ardcolm, Kilcomb

St Sillóg (2): Kilmakilloge, Kilmallock

St Colmán of Mid-ísil (2): Kilmyshall, Kilrush

St Abbán (1): Adamstown.

Unfortunately, for the purpose of historical research, there has been a tendency to transfer all 'pattern' days to the summer months. This means that in time the connection with the original saints' feast days and eventually with the saints themselves will be lost.

In the absence of 'pattern' days, some of the dedications are impossible to sort out. For example, five Garbháns are listed in the Martyrologies but it is not known to which of them Kilgarvan was dedicated. In other cases knowing the 'pattern' date has enabled the dedication to be confirmed. This applied at Kilcavan, Kilcomb, Kilcormick, Kilcowanmore and Kilmannon.

The close connection between southeast Ireland and Wales is reflected in church dedications to David, Degumen, Dubhán, Brecaun and Brioc. While David was well known to the early Irish Church he was also a patron of the Normans who invoked his aid before engaging in battle with the Irish (Orpen, 1892, 57).

From their listing in the Martyrologies it is known that the early Irish Church held certain foreign saints in high regard. Thus, we find churches dedicated to St Peter, St John, Michael the Archangel, St Eusebius, St Stephen, St Agatha and St Martin of Tours.

By the twelfth and thirteenth centuries the cults of the universal saints were taking over from the local saints (Geary, 1994, 175). In Ireland this trend was enhanced by the arrival of the new religious orders and the Normans who brought devotion to their own special saints. The canons regular of St Augustine, who came to Ireland around the middle of the twelfth century, dedicated churches and wells to Mary, the mother of Jesus, but she was also venerated in the early Irish Church as shown by her listing in the Martyrology of Óengus. Churches were also dedicated to Mary Magdalene, St James, St Nicholas, St Anne and St Catherine around this time. In fact, they sometimes replaced the older Irish dedications as at Rathnure, Templeludigan and Tomhaggard.

Holy wells are frequently associated with early church sites, but they also occur in isolation. Their origins go back to the pre-Christian period, as do many of the rituals observed at them up to recent times. Early Christianity used many elements of the older religions, including the sacredness of natural springs, in order to win more converts. This, apart from the convenience of having a ready source of water for baptisms and domestic use, probably led to the location of some churches near such springs. In Co. Wexford the church and holy well have the same dedication in twenty-five percent of cases: in other cases the church or holy well dedication only is known, see Appendix 3.

Stone crosses, cross slabs and ogham stones

Another indication of an Early Christian origin for a church site is the presence of stone artifacts such as crosses, decorated stone slabs and ogham stones. Parts of high crosses are found at Ferns and Taghmon, in both cases probably dating to the eighth or the ninth century. A cross at Rossminoge North may date to the same period. There are also crosses, possibly from the Early Christian period, at Kildoran, Kilmokea and Adamstown.

Stone slabs were popular as grave markers from the seventh century onwards. At Killell in Bulgan townland, Glynn, a cross-carved slab was found which Kelly (1988, 100) dates to the sixth or seventh century. Examples with incised crosses are found at Clone, Ferns, Kilcowanmore, Kilgorman and Killell. No examples with names inscribed are found in Co. Wexford. At Killannduff a Latin cross, measuring only 0.53 metres across the arms, was found on which there are crosses in relief on one face. The other face shows a raised rectangle. This is now in the County Museum, Enniscorthy. At Killabeg a cross was inscribed over an ogham inscription (Macalister, 1945, 49-50). Parts of an ogham stone were also found at St Brecaun's church, Hook Head.

Architectural features
Co. Wexford has very few architectural church features dating to the Early Christian period. At St Dubhán's church at Churchtown on Hook Head a small nave and antae were incorporated into a later medieval church. Dating from the twelfth-century Romanesque period are the slight remains of churches at Templeshanbo and Kilmakilloge. Also from the later period is St Mary's abbey, Ferns, which was built around 1160 and rebuilt in 1169.

Church sites mentioned in early literature
Mention in early literature sources such as the Martyrologies and the Lives of the saints provides positive evidence for an Early Christian origin for some church sites in the county. Unfortunately, many of the places referred to cannot be identified. The earliest reference, found in a Fragment in the Book of Armagh, compiled around 807, mentions a supposed visit by St Patrick to Donaghmore (de Paor, 1993, 206).

The Martyrology of Tallaght, which was compiled around 800, but which has some additions from the 900s, lists the following churches: Adamstown (Magh Arnaidhe), Ferns, Rathaspick, Rossminoge, Taghmon, Templeshanbo.

The Martyrology of Óengus, compiled in the early 800s, lists the following churches: Ardcavan, Beggerin, Ferns, Kilmakilloge, Rossminoge, Taghmon and Templeshanbo.

The Martyrology of Gorman, compiled between 1166 and 1174, lists the following churches: Adamstown (Magh Arnaidhe), Ardcavan, Beggerin.

The Martyrology of Donegal, compiled by Brother Michael O'Clery, one of the Four Masters, and completed in 1630, lists the following churches: Adamstown, Ardcavan, Beggerin, Ferns, Kilgorman, Kilmakilloge, Kilmuckridge, Rathaspick, Rinn Dubháin (St Dubhán's) on Hook Head, Taghmon, Templeshanbo. In the Annals of the Four Masters, Ardcolm is mentioned for the year 890 when Ciarán, son of the abbot of Ferns, died. It was probably founded much earlier.

The Lives of the saints were mostly written down between the ninth and the thirteenth centuries, but the places referred to were probably in existence during, if not before, the lifetime of the saint:

Ibar	Beggerin
Abbán	Adamstown, Beggerin, Camaross, Templeshanbo
Munnu	Taghmon
Caomhán	Ardcavan
Aidán	Ardamine, Clongeen, Clonmore (Bree), Ferns, Taghmon, Templeshanbo

Norman records: several documents dating from the medieval period show that the bishop of Ferns quickly disputed the ownership of certain lands in Co. Wexford which had been appropriated by the newly arrived Normans. These lands would have included several churches dating to the Early Christian period. Between 1228 and 1232 the bishop successfully reclaimed churches in south Wexford at Kilmore, Tomhaggard, Brandane, Carrig (on-Bannow), Kilcowan, Kilturk and Fethard (Hore, ii, 32). Colfer (1986, 46) suggests that the manor of Kinnagh, and presumably the church, were also owned by the bishop in pre-Norman times.

In the 1220s the Norman, Philip de Prendergast, accepted the bishop's claim for large tracts of land at Templeshanbo, Killalligan, Clone and a smaller portion at Killegney.

That the bishop held lands at Ferns, Enniscorthy and Templeshanbo, which also contained church sites, is shown by the fact that in 1226 Henry III granted weekly markets and annual fairs to him in these places (Hore, vi, 342). In the same year Gerald de Prendergast granted the church of St Senán, Enniscorthy, to the priory of St John, Enniscorthy.

Bullaun stones

These are boulders or large stones with one or more bowl-shaped depressions. They are mostly associated with Early Christian sites and may have served as holy water or baptismal fonts or communal mortars used for grinding grain. Their location on ecclesiastical property may have saved them from loss or destruction. They are found at the following sites: Ballycanew, Ballynastraw Oylegate), Clone, Coolstuff, Courthoyle, Garraun Lower, Kildenis, Kildoran, Killiane Little, Killynann, Kilmacree, Kilmannon (now in Bannow), Kilmokea, Kilnahue, Kilrush, Morrisseysland, St Kieran's, Shelbaggan, Templeshanbo, Templeshannon and Toome.

Bullaun stones are also found at several sites which have no indication of being used for ecclesiastical purposes in the Early Christian period.

Sites fulfilling specific numbers of identifying criteria
Sites fulfilling five criteria: Kilmakilloge, Templeshanbo

Sites fulfilling four criteria: Adamstown, Beggerin, Clone, Ferns, Kilcowan, Killiane Little, Kilmokea, Kilnahue, Kilrush, Taghmon

Sites fulfilling three criteria: Ardcavan, Ardcolm, Ballycanew, Clongeen, Donaghmore, Kerloge, Kilcavan, Kilcormick, Kildavin, Kildenis, Kildoran, Kilgarvan, Kilgorman, Killegney, Killell, Killinick, Killurin, Kilmallock, Kilmannon, Kilmore, Kilmuckridge, Kiltennel, Kiltilly, Kilturk, Rathaspick, St Vauk's, Shelbaggan, Templeshannon

Sites fulfilling two criteria: Ardamine, Ardcandrisk, Ballybrazil, Brandane, Bush, Carrick (on-Bannow), Clonmore, Coolhull, Dairinis, Fethard, Kayle, Kilbride (Ballylusk), Kilbrideglynn, Kilcashel, Kilcavan Lower, Kilcomb, Kilcannon, Kilcarbry, Kilcloggan, Kilcowanmore, Killabeg, Killag, Killagowan, Killann, Killannduff, Killilla, Killincooley Beg, Killisk, Kilmacot, Kilmurry, Kilmyshall, Kilnamanagh, Kilpatrick, Kilscoran, Killynann, Kilmacree, Kilrane, Kinnagh, Monamolin (Rathnure), Monamolin (Kilmuckridge), Morrisseysland, Rathmacknee, Rossminoge North, St Brecaun's, St Dubhán's, St Kieran's, Screen, Tacumshin, Templeludigan, Tomhaggard, Toome.

For Wexford town see Appendix 4.

Dating the sites
Most Early Christian ecclesiastical sites cannot be accurately dated. However, using the available historical and archaeological information it is possible to put an approximate date on the foundation of some Early Christian churches in the county.

Among the earliest ecclesiastical sites, possibly dating to the fifth century, are Beggerin (founded by St Ibar), Adamstown and Morrisseysland (founded by St Abbán) and Ardcavan (founded by St Caomhán). Donaghmore also belongs to this early period as the word *donagh* or *domnach* had gone out of use by the seventh century.

In the late sixth or early seventh century churches were founded at Taghmon by St Munnu and by St Aidán at Ferns, Clongeen, Clonmore and Templeshanbo. Ogham stones found at Portersgate (St Brecaun's) and Killabeg indicate a date in this period and a cross slab at Killell, Glynn, is also thought to date to the sixth or seventh century. At St Vauk's, Carne, radiocarbon dates for wooden post holes also assign a church there to this period.

The Martyrology of Tallaght lists churches at Rathaspick and Rossminoge, showing that they were also in existence before that date. From the

Martyrology of Óengus Kilmakilloge can be added to the list, and in the Annals of the Four Masters Ardcolm is mentioned in the year 890.

Most of the churches in Wexford town must post-date the establishment of the town by the Vikings in the ninth and their conversion to Christianity in the tenth century. They are most likely to date to the eleventh or twelfth centuries. St Doologue's cannot be earlier than its patron, Olaf, the saint-king who ruled Norway between 1015 and 1028.

Other possible ecclesiastical sites

Although not included in the definitive list of Early Christian ecclesiastical sites for the county the following locations show at least one of the foregoing criteria for identifying such sites. (For a complete description of these sites see Appendix 4.)

Sites with circular, subcircular, oval or D-shaped enclosures
Ambrosetown, also medieval parish church site
Chapel, also medieval parish church site
Doonooney, also medieval parish church site
Horetown, also medieval parish church site
Lady's Island, also medieval parish church site
Whitechurchglynn, also medieval parish church site

Sites dedicated to early Irish or Welsh saint
Ballyboher-Munnu, also medieval parish church site
Ballyconnick-Degumen, later St Anne, also medieval parish church site
Ballynaslaney-David, also medieval parish church site
Ballybrennan-Kevin of Glendalough, also medieval parish church site
Rosslare Burrow-Brioc
Killurin, Chapel Carron-Cairín
Churchtown, Mulrankin-David, also medieval parish church site
Drinagh-Caomhán of Dairinis, also medieval parish church site
Kilbegnet
Kilmacoe
Kiltealy
Mayglass-Fintan of Clonenagh, also medieval parish church site
St Ivor's-Ibar, also medieval parish church site

Mentioned in early literature
Ballyanne, also medieval parish church site
Camaross
Glascarrig
Inch, also medieval parish church
Limerick

Sites with bullaun stone
Ballymaclare
Ballynastraw
Coolstuff
Courthoyle Old
Garraun Lower
Killowen
Killynann
Kilmacree

Bullaun stones found at non-ecclesiastical sites
Ballynastragh Demesne, Gorey
Fence, Lady's Island
Garryduff, Monagear
Kyle, Bunclody
Maudlintown, Bannow
Scurlocksbush, Oylegate

Site with cross-inscribed pillarstone
Millquarter, Old Ross, also medieval parish church site

Tradition
Ballinaleck

Other indicators of an Early Christian origin

Parishes began to be created in Ireland in the twelfth century. It is evident that existing centres of worship would have been chosen as the church sites of the new parishes. In Co. Wexford this happened in at least sixty percent of cases. Similar correlations have been found in Co. Clare (Ní Gabhláin, 1996, 57) and Co. Dublin (O'Brien, 1988, 521). Survival as medieval parish churches, and the fact that they were enclosed by earthen banks, in some places revetted by stone, helped to ensure the preservation of these sites to the present day.

Another feature indicating an ancient site is a raised area, from constant burial over a long period of time. Eight graveyards have this feature – Ballycanew, Kilgorman, Killincooley Beg, Killinick, Kilmallock, Rathaspick, Screen and Toome.

Location of churches in relation to ráths

If ráth distribution reflected population density from around AD 600 to 900, one would expect a corresponding number of churches to serve that population. This is clearly not the case in Co. Wexford, where the densest concentration of ráths, that is, around Rathnure, has only a few churches. Given the difficulty of identifying the early ecclesiastical sites, plus the fact that all the churches were made of timber and would leave no trace when abandoned and that many may not have been surrounded by an earthen enclosure, perhaps it is not surprising that the relationship between ráth/population density and ecclesiastical sites is enigmatic.

From the Early Christian sites identified it seems that most were not located close to clusters of ráths. In fact, most are in relatively isolated locations. Similar patterns were found by Stout (1997, 100) and by Herity in Co. Roscommon (1987, 135-6). It would seem that landowners were reluctant to part with valuable land close to ráths and usually gave poorer quality land for church sites. There are some exceptions in the county as at Kiltilly and Kilcloggan where ecclesiastical sites are found close to ráth clusters containing a bivallate ráth. This points to a church probably owned and controlled by the noble family of the bivallate ráth but serving the local population.

It is important to point out that much remains to be discovered about the settlement patterns in this period. For example, most people, particularly those not holding property, may have lived in unenclosed clusters of houses which have left no trace.

The higher density of ecclesiastical sites in the Forth and Bargy areas is very noticeable. It may be related to the large number of parishes formed in that area by the Normans, who then retained an earlier site for the church in each parish.

14

The Viking settlement in Wexford

For some reasons which are as yet obscure, hardy warriors from Scandinavia began to raid into various parts of Europe towards the end of the eighth century. They were called Vikings, a name of Norse origin whose meaning is not fully understood. In Old Norse the word *vik* meant a sea inlet. It has been suggested (Hodnebo, 1985, 44) that Viking may have referred to the inhabitants of the coastal areas around Oslofjord, now known as the Skaggerrak. These Vikings were skilled seamen whose boats could enter shallow sea inlets and penetrate inland on the bigger rivers. Ireland and particularly rich Irish monasteries were targeted by Vikings mainly from Norway

The earliest raid was in 795 when they raided the church on Rathlin Island and the island monasteries of Inismurray and Inisbofin. By 821 they had reached Loch Garman when they plundered the churches of Beggerin and Dairinis in Wexford harbour. The Tripartite Life of St Patrick (Stokes, 1887, 192-3) has an interesting reference to this raid: 'In the thirties and forties are the churches which Crimthann, king of Leinster, gave to Patrick in the east of Leinster, and in Uí Cheinnselaig; including Inis Fáil (Beggerin) wherein are Mo Chon-óc and Mo Chat-óc. Erdit and Augustin are in the lesser island, and, since it was taken by the pagans, their shrines are in Slébte (Sletty)'. The Tripartite Life, compiled around 895 to 900, is clearly a propagandist document, compiled to further Armagh's claims to jurisdiction over all churches in Ireland and hence must be treated with extreme caution. Nevertheless, the above quotation refers to an actual Viking raid which we know from the Annals took place in 821. Is it possible that the Vikings established their first base in Wexford harbour on Beggerin Island and not at the mouth of the Bishopswater stream, as suggested by Hadden (1968, 10). It should be noted (Map 10) that, before the reclamation of the North Slob in the middle of the last century, the channel which would have been used by boats entering the harbour ran close to the island.

The Vikings attacked Taghmon in 828 but were repulsed with help from Cairpre, king of Uí Cheinnselaig, son of Cathal, who had defeated Ferns in 817. However, they plundered both Taghmon and Ferns in 835.

The broad haven of Wexford harbour was well-known as a centre of monastic activity long before the arrival of the Norse. The bay itself was considerably broader: the areas now covered by the North and South Slobs consisted of mudflats with islands of glacial drift, such as Beggerin and Dairinis. Shifting channels and sand bars presented navigation difficulties similar to today's, but these would not have been a problem for the shallow-draught Viking boats. The river and outgoing tidal waters scoured out the Crescent area, creating the deep pool which for centuries was the centre of trade and shipping in the port. The picture of the waterfront, then, is of extensive mudflats to the south around the mouth of the Bishopswater river. North of the rocky eminence on which St Iberius church now stands the beach reached up to the Bullring and beyond.

Even before the Norse established Wexford town there may have been trade through the harbour. Centuries earlier the saints Finnian and Senán had been embarking here for Wales. Hadden (1968, 7) postulated the existence of a market from early times which he located around the present Cornmarket area.

The first indication of a settlement at Loch Garman is dated to 892, when the Annals of the Four Masters record the defeat of the Vikings of Wexford, Waterford and St Mullins by an Irish chieftain named Riagán. This was probably the Riagán who was king of Uí Cheinnselaig between 880 and 893. No doubt Wexford began as a tiny enclave, a safe haven in which the Vikings could spend the stormy winter months. Hadden (1968) visualized the Norse entering by the Bishopswater river and hauling their long-ships ashore just below the knoll or mound on which the present military barracks is situated.

Wexford town

A second wave of Norse raids began early in the tenth century. Taghmon and Ferns were plundered in 921 and Ferns was again attacked in 935. These raids may have been carried out from the Wexford base camp. In 933 the Annals of the Four Masters record how Cinnaedh, son of Cairbre, lord of Uí Cheinnselaig, was slain by the foreigners of Wexford in a nocturnal attack. Possibly the small colony was being beseiged by the Irish and counter-attacked at night. By this time the Vikings may have established themselves around the deep pool at the Crescent which would have been an accessible and convenient place for their ships. From this focal point the town gradually expanded.

While the Vikings may have come to Ireland as raiders, by the beginning of the tenth century they were beginning to engage in trade. In fact it is now agreed that their trading activities contributed greatly to the expansion of commerce in Europe at this time.

The Vikings had good reasons for settling in Wexford. That the harbour

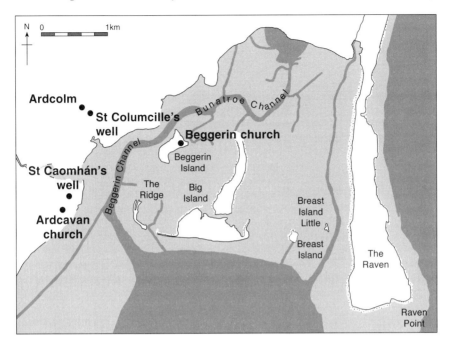

Map 10 Wexford harbour before reclamation of the sloblands in the nineteenth century. Note the channel giving access to Beggerin Island. The Vikings probably used this route to attack the island in 821 and may have established themselves there before settling on the mainland.

was well known is shown by the poem written by the eleventh-century poet Eochaidh Eolach Ó Ceirín (Gwynn, 1913, 169-83):

> King of loughs is this lough in the south,
> Loch Garman of the famous poets,
> Wide and winding haven of the ships,
> Gathering place of the buoyant boats.

The harbour provided a safe haven for their ships, it was a convenient place from which to trade with Bristol and other ports on the west coast of Britain, and the rich Wexford hinterland was a ready source of agricultural produce for such trade. In exchange for the hides of cattle, wolf and pine marten and other agricultural produce, the Norse supplied silks, slaves, wine, figs, olives and other exotic goods. Wine would have been an important commodity for consumption by the well-off and for use in the celebration of the Eucharist. They called their town Ueigsfjord, meaning 'the fjord of the water-logged island and land', later to be become Wexford, and one of its streets, Kayser Lane, 'the lane to the ship wharf'.

However, according to Oftendal (1976, 133) the original meaning of the element *ueig*, found in several Norwegian place-names, is not quite clear. It may have meant 'water-logged island or piece of land'. There is an island named Vegund, in Borgund, in the Sognefjord, in western Norway, originally in Old Norse *Ueig-sund*, 'the sound of the island Ueig', the word Ueig having become Veg in the course of time.

Two Viking silver hoards have been found in Co. Wexford. A hoard of Hiberno-Norse coins, dating to around 1050, was found at Dunbrody abbey (Dolley, 1966, no. 164, in Graham-Campbell, 1976, 64). Another hoard, this one consisting of seventeen silver ingots, was found at 'Blackcastle, near Wexford' in the last century (Armstrong, 1915, 291). The only Black Castle known in Co. Wexford is at the Norman town of Clonmines, some fourteen miles from Wexford. Only one ingot, now in the National Museum, is still extant. This is about six centimetres in length and weighs about thirty-seven grammes. The total weight of the hoard would have been around one pound which would have represented a considerable amount of wealth. (I am indebted to Dr John Sheehan, University College, Cork, for this information.) Ingots functioned as convenient ways of storing silver bullion in the Viking Age. It is difficult to assess the significance of the Clonmines find. Its location suggests that it may derive from the Viking town of Wexford. But much Viking silver appears to have been acquired by the Irish from the Vikings through raiding and trading, and it is possible that the hoard represents wealth buried by Irish hands. It is possible that the silver was originally derived from the nearby lead/silver mines at Barrystown, Wellingtonbridge.

We can only conjecture on the nature and pace of development of the settlement up to the eleventh century. We now know that in that century houses existed at the lower end of Bride Street; Hadden's lament that all the Viking houses 'have perished' was premature. In 1987, when businessman Colman Doyle began clearing a site at the corner of Bride Street and Main Street, Dr Brendan Swan detected some timbers protruding from the wet, sticky organic material. With the agreement of Mr Doyle the National Museum was informed. The excavation which followed revealed the remains of houses dating from 1,000 to around 1,300 (Bourke, 1995, 34-6). These houses were rectangular in shape, averaging 7.60 by 5.60 metres in size, with post and wattle and plank walls and thatched roofs. Inside a central aisle ran from front to back, with sleeping areas on each side. Rushes, ferns, moss and wood chips were used to cover the floor. These houses, in fact, were not unlike those used by the Irish at that time. The excavation also showed that the present Main Street follows the same alignment as houses built in the late eleventh/early twelfth centuries (Bourke, 1988-9, 59).

Certainly by 1169 Wexford was a thriving town. In the first issue of the *Journal of the Old Wexford Society*, as it was then known, Hadden (1968, 1-6) developed a model of a settlement, probably enclosed by an earthen bank and ditch, running from the military barracks across the high ground of Clifford Street and School Street and thence down Anne Street to the waterfront. Based on parish boundaries (Colfer, 1990-1, 9) included St Iberius parish within the Norse town, thereby extending it as far as the Bullring. Hadden (p.12) paints a fascinating picture of the busy seaport and its connections to its hinterland.

> To establish its commerce with the countryside the new seaport sent out link roads to connect with the ancient Market thoroughfare.
>
> From the shipwharves in the Pool, Kayser Lane and Peter's Street ran straight uphill, cutting across Main Street and the long diagonal of High Street to the high level gates at the back of the town – Kayser Lane to join John Street and go out with it, bypassing the dip down to the Market entrance, and on by Coolcotts to the Slaney valley and the west country; Peter Street to join the south west market trail at Talbot Street, and go out with it by the ford of Slippery Green to the southwest.
>
> From the fisheries around the Bishopswater and Oyster Lane area ran two corresponding link routes; one up Bride Street to join the Market trail at the ford of Slippery Green; the other up the long diagonal of Mary's Lane – Patrick's Lane – and High Street to join the Kayser Lane and go out with it to the west country.
>
> All three trade routes sent out branches along the Main Street trail – southward to the barony of Forth, northwards to the Market Place and the Ferry.

An eye-witness description of the Norman attack on the town given by Giraldus Cambrensis (Scott and Martin, 1978, 33) shows that it was sufficiently defended to withstand the first onslaught. The presence of three ships from Bristol with cargoes of wheat and wine shows a busy trading port.

While the town undoubtedly prospered, the Annals give only a few tantalizing references to its inhabitants. Thus, the Annals of the Four Masters record how, together with the Norse of Waterford and Dublin, the Wexfordmen attempted to plunder Cork in 1088, only to be repulsed with great slaughter. Their relationship with Diarmait Mac Murchada was sometimes fraught. Although they helped him to attack Waterford in 1137, they were not reliable allies, as in 1161, Domhnall, Diarmait's son, was forced to defeat them, this at a time when Diarmait was at the height of his power. Again in 1169 they resisted Diarmait's first Norman attack on the town of Wexford.

Viking settlement in the county

It is not known at what period the Vikings of Wexford town began to acquire estates in the surrounding countryside. Contact through commerce would have familiarized them with the native Irish; later, perhaps, a desire to control the source of their trade in agricultural products as well as to increase their profits would have led them to acquire their own farms. But how was this land acquired? Was it rented or taken by force? Had the system broken down to such an extent that they were allowed to purchase property? How big a factor was intermarriage with Irish landowners and subsequent inheritance of property?

However it happened, there is no doubt that the Vikings eventually became large landholders. This is borne out by an inquisition into their condition in 1283 which stated 'that in the time of the Marshals, Lords of Leinster (1207-45), there were within the county of Wexford five score foreign Ostmen (Vikings) very rich, having many beasts' (Hore, v, 93-4). The inference must be that in the pre-Norman period there was an even greater number of them in the Wexford hinterland.

The location of some of these rich farmsteads can be inferred from an examination of place-names containing a Norse element. Map 11 shows that they were based mainly along the south and southeast coast of the county, with a few inland exceptions. One Norse element found is *-gate*, meaning a road or path. Thus place-names such as Libgate, Bunargate and Mountaingate probably indicate the presence of Norse settlers in these areas. The word 'scar', meaning a rock, is found in Scar itself, as well as in Selskar (Seal's Rock) and Tuskar, and possibly Skeetar. The name Arklow, a townland in the parish of Ballycullane, consists of the Norse personal name Arnkell or Arnketill, combined with *lo*, which, in Old Norse, denoted a lowlying meadow near water, a description which matches the site at Ballycullane. Bannow may also fit into this category. The suffix *-ore*, meaning 'sandy point' also indicates a Norse connection, for example, Carnsore and Greenore. The word *gall* meant stranger, that is, a Viking; hence the place-name Knockangall indicates their presence in the Piercestown area. Knottown and Saltee are also probably of Norse origin. Saltee is also probably Norse, meaning Salt Island, *ey* being their word for island. The name Doyle comes from *dubhgall*, meaning 'dark foreigner', as in Ballydoyle, and is of Danish origin.

A townland called Ting, the only one in Ireland, is located in Piercestown parish, about six miles south of Wexford town. The tingmote was the meeting place of the Vikings but no archaeological evidence of one has as yet been found in the townland or the surrounding area, despite a thorough search of the ground and the aerial photographs.

The Vikings converted to Christianity during the first half of the tenth century. There appear to have been several Norse churches in the vicinity

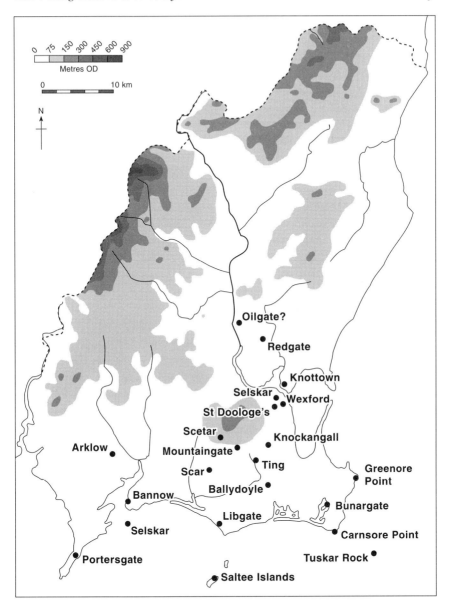

Map 11 The distribution pattern of Viking place-names shows that they confined themselves mainly to south Wexford. Most names ending in -gate, meaning a road, such as Libgate and Bunargate, and -ore, meaning sandy, such as Carnsore and Greenore, are of Norse origin.

of Wexford town. St Doologue's, dedicated to St Olaf, a Norse saint/king, was located around Stonebridge; St Michael the Archangel, being the patron saint of sailors, was a favourite of the Norse and churches dedicated to him were located at Castle Hill Street and Bush, Tagoat. (Kilmichael, in north Wexford, may have been founded by the Norse of Arklow). A church and well dedicated to the Holy Trinity, also favoured by the Norse, was located southeast of the present military barracks (hence the name Trinity Street).

Viking influence, in the form of interlacing, has been found on a tenth-century cross-decorated stone on Beggerin Island (see p. 144, above). It is possible that Vikings were then living in the monastery on the island. Certainly, by the time of the Norman invasion they were in control of the island, as it was there they imprisoned Robert Fitzstephen in 1171.

The final reference to the Norse of Wexford is contained in an inquisition of 1307 which states that at Rosslare 'the issues of the coney borough (rabbit warren) and herbage thereof, woods, labours of the Ostmen with other small exits, are worth yearly £9 9s. 2d.' (Hore, 1920, 66).

The Viking influence on Wexford

Up to recently the Vikings have been seen as a malign influence in Ireland. This is partly due to the fact that the accounts of their activities were written by monks who were keenly aware of the attacks being made on the monasteries. However, it is now established that the Irish themselves were not averse to plundering the monasteries.

Although Wexford did not escape unscathed from Viking raids, the overall effect of their presence has to be seen as beneficial. It led to the foundation and development of the town as an important trading centre; it encouraged trade in agricultural products which benefited the farmers; it made exotic goods available to Wexford inhabitants; and it probably helped to improve and extend the road network in the county. In addition the Vikings introduced the use of coinage to Ireland and to Wexford. Byrne (1987, 21) has stated, perhaps with slight exaggeration, that it was the economic strength derived from the trade between Wexford and Bristol which underpinned the Mac Murchada power base.

Despite their involvement in the affairs of the county for several hundred years and living in close proximity to the Irish it seems that the Vikings maintained, and were perceived to maintain, a separate identity, even into the fourteenth century. They are described in the Annals as the Norse of Wexford in 1088 and 1137 and as 'foreigners' in 1161. In the inquisitions of 1283 and 1307 (Hore, v) they were apparently still easily identified as Ostmen or Vikings. After that they pass out of the documentary sources, their former presence now attested by a few place-names, the winding, narrow streets and the name of the town they founded over a thousand years ago.

15

Early place-names, townland names and Gaelic estates from literary sources

Many Co. Wexford place-names date back to the Early Christian period (400-1169) and are therefore rooted in the Irish language, but over the centuries these names have been altered almost beyond recognition. The imposition of English spelling forms on many of our place-names has obscured their original meanings and Irish scholars have been grappling with this problem since the last century. An tAthair Seamas de Val, has sought to elucidate the origin and meaning of the place-names of the county and his comprehensive account was published in *Treasures of the county Wexford landscape* (Culleton, 1994) and has been extensively used in this study.

Place-names are an invaluable source of information on settlement patterns in ancient times. The element *baile* (bally-), for example, indicates a Gaelic estate, thus Ballyregan was the estate of an Ó Riagáin family. The words dún and ráth tell us that places with these elements in their names were once the location of fortresses or homesteads of nobles and strong farmers. Many ráths have been removed from the landscape, particularly in this century, and the only clue to their former presence may be in the inclusion of the word itself in a modern townland name. Similarly the word 'kill' (Irish *cill*) indicates the presence of a church during the Early Christian period.

Ancient place-names also relate to landscape features; a rocky place (*carraig*), a moor (*easc*), a hill (*cnoc*) would certainly have been given specific names in the Early Christian period. For example, Lacken Hill, near New Ross, was called *leacán*, the place of the flagstones, in the *Leabhar branach*, the Book of the O'Byrnes, in a poem composed in the mid-sixteenth century (Mac Airt, 1944, 62). Geologically the hill is composed of flaggy shale bedrock. Carnsore was originally Carn, meaning a monumental heap of stones. This probably refers to the portal tomb which supposedly was located at Carnsore Point before it fell into the sea (Ordnance Survey, six-inch sheet No. 53, 1841), or to the abundance of rounded boulders of Carne granite which were scattered over the area during the Ice Age.

The Norse influence, particularly in south Wexford, is evidenced in place-names ending in -gate, such as Libgate and Bunargate and in words ending in -ore, for example, Carnsore and Greenore (see p. 169, below).

The literary sources
The earliest literary sources for Co. Wexford place-names are the Martyrologies of Tallaght, Óengus, Gorman and Donegal and the annals. Some names are also mentioned in the Lives of Abbán, Aidán, Munnu, Finnian and Moling. Many names are listed in the monastic charters. The earliest charter covers Diarmait Mac Murchada's grant to the canons regular of St Augustine at Ferns around 1160. It may also be acceptable, but not without some reservations, to include many place-names listed in the earliest Norman charters as being of pre-Norman date. This can be done by making the following assumptions: 1) that these names are genuinely Gaelic in origin and meaning; 2) that, in any case, the early Normans tried to use the existing Gaelic names, admittedly with some difficulty; and 3) that names of obvious Norman origin such as words ending in 'town' (*tun*) are eliminated.

A charter was granted to the Cistercian Order in 1200 by William Marshal to found Tintern abbey (Hore, ii, 19). A charter was granted between 1207 and 1213 for the foundation of Dunbrody abbey when the Cistercian Order was given land by Hervey de Montmorency (Hore, iii, 37). Ferns, Enniscorthy and Templeshanbo are listed in a grant of Henry III to the bishop of Ferns in 1226 (Hore, vi, 342).

Ballyregan, Clone, Killegney, Killalligan and Lishote are listed in a dispute between the bishop and Phillip de Prendergast around 1230 (Hore, vi, 343).

In an agreement between the bishop and the see of Canterbury concluded between 1228 and 1232 several place-names in south Wexford are listed (Hore, iv, 311).

In 1231-4 a deforestation charter was granted by Richard Marshal for the forests of Ross and Taghmon (Orpen, 1934) and this charter provided a rich source of place-names, as well as topographic information on south Co. Wexford. Another source of names is found in the documentation relating to the partition of Leinster after the death of the last son of William Marshal in 1246. The following places are listed for Co. Wexford: Banno, Tamenie (Taghmon), Fernes, Karrec, and Roselar (Rosslare) (Hore, v, 38).

The final source used to examine place-names is the list of knights' fees for 1247 (Brooks, 1950) which names many of the places allocated to the early Normans. (For complete list, see Appendix 6).

Although the Norman occupation of a large part of Co. Wexford had lasted for almost eighty years there is little evidence for the introduction of Norman elements into the place-names, apart from a few names ending in 'town' such as Pettitstown. They did, however, list existing place-names in their charters and land grants, usually in a corrupt form, not surprisingly, given their lack of knowledge of the Irish language.

The number of pre-Norman place-names available for study is limited and confined to relatively small areas, chiefly in south Wexford. Despite the small number, by classifying the place-names into specific categories some useful information can be derived.

Baile (bally-) as place-name/townland name

Although the word *baile* was in use between 900 and 1200 in prose and poetry it was not documented in place-names until the middle of the twelfth century (Flanagan, D. and L., 1994, 21-2). Its earliest use, in this way, was in the foundation or endowment charters for the new religious orders being brought in from Continental Europe to help revive the religious life in Ireland. It is not known at what period, previous to its use in charters, that *baile* came to denote a territorial unit.

The earliest known use of *baile*, meaning land, for Co. Wexford is found in Diarmait Mac Murchada's charter to the canons regular of St. Augustine for the abbey of Ferns. This is dated to around 1160. The only existing copy was printed in Latin in Dugdale (1673), reputedly from an ancient copy by Sir James Ware, the famous seventeenth-century scholar and collector. According to Hore (vi, 180), who searched in vain for the original charter, there is a copy, made in 1655, in Latin, in the British Museum (Add. Mss No. 4797, p. 129). Although it is thought to be a thirteenth-century forgery by Price (1963, 119), this may not invalidate the authenticity of the place-names mentioned in it. The charter quite specifically equates *baile* with land, stating that he (Mac Murchada) has granted

> the following lands, namely Balisifin, Balilaccussa, for one village; Borin and Roshena and Kilbride for two villages; the lands of Fereneghegan and a certain cell at Thaghmoling, being the chapel of St Mary with all belongings, with the lands of Ballygery, with all the fisheries and my chapel ...   [Hore, vi, 180]

Clearly by this time Co. Wexford was divided into territorial units, many of whose names included *baile* as an element.

Many early place-names have been preserved, albeit often in a changed form, in the modern townland name. The word 'townland' to denote a unit of land was first used in Ireland in the Civil Survey of 1654 (Simington, 1953) to denote 'town and lands of ...' which according to Price may in time have become shortened to 'townland'. It bears no relation to the modern word 'town' but like the Irish word *baile* refers to place. According to Price (1963, 125) the word 'townland' is derived from the Old English 'tun land' and meant 'the land forming an estate or manor'.

Since *baile* in many cases infers a land unit and 'townland' always does so, the two terms are to a large extent interchangeable. Thus, the *baile* of the early documents, may, for all practical purposes be considered equivalent to a townland.

The names of the owners of at least fourteen of such *bailte* are preserved in the modern townland names as shown in Table 6.

Table 6 Gaelic place-name/townland name with *baile* followed by a family name (knights' fees, 1247 in Brooks, 1950)

Place-name	Family name	Medieval parish
Ballybrazil	Ó Breasáil	Ballybrazil
Ballybrennan	Ó Braonáin	Clonmore
Ballybrennan	Ó Braonáin	Ballybrennan
Ballycanew	Mac Conmhai	Ballycanew
Ballyconnick	Mac Conmhaic	Ballyconnick
Ballygarvey	Ó Gairbhith	Kilscoran
Ballyhealy	Ó Dubhaile	Kilturk
Ballylane	Ó Lonáin	Old Ross
Ballymacane	Mac Eachthighern	Tacumshin
Ballymagir (Richfield)	Mac an Ghirr	Killag
Ballyregan	Ó Riagáin	Kilbride
Ballyregan	Ó Riagáin	Ballymore
Ballyregan	Ó Riagáin	Rossminoge
Ballyregan	Ó Riagáin	Artramon

According to MacLysaght (1980, ix) surnames or hereditary family names came into general use in Ireland towards the end of the tenth and beginning of the eleventh century as a result of population increase. Each member of a family adopted the name of their father or grandfather or even a famous ancestor, prefixed by their first names. If the father's name was taken, the word Mac was prefixed, if an older relative's name was taken the prefix Ua or Ó signifying grandson was taken.

It can be taken that those Co. Wexford families whose names have survived were of considerable social and economic importance. Four of these townlands are named after an Ó Riagáin family.

It is perhaps not surprising that *baile* is prominent in the knights' fees listed in Appendix 6 since these fees deal with definite properties. This prominence may also reflect the Norman custom of using the local names of the places in which they settled, thus continuing the practice to which they were accustomed before coming to Ireland. It seems unlikely that they imposed their own names, except in a few easily recognized instances, for example, Ambrosetown, Pettitstown, or that they had learned the native language quickly enough to bestow Irish names on places at this time.

Place-names with 'kill' (*cill*)

Apart from *baile* the most common element of place-name/ townland name is the word *cill*, meaning church. The word 'kill', or more correctly in the original Irish, *cill*, is derived from the Latin word *cella* and has an ecclesiastical connotation relating to either a church, graveyard or monastic site. A complicating factor in elucidating cills is that the Irish word for wood is *coill* and since both are frequently anglicized 'kill' the two words can easily be confused. Although over fifty ecclesiastical sites with 'kill' from Co. Wexford have been shown to date to the Early Christian period references to only eight are found in the early literature (Table 7).

Table 7 Early place-name/townland name containing 'kill' (*cill*)
(knights' fees, 1247 in Brooks, 1950)

Norman name	*Modern townland version*
Kilanegry	Killegney
Kilbrideglynn	Kilbrideglynn
Kilkevan	Kilkcavan
Kilcony	Kilcomb
Kilcougan	Kilcowan
Kilmore	Kilmore
Kilmucres	Kilmuckridge
Kylluskerd	Killesk
Kilrothane	Kilrane

Dún in place-names

While both the terms *dún* and *ráth* seem to have been applied to defended sites, the word *dún* appears to have referred to more strongly defended and therefore more important places. It often appears in the anglicized form of 'doon'. A feature of the Co. Wexford sites listed in the early literature is that, with one exception, they are combined with individual names (Table 8). The exception is Dúnrodgel, whose location is unknown and whose meaning is uncertain. Apart from those listed in the early literature there are nine other place-names with dún or don in Co. Wexford. These survived as modern townland names But the sites which gave rise to the name are almost certainly of Early Christian or even earlier date. There is some slight evidence, in fact, that the promontory forts at Baginbun (Dundonnell) and Duncannon may date back to the Iron Age, that is to between 500 BC and AD 400.

Table 8: Place-names with dún element incorporating personal names

Dúnbrodik (Dunbrody)	Broth's fortress
Dúncormick	Cormac's fortress
Dúnculip (Dungulp)	C——?'s fortress
Dúndonnell (Dúndonald)	Domnall's fortress
Dúnmechanan (Duncannon)	Conan's fortress (Cana>Canog>Canann)

Ráths

Ráths are the most ubiquitous monuments on the Irish landscape and, generally, were the dwelling places of nobles and farmers mainly between the years 600 and 900. In Co. Wexford alone they once numbered over 600 (Moore, 1996, 28). Only nine have been listed in the early literature for the county, of which only Rathumney (Rathubenai) can be identified.

Of around seventy modern townland names in the county containing the word ráth, several commemorate people who once owned them or were associated with them, for example, Rathaspick, 'the ráth of the bishop'. In a few cases these are of Norman origin, for example, Raheenarostia (Roche's little ráth), Rahale (Howell's ráth) and Raheenvarren (Warren's little ráth). Mostly the name included the name of a tree, for example, Rathnure, meaning ráth of the yew tree, or indicated the size of the enclosure, for example, raheen, the little ráth. It is possible that not every ráth was continuously occupied, many may have decayed as families died out or moved to a new place.

In some cases the prefix 'ráth' in the name is the only indication that such a structure ever existed in the vicinity.

Natural landscape features

Of the number of names referring to landscape features listed in the county only thirteen can be identified. Of these seven refer to rocky places (*carrig*), three refer to river crossings (*ath*), two refer to hills (*cnoc*) and one refers to the Slaney river.

Antiquity of place-names

It is not possible to put precise dates on the origin of most place-names. Joyce (1913) believed that words with the elements *dún*, *ráth* and *kill* date back to the Early Christian period, but that most place-names originated

Table 9 Identifiable place-names referring to natural landscape features

Old name	Modern name
Accefade	Aughfad
Admoinger	Aughermon (Orpen and de Val differ on the translation). Orpen gives *Ath mona gcorr*, the ford of the bog of cranes, while de Val gives *eachar Munnu*, St Munnu's field.
Archlar	Aughclare
Carn	Carne, a monumental heap of stones
Carneauth	Carnagh, *carn-mhagh*, the plain of the cairn(s)
Cnokrod	Cnocrua, Knockroe
Leacán	Lacken Hill, the hill of the flagstone
Glaskarec	Glascarrig
Karcbren	Carrigbyrne – Bran's rock, Carraig Bhriain or Bhroin
Karrech	Ferrycarrig
Karrechogan	Carrigogan, Carrigadaggan – rock of the fort
Sceter	Skeetarpark (*scer* is Norse for a sharp rock)
Sláine	Slaney

during the twelfth to fifteenth centuries. It is possible to put a *terminus ante quem* on at least some of these names. For example, the word donagh, as in Donaghmore, which is derived from *domhnach* meaning church, went out of use in the seventh century.

Norse words such as Scar, Saltee, Keeroc, Wexford, Carnsore, Greenore and those ending in -gate came into the Irish language only after the tenth century when the Norsemen began to settle in the county. Over one hundred and fifty place-names names, and these from a limited area of the county, with some slight reservations, can be attributed to the pre-Norman period.

Gaelic estates

Apart from commonage, the land of Ireland has been in some form of limited, if not outright, ownership since at least Early Christian times. This is made clear from the brehon laws of the seventh and eighth centuries where property rights, inheritance and trespass were well defined (Kelly, 1997).

Ownership resided in: 1) the kings and nobles, who held their own private estates and who also rented out land and stock to their clients; 2) the independent landowning classes of farmers, that is, the ocaire and boaire; 3) the king's advisors and learned men such as judges, bards and genealogists; 4) the monasteries and the Church who could also rent out land to their tenants. Ownership, however, would not have been outright but was subject to certain restraints within the kin group. For example, land could not be freely disposed of as family members had certain inalienable rights in the property. However, it seems that by the twelfth century the land previously owned by the farmers had been taken over by the nobles to whom the farmers paid a rent for its use (Kelly, 1997, 428). This rent or tax was paid in the form of food, tribute, hospitality, and military obligation. The amount of these taxes was related to the size of the territorial unit held. According to McErlean (1983, 330) 'such a unit (townland) may have been held by an individual family of the sept but it must have been worked by a larger group'. This group would have consisted of other family members as well as servants, serfs and slaves.

The largest territorial units, the Gaelic estates, were held by kin-related septs, while smaller units such as the *baile* were held by individual family members. Units varied in size depending on the size of the estate, the number of family members and the quality of the land occupied. Larger units were usually found on poorish land.

An enigmatic feature of townland size in the county is the preponderance of smaller townlands along the east and southwest coasts. The explanation is probably related to the Norman settlement pattern in the county. Before their arrival the extent of the Gaelic estates in these areas would have corresponded closely with the rest of the country. Those areas of smaller townlands occur nearer the coast and appear to have been densely colonized by new settlers brought in by the Norman lords to farm their lands. To accommodate these, the estates of the Gaelic families were taken over and divided among the Normans and possibly some remaining Irish. This led to smaller land units in these areas in contrast to the north of the county where the Irish were allowed to remain but subject to Norman overlords.

Ancient boundaries
The Gaelic land ownership system required a clear definition of the territory held by each sept and kin group and the need for strong, permanent fences around their territories. According to Joyce (1913, ii, 262) various landmarks were assigned to serve as boundary markers between large districts, some natural, some put down artificially:

> Among these are a 'stone mark' i.e. a large pillar stone; 'an ancient tree' of any kind, or the stump and roots of an old oak, after the tree had fallen or disappeared; 'a deer mark' namely the hair-marks left by deer or cattle on the trees of a wood, or the hair-marked footpath made by them along a plain; a 'stock mark' i.e. stakes in the earth, or the ruin of a mill or an old bridge under water; 'a water mark' i.e. a river, lake or well; 'an eye mark' i.e. a straight line fixed by the eye between any two of the preceding apart; a 'defect mark' i.e. a place

or line along which there was no cultivable land such as a declivity, a sedge, a stony vale, or the track of a disused road; a 'way mark' i.e. a king's road or a carriage road or a cow road; a 'mound mark' i.e. a mound or ditch or foss or any 'mound whatever' such as that round the trunk of a tree.

According to Andrews (1955-6, 11) boundaries following ridge tops, streams or bog are more likely to be older than those composed of straight lines. For smaller areas the laws stipulated four types of fences. These were a ditch, a stone fence, an oak tree and a post and wattle fence (see p. 26, above).

Mapping and naming the townlands

The earliest maps showing land divisions for Co. Wexford are those of the Down Survey, so-called because all measurements at parish level were to be carefully 'layde downe' on paper at a scale of forty perches to one inch. The purpose of these maps was to enable land confiscated under the Act of Settlement of 1652 to be divided among the Cromwellian beneficiaries.

The earliest maps delineating and naming the townlands were produced in 1840 by the Ordnance Survey. These were at a scale of six inches to one mile. The boundaries shown were surveyed in 1826-41, based on Grand Jury records and local estate maps. Many new townlands were created by the Ordnance Survey, chiefly by subdivision of large townlands. For example, Annagh, in north Wexford was subdivided into Annagh, Annagh Central, Annagh Hill, Annagh Long, Annagh Lower, Annagh Middle, Annagh More, Annagh Gap and Annagh Upper. Other townlands were divided into Big and Little, East and West and Upper and Lower. In the end over 2,000 townlands were delineated. In the 1960s the Down Survey maps were super-imposed on the six-inch Ordnance Survey maps by the National Library, Dublin. These maps show that the boundaries of some land units had not changed in 1655-9 and 1826-41.

16

Origins of Ferns diocese and parishes

Although diocese were not formally established in Ireland until the
synod of Rathbreasail in 1111, the origin of Ferns diocese can be traced
back to the late sixth century. The Life of Aidán relates how Brandubh, the Uí Cheinnselaig king of Leinster, granted extensive lands to
Aidán:

> And afterwards the king granted extensive lands to Máedóg, and the
> king, Brandubh, as well as the laics and clergy, decreed that the
> archepiscopacy of all the Lagenians should always be in the see and
> cathedral of St Máedóg. (Plummer, 1910, vol. ii, 141-63).

The diocese defined
Following the reform of the Church under Pope Gregory VII (1073-85) the
Irish Church came under pressure from Rome and Canterbury to implement
the reforms of the Continental Church. An idea of the necessity for such
reform is gained from a letter written by Lanfranc, archbishop of
Canterbury, to Turlough Ó Briain of Munster in 1074. In this he accuses
the Irish of flouting church marriage laws by abandoning their lawful wives
to take on another woman, even a relation. He states:

> To speak truth, however, among many pleasing things, some things
> have been reported to us which are not pleasing. It is reported that
> in your kingdom a man will abandon his lawfully wedded wife at his
> own will without any canonical process taking place and with a temer-
> ity deserving of punishment, takes to himself some other wife who
> may be of his own kin or of the kindred of the wife whom he has
> abandoned, or whom another has abandoned with similar wickedness,
> according to a law of marriage which is rather a law of fornication;
> that bishops are consecrated by one bishop only; that many bishops
> are ordained in towns and cities; that at baptism children are baptised

without consecrated chrism; that holy orders are conferred by bishops for money. [Watt, 1972, 6]

Another major problem was that the monasteries were controlled by
powerful families who retained the right to appoint bishops and abbots.
There was no central church organization or administration. That many
problems persisted into the next century is shown by a report on a synod
held at Drogheda in 1152 (AFM) when it was decreed that clergy should
put away concubines and lemans (lovers or paramours): they were not to
demand payment for anointing or baptizing or to take payment for church
property.

At the synod of Rathbreasail, Co. Tipperary, in 1111 the boundaries of
Ferns diocese were vaguely defined (Keating, ed. Dinneen, 1908, 299) as
being from Mount Leinster to the sea and from Beggerin in Wexford
Harbour to Mileadhach (Great Island). In effect this constituted the twelfth-
century territory of Uí Cheinnselaig, apart from Idrone and Fothart, which
were separated from the rest of the territory by the Blackstairs Mountains,
and whose ruling families, in any case, were not of the direct Uí
Cheinnselaig line. As Byrne (1984, 101) has pointed out 'the native sources
name the diocese by their territories rather than their episcopal sees'. The
Uí Cheinnselaig territory was given a choice of two sites for its see, Ferns
and Wexford, but the power of the Mac Murchada ensured that Ferns
would prevail. The parishes of Castletown and Coolgreany in the northeast
of the county are in Dublin diocese. This area originally belonged to the Uí
Enechghlais who had settled in southeast Wicklow and northeast Wexford
(Smyth, 1982, 16). The area later came under the control of the Vikings.
Hence, that part of Co. Wexford was not in Uí Cheinnselaig territory and
therefore did not come under the jurisdiction of Ferns but of Glendalough
diocese, which was incorporated into the Dublin diocese 1211. The churches of Kilgorman and Kilbegnet were probably attached to the monastery of
Glendalough from an early date. Parts of Clonegal and St Mullins parishes
are also in Wexford county but in the diocese of Kildare and Leighlin.

Bishops at Ferns
A list of the rulers of Ferns is given in the Annals of the Four Masters,
Colgan (1645, 223), O'Donovan (1840, 54) and Flood (1916, 226). This list
includes bishops, abbots, coarbs and erenaghs who ruled the monastery at
various times.

Unfortunately, all these names have sometimes been taken to have been
bishops of the diocese. The following list of bishops at Ferns is taken from
the Annals of the Four Masters:

Table 10 Names and year of death of bishops of Ferns, 598-1223

Aidán	624/25	
Mo Ling Luachair	696/97	In the Life of Aidán, Mo Ling succeeded him
Máel Dogair	678	as bishop of Ferns. Also in Moling's Life
Commán	678	(O'Leary, 1913, 25) he was consecrated bishop
Díraith	693	of Ferns after the death of Aidán but more like-
Cilléne	715	ly this would have been sometime later as
Diarmait Ua Rodacháin	1050	Moling would have been too young at that time.
Cellach Ua Colmáin	1117	
Máel Eoin Ua Dúnacáin	1125	
Brigtén Ua Catháin	1172	
Joseph O hAodha	1183	
Ailbhe O Máel Muaid (O'Mulloy)	1186-1223	

This list shows that from the time of St Aidán up to 1183 the names of only eleven bishops were recorded. This does not mean that there were no bishops during this period at Ferns but rather that those keeping the records of the monastery were monks to whom the deaths of the abbots were more worthy of being recorded than those of the bishops; hence the latter went unrecorded. The extent of the bishop's jurisdiction was probably also limited; for example, it may not have extended into the southern part of Uí Cheinnselaig. He was regarded as a 'holy man' with few, if any, administrative duties. Nevertheless, bishops were needed to perform reserved episcopal duties such as ordination of priests.

The secularization of the early Irish Church is clearly illustrated in the case of Ferns. Apart from a short break after the death of Aidán in 624/25, the see was ruled by a bishop up to the death of Cilléne in 715. From then until 1050, almost three and a half centuries later, no bishop is recorded.

This is in line with what was happening elsewhere in Ireland as power and authority passed from the bishops to the abbots of the powerful monasteries. Only after the re-organization of the Irish Church at the synod of Rathbreasail does the diocesan and episcopal structure become re-established. Even then, the succession of bishops of Ferns is not clear and the dates for their deaths are not well authenticated.

There are several references to bishops of Wexford. In the foundation charter of Dunbrody abbey Joseph Ó hAodha is so called. Also, Hore (vol. vi, 179) relates that 'In a Bull of Pope Lucius III to John Comin, Archbishop of Dublin, from Velletrum, April, 1182, this See is called the bishopric of Wexford. We also find David, Bishop of Loch Garman, mentioned in the Annals of Loch Cé, under date 1209.'

It seems likely that the temporary transfer of the bishop's residence to Wexford resulted from the destruction of Ferns by Diarmait Mac Murchada in 1166.

Formation of parishes

The concept of the parish church was expounded by Archbishop Hincmar of Rheims, writing between 858 and 860 who stated 'the main pastoral work of the church in the country will be carried on from a church which is served by a single priest assisted by a few clerks in minor orders, and whose parish extends only to one village or a few adjacent villages' (Otway-Ruthven, 1964, 112).

However, the major church reforms sweeping Europe from the eleventh century onwards were to alter forever the organization of the Church at local as well as diocesan level. At the synod of Rathbreasail, Gilbert, bishop of Limerick, submitted a programme for church re-organization based on the parish and the diocese. It is generally thought that organization of the diocese into parishes could only have been in its early phase when the Normans arrived in 1169. But the territorial divisions on which they were based must already have been in existence.

Many of the ecclesiastical sites in the county became the focus of the new parishes. Whether or not these churches had continued to service their communities continuously from earlier times is impossible to tell.

Creation and demarcation of the earliest parishes probably came about as follows:

1. From church lands: Following the church reforms of the twelfth century the lands belonging to the monasteries became vested in the bishops, although not always without resistance from the new Norman overlords. The number and extent of these properties cannot be rigidly established but possibly as much as one third of Ireland was in church hands in early medieval times. Records show that in the early Norman period in Co. Wexford the bishops held six manors in the south of the county – Fethard, Kinnagh, Ballingly, Mayglass, Pollregan and at Ferns (Brooks, 1950). Five of these became parishes, the exception being Pollregan. According to Colfer (1987, 74) the bishops also held extensive lands in other districts, possibly by lay tenants. These may also have become parishes.

2. From family estates: The land of Ireland not held by the Church consisted of estates in the hands of the nobility. Many of these may already have been supporting a church and priest and the transition to a parish structure may have been fairly simple. The names of some of these Wexford Gaelic families can be traced back to their estates through place-and townland names which have been found to pre-date the Norman invasion.

3. From subdivision or amalgamation of *bailte* (townlands or Gaelic estates) into Norman manors: The Norman knights who came to Ireland were given

Table 11 Gaelic families which gave their names to medieval (civil) parishes

Family name	Medieval parish	Part of modern parish of
Ó Breasáil	Ballybrazil	Suttons
Ó Braonáin	Ballybrennan	Tagoat
Ó Conmhai	Ballycanew	Camolin
Ó Conmhaic	Ballyconnick	Rathangan

lands which were called manors. The demarcation of these land grants was based on territorial units, or estates, already in existence. These manors then formed the parishes of the conquered areas. The extent of the manor depended on what was known as a knight's fee, which was generally equivalent to a rent of forty shillings per year. The extent of the knight's fee and hence of the manor could vary from as little as one-twentieth of a fee to several fees. In his seminal paper on Anglo-Norman settlement in Co. Wexford (Colfer, 1987, 73) has shown that 'of the sixty-one recorded knight's fees, twenty-nine formed the bases for a medieval parish. In nineteen instances (thirteen in the southern half of the county) the boundaries of manor and parish appear to coincide.'

Table 12 Medieval parishes and Norman manors coincident
(Colfer, 1987, 95-9)

Adamstown	Carne	Killesk
Ambrosetown	Duncormick	Kilrane
Ballyanne	Glascarrig (Donaghmore)	Leskinfere
Ballybrazil	Kilcavan	Mulrankin
Ballybrennan	Kilcomb	Rossdroit
Ballycanew	Kilcowan	
Ballyconnick	Kilcowanmore	

4. Apart from the three categories suggested above it is accepted that from earliest times many community-based churches existed. It is not unlikely that many of these functioned in the same manner as the later parish churches and also formed the basis for such parishes.

A glance at the medieval parish map (Map 12) of the county shows a marked difference in parish size between the south, the east, the west and northwest. This reflects the Norman impact on land organization, the smaller parishes of the south and the east being due to the influx of tenants which

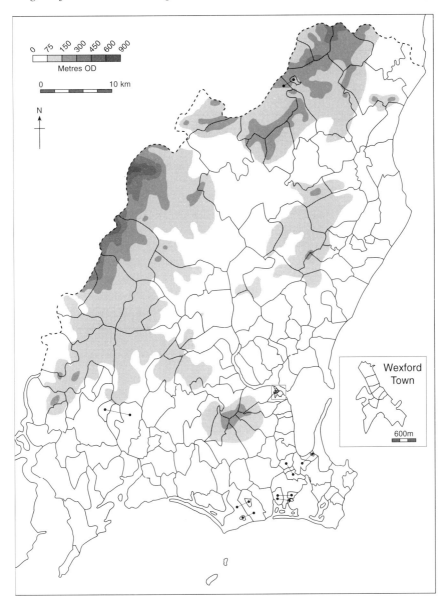

Map 12 Parishes began to be formed in the twelfth century based on existing Gaelic territorial divisions. To provide for the influx of Normans after 1169, the Gaelic estates in south Wexford were subdivided into smaller units. These then became the basis for a large number of small parishes in contrast to the bigger parishes in the northern area (map based on Colfer, 1987).

necessitated the break up of the larger Gaelic estates into smaller units, while the west and northwest largely retained their Gaelic estates, but under Norman overlordship. What seems certain is that the existing well-defined territorial boundaries of Gaelic estates and farms (townlands) enabled the Normans to rapidly establish their manors and corresponding parishes.

In a paper on 'Ancient crosses in the barony of Ballaghkeen' Ranson (1948, 97-104) showed how stone crosses were used to mark the boundaries of the medieval parishes of Ballyvalloo, Killila, Ballyvaldon, Killincooley, Kilmuckridge, Donaghmore, Ardamine and Kiltennel. Although he places them in an Early Christian context, the dating of the crosses and hence of the formation of the parish is problematic. Harbison (pers. comm.) says that these crosses can only be ascribed to the medieval period and cannot be presumed to be pre-Norman. Such crosses were widely used to mark parish boundaries in medieval Europe and were considered to place the territory under heavenly protection.

Apart from the three possibilities for parish formation outlined, mention must be made of the Norse impact in Wexford town and county. Colfer (1990-1) has speculated that there were four parishes within the Hiberno-Norse town of Wexford. These were St Doologue's, St Mary's, St Patrick's and St Iberius'. The Norse also appear to have owned estates around Wexford, particularly in the Rosslare-Ballymore area, which may have formed the bases of these parishes.

17

Co. Wexford at the end of the Early Christian period

Co. Wexford in the twelfth century was a prosperous place. The landscape was a mosaic of pasture, with cattle and sheep grazing, tilled fields of wheat, oats, barley and rye, and mudwalled, thatched houses with their vegetable gardens and orchards. Numerous mills, both horizontal and vertical, powered by streams, ground the grain to make bread and gruel. Many small areas of forest were interspersed through the farmland. But large areas of the county were still forested, particularly from west of Enniscorthy to Bunclody, the Slaney valley, between New Ross and Taghmon and Ferrycarrig and probably the poorly drained land along the east coast. The low-lying areas were wet and marshy but were a valuable source of summer grazing.

Wexford was a thriving centre of trade and shipping, while Ferns and other ecclesiastical sites also functioned as market places. The general population may have lived in small clusters of houses, although there is as yet little evidence for this type of settlement. A network of roads facilitated transport of goods and people throughout the county.

Many places had now been given specific names, derived either from families or landscape features. People, too, had now adopted surnames, using their father or grandfather's first name.

Emphasizing the continuity of landscape occupation during the previous millennia for its twelfth-century inhabitants were prehistoric monuments such as standing stones and stone alignments and promontory and hill forts. But the most ubiquitous monuments, over 600 of them, would have been the ráths, by that time mostly unused and overgrown. Numerous also would have been the ecclesiastical enclosures, mainly circular, some now without churches, others becoming the centres of the new parishes being created as part of the general Church reforms.

The political situation on the eve of the Norman landings

While the pastoral scene appeared peaceful the political machinations of the reigning families were less so. Power no longer rested with the petty kings of the *tuatha* but was centralized in the higher regional and provincial kings. In Wexford that power centre was Diarmait Mac Murchada's capital in Ferns. But his power extended well beyond the confines of the county. He was also king of Leinster and Norse Dublin and sometime ally of the most powerful kings in Ireland. Although there is some doubt about his age, Diarmait was probably born in 1110. In either 1126 or 1131, through the lack of any other acceptable candidate, he was elected king of Uí Cheinnselaig and Leinster. That he was a scion of one of the most power-ful families in Ireland, a great-grandson of Diarmait Mac Máel na mBó, who had subdued Munster and Norse Dublin, would quickly have been impressed on the young king.

No sooner had Diarmait been elected king of Leinster than he was deposed by Turlough O'Connor, the powerful king of Connacht. Even worse was to follow in 1128 when Tigernan O'Rourke, at the instigation of O'Connor, ravaged and plundered Uí Cheinnselaig. The lesson was clear lost on a man of Mac Murchada's calibre. It was also the start of a bitter per-sonal enmity between the two men.

Diarmait did not long remain subdued. With the decline of O'Connor's power he asserted his claim to the kingship of Leinster. But over the fol-lowing years this claim was often disputed. The fact that his family had held it almost continuously from 1042 did not prevent other families such as the Uí Fáilge and Uí Faeláin of North Leinster and the O'Tooles of Wicklow from pressing their claims. Even strategic marriages to Sadb Mac Faeláin and Mor O'Toole did not completely eliminate the threat. Taking hostages was a way of keeping control, and at one time Laurence O'Toole, his broth-er-in-law, and later a canonized saint, was such a surety.

In 1134 Diarmait's attack on Ossory was repulsed but later that year with the help of Norse Dublin he attacked Ossory and Munster, defeating O'Briain of Thomond and taking Norse Waterford. In the same year Diarmait fought alongside O'Rourke, O'Connor and Máel Sechnaill at the battle of Moin Mor, near Fermoy, where they routed the forces of Turlough O'Briain of Thomond.

In 1152 the duplicity of O'Rourke in his dealings with the high king finally drove O'Connor and Mac Lochlainn to invade his kingdom of Bréifne and to set up a rival king in his place. Politically O'Rourke was at his nadir. Now Diarmait inflicted another blow, if not to O'Rourke's lovelife, at least to his honour. He took O'Rourke's wife, Dervorgilla, together with her cat-tle and furniture, to his capital at Ferns. The Annals of Clonmacnoise, never too well disposed to Mac Murchada, gave the following version of the event:

> Dermott Mac Murrough, king of Leinster, tooke the lady Dervorgill, daughter of the said Morrough O'Melaghlin and wife of Tyernan O'Royrck, with her cattle with him, and kept her for a long space to satisfy his unsatiable carnall and adulterous lust. She was procured and enduced thereunto by her unadvised brother McLoghlin for some abuse of her husband Tyneernan don before.

By other accounts the arrangement was mutual, if shortlived. Within a year she was back in Bréifne and O'Rourke was gradually restored to power.

By 1159 two powerful rival camps had become established in Ireland, on one side O'Connor and O'Rourke, on the other Mac Lochlainn and Mac Murchada. In a major battle at Ardee, Co. Louth, the Connacht alliance was defeated. O'Rourke was again deprived of his possessions in Meath. Mac Lochlainn and Mac Murchada were now at the height of their powers and a period of relative peace ensued. But in 1166 Mac Lochlainn made a fatal mistake: he broke a solemn agreement, witnessed by the archbishop of Armagh, by blinding an enemy. This was the signal for general warfare against Mac Lochlainn and his ally Mac Murchada. O'Connor, with his allies, including O'Rourke, marched into Uí Cheinnselaig and defeated Mac Murchada, who burned Ferns at their approach. He was forced to hand over four hostages and to relinquish his kingship of Leinster, though not of Uí Cheinnselaig.

Worse was to follow. Mac Murchada's great ally, Mac Lochlainn, was now beset by enemies and died ignominiously in a skirmish in a bog in Co. Armagh. Mac Murchada's enemies, O'Rourke and Máel Sechnaill, with the Norse of Dublin, marched into Uí Cheinnselaig. Mac Murchada was left defenceless, deserted even by his own chiefs, including Ó Brain, chief of the Duffry, west of Enniscorthy, who had been expected to guard the Fid Dorcha (dark wood), the strategically important pass through the Blackstairs mountains between Clonegal and Bunclody. Diarmait fled, Ferns was destroyed, he himself was deposed, and his kingdom was divided between his brother Murchad and the king of Ossory.

The Annals explain his fall from favour by claiming that Diarmait was banished 'being, before, for his pride, tyranny and bad government, hated by the Leinstermen themselves' (Ann. Clon.). The Annals of Tigernach state that the 'Leinstermen and Foreigners revolted against Mac Murchada for his own crimes'.

With few friends left in Ireland, Diarmait set sail for England in August 1166. Only the previous year he had allowed the Dublin fleet to help the king of England, Henry II, in Wales. Now was the time for the king to reciprocate.

Diarmait Mac Murchada and the Church

The Church in the twelfth century was pressing ahead with reform. The old monastic system no longer served that function and was replaced by the diocesan arrangement. The number of dioceses had been reduced and their boundaries fixed, and parishes were being organized, however slowly. But among the higher clergy there was a belief that the Irish Church needed outside help in the process of rejuvenation. For this purpose religious orders from Continental Europe were being invited in and given land and other assistance to found their abbeys and priories.

In such patronage Mac Murchada played a leading part, encouraged, no doubt, by his distinguished brother-in-law, Laurence O'Toole, archbishop of Dublin. One of his earlier encounters with the church had not been auspicious. In 1132 he stormed the abbey in Kildare, deposed the Uí Fáilgi abbess, Mor, and forced her to marry, thereby making her unsuitable to be an abbess (Ann. Clon.). The Annals of Loch Cé have a somewhat cruder version, stating that she was 'put into a man's bed'. In her place he put a member of his own family. In fairness it must be said that Mor herself had also been intruded violently at the expense of Mac Murchada's own sister-in-law, one of the Mac Faeláin. Control of the abbey of Kildare was, of course, essential for anyone with pretensions to the kingship of Leinster.

In 1146 Diarmait founded an abbey for nuns of the canons regular of St Augustine, near the present St Andrews' church (now a tourist office) in Suffolk Street, Dublin. In 1148 he granted a charter to the Cistercian Order to build an abbey at Baltinglass, Co. Wicklow. For this he was awarded the distinction of a personal letter from the famous St Bernard, abbot of the Cistercian monastery of Clairvaux. A translation of this letter, written in Latin, in the Konventbibliothek, Vienna, was first published in Nicholas Furlong's book, *Dermot, king of Leinster and the foreigners* (1973, 62):

> A letter from the community to Dermot, king of Ireland, Bernard, abbot of Clairvaux, sends greetings and good wishes to the noble and glorious king of Ireland.
>
> Your renown has reached this country, and we rejoice exceedingly in the good reports of you: that you received with regal generosity the poor of Christ- or rather, Christ himself in the person of these poor. It is truly a matter of amazement to us that a king who reigns over a barbarous people should pursue the works of mercy with such generosity. Those whom you have welcomed are our own very offspring, and you may cherish yourself in them and regard them as your own.
>
> Accordingly, we thank your regal majesty, praying for you and your kingly salvation, that the Lord our God may give you peace in

your days. And that you may carry out more freely and more completely what you have initiated, we make you a participant in all the
good works which we perform in our house and our Order, and we
pray that when you depart your kingdom, it will be for an eternal one.

The similarity in carved detail between Baltinglass, Glendalough and
Killeshin has led to the belief that Mac Murchada may also have endowed
the latter two churches (O'Keeffe, forthcoming).

In 1150 Diarmait brought existing convents at Aghade, Co. Carlow, and
Kilculliheen, Co. Waterford, under the Augustinian rule. Around 1160 he
granted a charter to the abbey at his capital Ferns, also under the canons
regular of St Augustine and dedicated to the Virgin Mary. In 1161 he
founded the monastery of All Hallows (on the site of the present Trinity
College, Dublin) also under the Augustinian rule. He donated land for
Duiske abbey, Graignamanagh, this time under Cistercian rules, as well as
confirming by charter land at Killenny, Co. Kilkenny, to the Cistercians.

The climax to Mac Murchada's benefaction to the Church came in 1162
when he presided over the synod of Clane. This synod was attended by all
the Irish bishops, including the archbishop of Armagh, and also presided
over by the papal legate. An interesting sidelight on the mores of the time
was Diarmait's possible espousal of at least two wives and his cohabitation
with Dervorgilla in his lustier days. While this was perfectly legitimate
under brehon law, it ill-fitted the decrees of the Church against concubinage
and the like. But no voice was raised against Mac Murchada or his patronage of the Church. This may not be unrelated to the fact that the bishop of
Ferns, Joseph Ó hAodha, was a kinsman of Diarmait.

Paradoxically, in 1156 Mac Murchada, with Norse Dublin and Domhnall
Mac Seachlainn of Meath, plundered east Meath 'both churches and territories and carried off many cows' (AFM). It should be remembered that
churches were often used by the laity to store valuables and also they may
have belonged to rich families who were enemies of the attackers. Churches
had been attacked for centuries by both the Irish and the Norse.

Diarmait Mac Murchada's court

In his charter for the foundation of Ferns abbey, Mac Murchada refers especially to taking 'the counsel and advice of the principal men of my Council'
in granting lands to the abbey (Hore, vi, 180).

Who formed this core of administrators, scholars and political and military advisors at Ferns? Notices in the Annals tell us that in 1117 Áed Mac
Cremthainn *ferleighinn* (learned man) was born. In 1127 Domhnall Dall Ua
Murchada, chief sage of Leinster, died and in 1129 Mac Muirgheasa, professor of Ferns died (AFM). This shows that a coterie of learned men had

existed at Ferns in Mac Murchada's youth. That Mac Murchada was interested in scholarship, even if only of a kind to enhance the family name, is
shown by his sponsorship of the compilation known as the Book of Leinster
by Áed Mac Crimthainn at Terryglass monastery, Co. Tipperary.

That Muiris Ó Riagáin was Mac Murchada's closest advisor is evident
from the *Song of Dermot and the Earl*, an Old French poem describing the
coming of the Normans to Ireland (Orpen, 1892). Indeed, the composer
states that the poem is based on information supplied by Ó Riagáin, who is
described as Mac Murchada's interpreter. He is first mentioned as being sent
to Wales to drum up support for Mac Murchada. Later we find him nego-
tiating with the Norse of Dublin on behalf of Mac Murchada and Strongbow.

The Ó Doráin family, hereditary lawyers of Uí Cheinnselaig, must also
have been close to the centre of power. They gave their names to the townlands of Glandoran, parish of Craanford and Kildoran (now Askinvillar),
parish of Ballindaggan. Their law school was probably located at Ballyorley
(pers. comm. Brian Cleary). The Ua Nualláin from Forth, Co. Carlow, were
also close allies. Auliffe Ó Cinaeda was obviously close to Diarmait, being a
member of the party that went with him to meet Henry II in France.
According to Scott and Martin (1978, 288) there was a branch of the Uí
Cinnaeda in south Wexford in the twelfth century. Cellach Mac Cinnaeda,
of Síl nOnchon, king of Uí Cheinnselaig, died in 947.

Florence, who is listed as the 'king's chancellor' in Mac Murchada' charter, must also have been an influential voice in council. The abbots of Ferns,
too, were probably in close contact with Mac Murchada. He would have had
a major, if not total, say in their appointment but, judging by his attacks on
church property, they exerted little restraint on his conduct, at least outside
of Uí Cheinnselaig.

Another person who may have been close to Mac Murchada was Áedh
Ó Caellaighe, with whose family he was fostered. Obviously among his most
trusted advisors would have been his close relations. These included his
brother, Murchad, and Domhnall Mac Murchada Caomhánach, his son born
out of wedlock. That the latter was a man of some metal is proved by the
fact that he defeated the Vikings of Wexford in 1161 (AFM).

Since he constantly had to call on his subkings to support him in arms,
it is likely that they were also called on for advice. As Ó Corráin (1972, 173)
stated, 'it is clear that most royal officials were, in fact, dependent nobles
and petty rulers'.

Mac Murchada's Wexford chiefs and their territories
At the time of the Norman landings Wexford was subdivided into about
eight minor kingdoms (Map 13). Although the rulers of these small kingdoms had lost most of their former autonomy, they were still not complete-

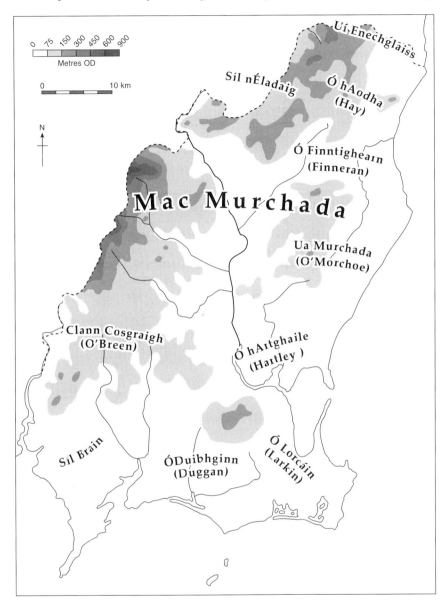

Map 13 The names and territories of the principal Gaelic families on the eve of the Norman conquest. This information is derived from the *Song of Dermot and the Earl*, a Norman account written around 1180, and an Irish poem from around 1400.

ly subjugated. This is borne out by the defection of Murchad Ó Brain of the Duffry and later by the forces of Uí Cheinnselaig and Norse Wexford besieging Fitzstephen at Carrick in 1171 (Scott and Martin 1978, 235). Also, Ó Riain of Idrone and his followers attacked the Normans and Mac Murchada's followers at their encampment at Dundonnell, later called Baginbun, now Ramstown, in 1170 (Orpen, 1892, 107).

In attempting to provide a guide to the chiefs of Co. Wexford and their territories in the immediate pre-Norman period it is well to note the cautionary words of Byrne (1984, 103) that 'all attempts to draw precise borders for this period must remain approximate'.

The earliest source of evidence on the ruling families and their territories is provided by the *Song of Dermot and the Earl*, written shortly after the Norman invasion from information probably given by Diarmait Mac Murchada's secretary, Muiris Ó Riagáin. From this Orpen (1892, 327) derived a list of Uí Cheinnselaig chiefs and their territories. The following were located in Co. Wexford:

Uí Deaghaidh: nearly co-extensive with the barony of Gorey; chief, Ó hAodha (Hay or Hughes). Under 1165 the Annals of Ulster list the death of Paitín Ua Aedha: 'the candle of Uí Cheinnselaig, killed by the O'Moore's of Laoighis for evil causes'. Paitín was a relation of bishop Ó hAodha and of Diarmait himself.

Dubhtire (the Duffry): the barony of Scarawalsh; chief, Ó Brain (O'Breen).

Uí Feilmeadha Deas (southern Offelimy): the barony of Ballaghkeen; chief, Ó Murchada (O'Morchoe and afterwards Murphy).

Benntraige: the barony of Bantry; Clann Cosgraigh.

Siol Brain: the barony of Shelburne.

Fearann-deiscertach: the barony of Bargy; chief, Ó Duibhginn (Deegan and Duggan).

Fothart an Chairn: the barony of Forth; chief, Ó Lorcáin (Larkin).

Fearann na-gCenél (Fernegenal): the barony of Shelmalier East; chief, O hArtghaile (Hartley or Hartilly).

Fearann means land or country; *Fearann deiscertach* = the southern country; *Fearann na gCenél* = the country of the tribe.

Most of this information is corroborated in a poem written by Giolla na Naomh Ó hUidhrin, who died in 1420 (O'Donovan, 1862, 4). The poet is described as a learned historian who gives an account of the principal families of Leinster and Munster and the districts occupied by them. Nicholls (1984, 552), however, has expressed strong reservations about its accuracy. The poem consists of 780 verses, beginning 'An addition of knowledge on sacred Erin'. The following lines (pages 91 and 93) refer to Co. Wexford:

O'hAodha over Uí Deaghaidh for me,
For whom the trees blossom after bending.

O'Muirte of great mirth
Is over the fair Cinél-Flaitheamhain,
Over Uí Mealla of swift ships,
The hero O'Finntighearn has sway.
A lordship profitable, weighty,
Has O'Murchada of smooth fair land,
The territory of Uí Felme, the hero has obtained,
In his turn of ancestral possession.

Another high noble tribe,
The Siol Brain, people of the Dubhthoire,
They have not got a portion of the plain of Corc,
The scions from the middle of the garden.

From the Bearbha to the Sláine eastwards
Is the extent of the territory of the Clann-Cosgraigh,
The host of Beanntraige of curling locks,
The hawk-like, slow-eyed, warlike host.

Lord of the Fearann-deiscertach
Which is not uneven to be mentioned,
To O'Duibhginn it is hereditary,
The host from the black pool of fair bushes.

Hero of Fothart of the carn,
A stately, modest, polished youth;
A hero of good deeds with darts,
The affluent chief Ó Lorcáin.

Crioch na gCenél, fair land,
Land of the sod of brown berries,
A harbour the fairest under the sun,
O hArtghaile is its hereditary chief.

Ó hUidhrin's poem includes two groups not mentioned by Orpen – the Cinél Flaitheamhain and the Uí Mella. Since the places listed are in a particular geographical sequence, going from north to south, this would place the latter somewhere south of the barony of Gorey. However, Nicholls (1969, 90) equates the Síl Mella with the Norman corruption of Schyrmal and places them south and east of the Slaney from Enniscorthy to the coast.

Table 13: Families and territories listed in Ó hUidhrin's poem

Family	Territory
Ó hAodh (Hayes, Hay)	Oday, Gorey
Ó Muirte	Cinel-Flaitheamhain?
Ó Finntighearn (Finneran)	Uí Mella
Ó Murchada (O'Morchoe)	Ballaghkeen
Ó Brain	Duffry, Enniscorthy
Clann Cosgraigh (Cosgrave)	Benntraige, Bantry
Ó Duibhginn (Deegan, Duggan)	Fearann-deiscertach, Bargy
Ó Lorcáin	Fothart, Forth
Ó hArtghaill (Hartley)	Fernegenall, Shelmalier East

Wexford on the edge

By the end of 1166 the once all-powerful ruler and church benefactor, Diarmait Mac Murchada, had been stripped of his kingdoms of Uí Cheinnselaig and Leinster. Together with members of his council he was actively engaged in seeking military help from abroad to redress the situation. Would he succeed? This question, no doubt, was exercising the minds of his subkings. Unlike Ó Brain of the Duffry they had always given him full support. But how should they and the Norse react to a foreign force, particularly if it landed in their territory? Mac Murchada, if successful, might reward his Norman adventurers with grants of land. But whose land? For Mac Murchada's Wexford chiefs the future looked uncertain.

Appendices

Kings	Branch	Died
Énna Cennsalach		483
Crimthann		?
Brandubh	Uí Felmada	605
Ronan	Síl Chormaic	624?
Áed Mend	Síl Chormaic	738
Diarmait mac Máel na mBó	Síl nOnchon	1072
Murchad	Síl nOnchon	1070
Domnall	Síl nOnchon	1075
Énna	Síl nOnchon	1092
Diarmait	Síl nOnchon	1098
Donnchad	Síl nOnchon	1115
Diarmait	Síl nOnchon	1117
Énna	Síl nOnchon	1126
Diarmait	Síl nOnchon	1171

Brandubh mac Echach, slain in 605	Uí Felmada
Conall mac Áeda	Síl nAeda
Crimthann mac Ailella	Uí Felmada
Dúnchad mac Conaill	Síl nAeda
Ronán mac Coluim, died 624	Síl Chormaic
Crundmáel mac Ronáin	Síl Chormaic
Cummascach mac Ronáin	Síl Chormaic
Colgu mac Crundmáel, *floruit* 647	Síl Chormaic
Colum mac espuic?	?
Bran hua Máele Dúin, slain in 712	Síl Máeluidir
Cú Congalt mac Con Mella, died in 724	Síl Máeluidir

Laidcend mac Con Mella, slain in 727	Síl Máeluidir
Élotach mac Fáelchon, slain in 732	Síl nÉladaig
Áed Mend mac Colgan, slain in 738	Síl Chormaic,
Sechnassach mac Colgan, died in 746 or 747	Síl Chormaic
Cathal hua Cináid?	?
Dondgal mac Laidgnén, slain in 761	Síl Chormaic
Dub Calcaig mac Laidgnén, slain in 769	Síl Chormaic
Cennselach mac Brain, slain in 770	Síl Máeluidir
Eterscél mac Áeda Mind, died in 778	Síl Chormaic
Cairpre mac Laidgnén, died in 793	Síl Chormaic
Cellach Bairne mac Dondgaile, slain in 809	Síl Chormaic
Cathal mac Dúnlaing, died in 819	Síl Máeluidir
Cú Congalt mac Cathail, died?	Síl Máeluidir
Cairpre mac Cathail, died in 844	Síl Máeluidir
Echtigern mac Guaire, slain in 853	Síl nÉladaig
Bruatar mac Áeda, slain in 853	Síl Chormaic
Cellach mac Guaire, died in 858	Síl nÉladaig,
Tadc mac Diarmata, slain in 865	Síl nOnchon
Donnacán mac Cétfada?	?
Cairpre mac Diarmata, slain in 876	Síl nOnchon
Dúngal mac Fáelain, died in 876	Síl nÉladaig
Flannacán mac Fáelain, died in 880	Síl nÉladaig
Riacán mac Echthigirn, died in 893	Síl nÉladaig
Faelán mac Guaire, died in 894	?
Dubgilla mac Eterscéoil, died in 903	Síl Chormaic
Tadc mac Faeláin, died in 922	Síl nÉladaig
Cináed mac Cairpre, slain in 935	Síl nOnchon
Brutar mac Dubgilla, murdered in 937	Síl Chormaic
Cellach mac Cináeda, slain in 947	Síl Máeluidir
Echthigern mac Cináeda, died?	Síl nOnchon
Donnchad mac Taidg, died?	Síl nÉladaig
Domnall mac Cellaig, slain in 974,	Síl nOnchon
Máel Ruanaid mac Domnaill?	?
Donnchad mac Cellaig	Síl nOnchon
Muiredach mac Riain, slain in 978	Síl Chormaic
Bruatar mac Echthigirn, died in 982	Síl nOnchon
Diarmait mac Domnaill, slain in 996	Síl nOnchon
Donnchad mac Diarmata, alias Máel na mBó, slain in 1006	Síl nOnchon
Máel Morda mac Lorcáin, slain in 1024	?
Tadc mac Lorcáin, died in 1030	?
Diarmait mac Máel na mBó, slain in 1072	Síl nOnchon
Domnall mac Murchada, slain in 1089	Síl nOnchon
Énna mac Diarmata, slain in 1092	Síl nOnchon
Diarmait mac Énna, slain in 1098	
Donnchad mac Murchada, died in 1115	
Diarmait mac Énna, died in 1117	
Énna mac Donnchada, died in 1126	
Diarmait mac Donnchada?	
Diarmait mac Murchada, died in 1171	

APPENDIX 3: CHURCH AND HOLY WELL DEDICATIONS, SAINTS' FEAST DAYS AND 'PATTERN' DAYS, WHERE KNOWN

Abbreviations Flood = Flood, 1916. Hore = Hore, 1862. O'D = O'Donovan, 1840.

Location	Church	Holy well	Feast day	'Pattern' day	Reference
Adamstown	Abbán	Abbán	16 March	1 Oct.	Flood
Ardamine	Aidán		31 Jan.		Flood
Ardcandrisk	—	Eusebius	—	26 Sept.	Flood
Ardcavan	Caomhán	Caomhán	12 June	12 June	Flood
Ardcolm	Columcille	Columcille	9 June	9 June	Flood
Askinvillar – see Kildoran					
Ballinclare – see Toome					
Ballybrazil	—	Crone	—	—	O'D
Ballybrennan – see Kilcowanore					
Ballycanew	Moling		17 June		Flood
Ballymore – see Screen					
Ballynaberney – see Kilrush					
Beggerin Island	Ibar		23 April		MD
Bola Beg – see Templeshanbo					
Brandane	Brendán		16 May		Flood
Bregorteen – see Kilbrideglynn			—		—
Bulgan–see Killell			—		—
Bush	Michael	Michael	29 Sept	29 Sept	Flood
Carrick, Bannow	St Mary	St Mary	—		Flood
Churchtown – see Kilrane					
Churchtown – see St Dubhán's					
Churchtown – see Tacumshin					
Clonatin – see Kilmakilloge					
Clone	Aidán	—	31 Jan.		Flood
Clongeen	Aidán	Aidán	31 Jan.	18 May?	Flood

Location	Church	Holy well	Feast day	'Pattern' day	Reference
Clone	Aidán	–	31 Jan.	–	Flood
Clongeen	Aidán	Aidán	31 Jan.	18 May?	Flood
Coolhull	Aidán (Máedóg)	Aidán	31 Jan.	10 Dec.	Flood
Donaghmore	Patrick	–	17 March	–	Flood
Ferns Upper	Aidán	Aidán	31 Jan.	–	Flood
Fethard	Aidán	–	31 Jan.	–	Flood
Glebe – see Monamolin, Kilmuckridge					
Grange – see Kilmore					
Great Island – see Kilmokea					
Kerlogue	Ellóc	James	25 June(Ellóc)	25 July(James) MO, O'D	O'D
Kilbride, Ballylusk	Brigid	Brigid	1 Feb.	–	
Kilbrideglynn	Brigid	Brigid	1 Feb.	–	
Kilcarbry	Cairpre	Cairpre	–	–	Flood
Kilcavan	Caomhán	Caomhán	12 June	12 June	O'D
Kilcavan Lower	Caomhán	Caomhán	12 June	12 June	O'D
Kilcloggan	Ellóc	Alloc	25 June	–	Martyrologies
Kilcomb	Columcille	–	9 June	9 June	O'D
Kilcormick	Cormic	Cormic	21 June	21 June	O'D
Kilcowan	Cuán	–	10 July	–	Flood
Kilcowanmore	Cuán	Cuán	3 Feb.	3 Feb.	Flood
Kildavin Lower	Davin	Davin	–	1 August	Flood
Kildoran	–	Dorán ?	–	–	O'D
Kilgarvan	Garván	Garván	25 Oct.	–	
Kilgorman	Gorman	Gorman	27 Aug.	–	MD
Killag	Degumen	–	22 June	–	Hore
Killagowan	Cronán	Cronán	26 July	22 June	O'D
Killann	Anne	Anne	24 April	26 July	O'D
Killegney	Eigneach	Our Lady	27 August	–	O'D
Killiane Little	Degumen	–	–	–	Hore

Killila	Brigid	1 Feb.	Brigid	1 Feb.	O'D
Killincooley Beg	Canóc	28 Sept	Canóc	28 Sept	Flood
Or Mochanóc, feast day 11 Feb. (Colgan)					
Killinick	Enóc?	4 Oct?	Enóc?	—	Martyrologies
Killisk	—	1 Feb.	Brigid	—	Flood
Killurin	Lurán	10 Aug.	Laurence	10 Aug.	Flood
Kilmacot	Mochuda	14 May	Mochuda	—	MD
Kilmacree	Caomhán or All Saints	—	Caomhán or All Saints	—	12 June
Flood, Hore					
Kilmakilloge	Sillóg	13 July	—	—	Flood
Kilmallock	Sillóg	15 Aug.	Mary	15 Aug.	Flood
Kilmannon	Monnena	6 July	Monnena	6 July	O'D
Kilmore	Patrick	17 March	Patrick	19 March (sic)	Flood
Kilmuckridge	Canóc	11 Feb.	Brigid	11 Feb.	Flood
Kilmurry	Mary	—	Mary	—	
Kilmyshall	Colmán	22 Sept (Colmán)	Mary Magdalene	22 July (Mary M.)	O'D
Kilnahue	Aidán ?	31 Jan.	—	15 August	Flood
Kilnamanagh Lower	Moling	17 June	Moling	—	Flood
Kilpatrick	Patrick	17 March	Patrick	—	
Kilrane	Ruán	15 April	—	—	Hore
Kilrush	Colmán	2 2 Sept.	—	—	Martyrologies
Kilscoran	Enóc?	4 Oct.	—	—	Martyrologies
Kiltennel	Sinchell	15 June	—	—	Martyrologies
Kiltilly	Teille	25 June	Mary	—	MT
Kilturk	Cuán	4 April	—	4 April	Flood
Kinnagh	—	11 Nov.	Martin	—	O'D
Meelnagh – see Killagowan					
Monomolin, K'ridge	Moling	17 June	Moling	17 June	Flood
Monomolin, Rathnure	Moling	17 June	—	—	
Morrisseysland	Stephen	26 Dec.	Stephen	—	
Rathaspick	Brigid	1 Feb.	Brigid	Hore	MO, OS map

Location	Church	Holy well	Feast day	'Pattern' day	Reference
Rossminoge North	Enán or MoEnnóc	—	30 Jan.	—	MT
Ryland Lower – see Kilmyshall					
St Brecaun's	Brecaun	—	—	—	—
St Dubhán's	Dubhán	Dubhán	11 Feb.	—	MD
St Iberius or St Ivor's	Ibar	—	23 April	—	Hore
St Kieran's	Kieran	—	5 March	—	
St Vauk's	Vauk	—	15 June	20 Jan.	Flood, O'D
Sanctuary – see Killinick					
Saunderscourt – see Kilpatrick					
Screen	Maelruan	—	7 July	26 Sept (Cyprian)	Flood
Shelbaggan	—	Agatha	5 Feb.	—	Moore
Shemoge–see Coolhull					
Tacumshin	Mumnu	—	21 Oct	—	Hore
Taghmon	Mumnu	Mumnu	21 Oct.	21 Oct.	Flood
Templeudigan	Lugidon	—	6 Jan.	—	Hore, MD
Templeshanbo	Colmán	Colmán	27 Oct.	—	Martyrologies
Templeshannon	Senán	Senán	1 March	—	Flood
Tomhaggard	Mosacra	Mosacra	3 March	3 March	Martyrologies
		Anne	26 July	26 July	Flood, MO
Toome	Moling	—	17 June	—	Flood

WEXFORD TOWN

Location	Church dedication	Feast day	'Pattern' day
Castle Hill Street	St Michael	29 Sept.	29 Sept.
Main Street	St Ibar (Iberius)	23 April	—
Selskar			
Stonebridge	St Olaf (Doologue)	29 July	—
Trinity Street	Holy Trinity	Sunday after Pentecost	—

APPENDIX 4: GAZETTEER OF EARLY CHRISTIAN ECCLESIASTICAL
SITES IN CO. WEXFORD
(The physical descriptions are mainly from Moore, 1996.)

Sites are identified as follows: townland (= td), modern parish, OS six-inch sheet number and record number in the *Archaeological inventory of Co. Wexford* (Moore, 1996).

Adamstown, Adamstown. Sheet 31. No. 1171. Site of medieval parish church of same name, dedicated to St Abbán. Abbán founded a monastery here, which was then called Magharnaidhe, in the late fifth or early sixth century (see Chapter 8). This area, then controlled by the Uí Bairrche, was later taken over by the Uí Cheinnselaig, who probably never allowed the monastery to become important. No abbots or erenaghs are listed in the Annals. An undecorated, ringless Latin cross, possibly of eighth-century date (Harbison, 1992, 377), stands within an oval-shaped graveyard. St Abbán's well is located about one kilometre to the south; his feast day is 16 March.

Ardamine, Middletown td. Riverchapel-Courtown. Sheet 12. No. 1275. Site of medieval parish church of same name, dedicated to St Aidán, feast day 31 January. He is reputed to have landed at a place called Ard Ladrann (Plummer, 1922, ii, 205) which is taken to be around Ardamine, and to have built his first church on land given by the local chief, Dimma (Diarmait). According to the Annals of Ulster, Colgu, king of Ard Ladrann, was slain in 722. The cross in the rectangular graveyard is post-Norman. This site was utilized as a motte and bailey by the Normans in the late twelfth century.

Ardcandrisk, Glynn. Sheet 37. No. 1173. Site of medieval parish church of same name, possibly Ard Cainross mentioned in Martyrology of Óengus as being on the shore of Loch Garman. Hogan (1910, 38) stated that neither the exact location nor modern place-name of Ard Cainross or Ard Cnamross are known but Camaross seems the most likely place. St Eusebius' well *c*.50 metres south had a pattern on 26 September which was abolished around 1790 (O'Donovan, 1840, i, 129). Four saints of this name are listed in the Martyrology of Óengus, three of them popes, the other a martyr. A Eusebius, described as bishop of Rome, has a feast day on 25 September. O'Hanlon (1875, x, 125-6)) states that the one venerated in the Irish church was a pope and a martyr, whose feast day is on 9 October, but the pattern date indicates the former. Subrectangular graveyard.

Ardcavan, Castlebridge. Sheet 38. No. 1174. Site of medieval parish church of same name, dedicated to St Caomháin of Dairinis, an island in Wexford harbour, now part of North Slob. The death of the erenagh is recorded for 1055 (AFM). Well dedicated to St Caomhán, pattern 12 June, his feast day. He is listed in the Martyrology of Tallaght as being in Airdne and in the Martyrology of Donegal as Caomhán of Ard Caomháin; both names refer to Ardcavan. Oval graveyard, 53 x 18-30 metres. See p. 126, above.

Ardcolm, Castlebridge. Sheet 38. No. 1175. Site of medieval parish church of same name, dedicated to St Columcille, who died in 597. St Columb's well, pattern 9 June, his feast day, 150 metres southeast. Kilcomb may also be dedicated to this saint. That this place was of some importance is shown by a reference to it in the Annals of the Four Masters for 890 when it is recorded that Ciarán, son of Maeldubh, abbot of Airdne Coluim (Ardcolm), died. There is also a reference to Airdne Coluim in the twelfth-century Martyrology of Gorman. Circular graveyard.
Askinvillar Upper. Sheet 18. See Kildoran.

Ballinclare td. Sheet 11. See Toome.

Ballybrazil, Suttons. Sheet 39. No. 1157. Site of medieval parish church of same name. Site of St Crone's well nearby, but, not knowing the pattern date, it is not possible to identify which Crone was venerated here. According to O'Donovan (ii, 69) the large rectangular graveyard is believed to be the oldest in the county. Wells dedicated to the Blessed Virgin and St Brigid were located in the townland. Graveyard within large, circular enclosure, 94 x 86 metres, defined by slight traces of a fosse or ditch.

Ballybrennan, Bree. Sheet 31. See Kilcowanmore.

Ballycanew, Camolin. Sheet 16. No. 1184. Site of medieval parish church of same name, dedicated to St Moling of St Mullins, Co. Carlow, feast day 17 June. Bullaun stone. Subcircular raised graveyard, 44 x 30 metres.

Ballymore, Sheet 33. See Screen.

Ballynaberney. Sheet 10. See Kilrush.

Ballyorley. Monagear. Sheet 21. No. 1159. Medieval parish of Kilcormick. Listed in the sixteenth-century fiants of Elizabeth I as the site of an Ó Doráin law school (I am indebted to Brian Cleary for this information). This school may date back to the Early Christian period, as the Ó Doráin family were hereditary lawyers of the Uí Cheinnselaig. The crop mark of a circular enclosure, 90 metres in diameter, also indicates an Early Christian date for this site,

Beggerin Island, Castlebridge. Sheet 38. No. 1160. Site of school and monastery founded by St Ibar, feast day 23 April. Two crosses, one now in the National Museum, the other in the County Museum, Enniscorthy. Oval graveyard within former island. See p. 143, above.

Bola Beg. Sheet 14. See Templeshanbo.

Brandane, Bannow. Sheet 45. No. 1427. Church dedicated to St Brendan, the Navigator (Flood,1916,143), feast day 16 May. The chapel at Brandane was mentioned in the Tintern Charter of 1245 (Hore, ii, 28).

Bregorteen. Sheet 36. See Kilbrideglynn.

Bulgan. Sheet 36. See Killell.

Bush, Tagoat. Sheet 48. No. 1206. Site of medieval parish church of St Michael the Archangel, who was revered in the early Irish church. Well dedicated to him, c.60 metres southeast, pattern 29 September, his feast day, until c.1830 (O'Donovan, 1840, i, 98). Circular graveyard, 30 metres diam. defined by earthen bank.

Carrick, Bannow. Sheet 45. No. 1424. Site of medieval parish church of Bannow, dedicated to St Mary. Lady's well c.200 metres southeast. This church is listed in the Tintern charter of 1245 (Hore, ii, 32). The fact that it was claimed by the bishop of Ferns between 1228 and 1232 indicates that it was pre-Norman church property. Rectangular graveyard within D-shaped enclosure.

Churchtown td. Sheet 48. See Kilrane.

Churchtown td, Hook Head. Sheet 54. See St Dubhán's church.

Churchtown td, Kilmore. Sheet 47. Probable site of church of medieval parish of Mulrankin, dedicated to St David. Rectangular graveyard.

Churchtown td. Sheet 53. See Tacumshin.

Clonatin td. Sheet 7. See Kilmakilloge

Clone, Monagear. Sheet 15. No. 1220. Site of medieval parish church of same name, dedicated to St Aidán (Flood, 1916, 36). Two bullaun stones, cross decorated slabs and a sundial. Clone was claimed as church property by the bishop of Ferns in the 1220's. The present church probably dates to the thirteenth century. The Romanesque window in St Peter's Church, Ferns, was probably taken from here, also the face corbels at St Máedóg's well in Ferns. Rectangular graveyard.

Clongeen, Clongeen. Sheet 40. No. 1221. Site of medieval parish church of same name, dedicated to St Aidán, pattern 15 May. St Maedog's well 30 metres northwest. St Aidán and the young Moling are reputed to have met at Cluain Cain Máedóg (see Life of Moling, Stokes, 1907, 3-57). Cain is also spelled 'caoin' (Dinneen, 1927, 161)), in this case meaning 'sweet' or 'pleasant', hence Clongeen translates as 'the sweet meadow'. Large circular enclosure, *c*.300 metres diam. indicated by the curve in the road and surrounding wall. There is also a well dedicated to St Aidán some 300 metres west. Rectangular graveyard.

Clonmore, Bree. Sheet 31. No. 1222. Site of medieval parish church of same name. It is said to have been founded by St Aidán who allocated it to St Diochalla Garbh (Plummer, 1922, ii, 209). In the Life of Aidán of Ferns and the early literature it became confused with the important monastery of Clonmore, Hacketstown, Co. Carlow, which was founded by a different Máedóg. Clonmore, Bree, has been dismissed as of little importance (Doherty,1987,14-15). Rectangular graveyard.

Coolhull, Bannow. Sheet 46. No. 1223. Site of medieval parish church of same name, dedicated to St Máedóg (Aidán), locally called Imoge or Shemoge (Suidhe Máedóg). St Imock's well, pattern 10 December, *c*.400 metres south, abolished *c*.1800 (O'Donovan, 1840, ii, 35-6). Circular graveyard.

Dairinis, Castlebridge. Sheet 38. St Caomhán of Ardcavan had a church on this island in Wexford harbour. St Finnian is reputed to have visited him on the island, possibly when he was journeying to Wales (Colgan, 1645, 191). Dairinis, along with Beggerin, was plundered by the Norse in 821, according to the AFM. It was referred to in the tenth-century *Vita tripartita* (Stokes, 1887, 192-3) which claimed that the churches there and on Beggerin were given to St Patrick by Crimthann, king of Leinster, which would have made them subject to Armagh. It was stated that Erdit and Augustin, presumably monks, were on the lesser island (Dairinis) from where their shrines were brought to the monastery at Sleaty, Co. Laois, to save them from the Norse, who had taken the Island.

Donaghmore, Ballygarret. Sheet 17. No. 1227. Site of medieval parish church of same name, dedicated to St Patrick. A pattern was held until 1820 (O'Donovan, 1840, i, 23). In a Fragment in the Book of Armagh St Patrick is said to have come to Donaghmore from Tara Hill, Gorey, to meet the poet Dubhtach moccu Lugir, to select a person from among his Leinster followers to be a bishop (de Paor, 1993, 206). In fact, the saint never came this far south but all churches named domnach, that is, donagh, were claimed by Armagh to be associated with St Patrick and hence under its jurisdiction. Rectangular graveyard.

Ferns Upper, Ferns. Sheet 15. 1445. Site of early monastery founded by St Aidán (Máedóg). Three granite, high crosses and the base of a high cross on the site. St Máedóg's well *c*.100 metres northwest. Graveyard within subcircular enclosure, 450 x 300 metres. See pp 134-40, above.

Fethard, Grange td, Templetown. Sheet 50. No. 1449. Site of medieval parish church of same name, dedicated to St Máedóg (Aidán). May have been well endowed as the bishops of Ferns disputed the Norman claim to their church lands in Fethard.

Grange Little. Sheet 52. See Kilmore

Kayle, Clongeen. Sheet 40. No. 1246. Site of church of medieval parish of Inch. Gwynn and Hadcock (1970, 386) identify this site as Inis Doimle, a monastery founded by St Bairrfhinn, son of Aedh, prince of Dublin. This saint is listed in the Martyrology of Donegal and the Book of Leinster for 30 January. He is said to have been a disciple of St Comgall of Bangor who had been granted land in Wexford by the king of Leinster. St Munnu was also a disciple of Comgall. That a connection persisted between St Munnu's foundation at Taghmon and Inis Doimle is shown by the reference in the Annals of the Four Masters to the death, in 953, of Dunlang Mac Donnagáin, who is described as abbot of both places. Site of Lady's well *c.*250 metres north. Subcircular enclosure with stone-clad earthen bank beside the Owenduff river. No evidence of burial. Hogan (1910, 463) locates Inish-daimle as Little Island, on the Suir. A hermitage or monastery is said to have been founded there by a St Bairrfhinn, a disciple of St Comgall.

Kerlogue, Wexford. Sheet 42. No. 1247. Site of medieval parish church of Killiloge, dedicated to St Ellóc. According to the Martyrologies he was an Irish saint with a feast day on 25 June. Kerloge is a corruption of Killiloge, which, in turn, is a corruption of Cill Ellóc. Site of church and well dedicated to St James, the apostle, at which a pattern was held on St James' day, 25 July, until around 1820. According to O'Donovan (1840, i, 136) some called it St Tulloge's well. Tulloge would have derived from (Mo)Ellóc through a series of changes as follows: Tellóc > Teallóg> Tulloge. Slight evidence of oval enclosure, 64 x 30 metres.

Kilbride, Ballylusk td, Killinierin. Sheet 2. No. 1158. Site of church dedicated to St Brigid. Oval enclosure, 80 x 62 metres. No evidence of burial. O'Donovan considered this to be an early ecclesiastical site.

Kilbrideglynn, Bregorteen td, Glynn. Sheet 36. No. 1205. Site of medieval parish church of same name, dedicated to St Brigid, pattern 1 February, abolished around 1780 (O'Donovan, 1840, i, 129). Kilbride is mentioned in the accounts of earl Roger Bigod, 1239-46 (Brooks, 1950, 49). This may be the church mentioned by Flood (1916, 183) which 'was appropriated to the Priory of Kilcloggan. In 1581 the Earl of Ormonde got "St Brigid's, Taghmon" but it subsequently passed to the Loftus family'. Small oval enclosure removed *c.*1970. Not visible at ground level.

Kilcashel, Barnadown td, Killaveney. Sheet 2. No. 1200. Graveyard within roughly oval enclosure, max. diam. 137 metres, with stone wall and earthen bank.

Kilcannon, St Mary's, St Aidan's parish. Sheet 20. No. 1165. Arc of circular enclosure, *c.*78 metres, extant. Holy well *c.*30 metres southwest of church remains.

Kilcarbry, Davidstown. Sheet 26. No. 1371. Holy well dedicated to St Cairbre. This may be the St Cairbre listed in the Martyrology of Tallaght as bishop of Moville, Co. Down, but Ó Riain (1985, 179) gives him as a Welsh saint. Old graveyard not used (O'Donovan, 1840, ii, 2). Not visible at ground level.

Kilcavan, Bannow. Sheet 46. No. 1248. Site of medieval parish church of same name, dedicated to St Caomhán of Dairinis, in Wexford harbour. St Caomhán's well, pattern 12 June, his feast day, *c.*600 metres southwest. Subcircular graveyard.

Kilcavan Lower, Gorey. Sheet 7. No. 1249. Site of medieval parish church of Kilcavan, dedicated to St Caomhán of Dairinis. St Caomhán's well nearby. O'Donovan (1840, i, 4) states that 'the pattern was held on 12 June until about 1810, when it was abolished because a man was killed at it'. Rectangular graveyard.

Kilcloggan, Templetown. Sheet 49. No. 1346. Medieval parish of same name. Dedicated to St Ellóc or Alloc. The townland name, pronounced locally as Killoggan, may be a corruption of the Irish name, Cill Allocan (the church of Alloc). No evidence of enclosure or burial. A holy well nearby, dedicated to St Alloc, is now called Toberluke, which is a corruption of the Irish words *Tober Alloc*. According to the Martyrology of Donegal St Ellóc was an Irish saint whose feast day is 1 January. But Ó Riain (1985,179) lists a Welsh saint of this name in Wexford. See pp 128-9, above.

Kilcomb, Ballyduff td, Ferns. Sheet 10. No. 1186. Site of medieval parish church, dedicated to St Colmcille. Pattern on 9 June, his feast day. Triangular graveyard.

Kilcormick, Oulart. Sheet 21. No. 1250. Site of medieval parish church of same name, dedicated to St Cormac. Pattern at well on 21 June (Flood, 1916, 51), probably dedicated to Cormac Ua Liatháin, abbot of Durrow, Co. Offaly, whose feast day is on 21 June. Subcircular graveyard, 61 x 55 metres, defined by earthen bank.

Kilcowan, Hooks td, Rathangan. Sheet 46. No. 1164. Site of medieval parish church of same name, dedicated to St Cuán (Flood, 1916, 176). This would appear to be the saint listed in the Martyrology of Oengus as 'Cuán of Airbre, in Uí Chennsalaig, and he is identical with Maethail Broccan in the Dési of Munster' (see p. 127, above). Airbre is also mentioned in a mid-twelfth century, anonymous poem about the tidal waters of the Barrow river: 'The waters of the noisy sea going westwards around the approach to Airbre-to listen, at rest, to the cry of the Garbh makes the time pass more swiftly for me' (Murphy, 1956,117). The Garbh refers to the rough tide sweeping up the Barrow. From these references it would appear that the area around the south Wexford coast was known as Airbre from at least the ninth to the twelfth century. Cuán's feast day is given for 10 July in the Martyrologies of Oengus and Gorman, but there is no holy well, and the pattern date, which would have helped to better identify the saint, has been forgotten.

Kilcowan church was reclaimed by the bishop of Ferns between 1228 and 1232 (Hore, ii, 32).

Hogan (1910, 21) stated that the place-name of Kilquan, as it is pronounced locally, is derived from Cuán. Within subrectangular graveyard. Bullaun stone. Holy well in Longridge dedicated to St MoChuán. The importance of this place is shown by the large circular enclosure, 136 metres diam. visible from aerial photographs.

Kilcowanmore, Ballybrennan td, Bree. Sheet 31. No. 1182. Site of medieval parish church of Kilcowan, dedicated to a different St Cuán than the Rathangan saint. St Cuán's well *c.*100 metres southwest.

The pattern at St Cuán's well, Kilcowanmore, was held on 3 February up to 1810 (O'Donovan, 1840, ii, 18). This is the feast day of St Cuanan or Cuanna, abbot of Moville, Co. Down. According to the AFM he died in 742. O'Hanlon (1875, ii, 275-6) has caused some confusion by failing to distinguish between Ballybrennan, Bree, and Ballybrennan, Tagoat. Fragment of early cross slab in subrectangular graveyard.

Kildavin Lower, Piercestown. Sheet 42. No. 1251. Site of medieval parish church of Kildavin, dedicated to a St Davin. Pattern at St Davin's well, 1 August, *c.*150 metres northwest. Subcircular graveyard *c.*47 metres diam.

Kildenis, Tinnacross td, Monagear. Sheet 20. 1305. Bullaun stone within enclosure. Circular area of which only half survives, 40 metres diam. No evidence of burial.

Kildoran, Askinvillar Upper td, Ballindaggan. Sheet 18. No. 1156. Medieval parish of Killann. The bullaun stone and nearby Doran's well, recorded in the last century, do not survive. Two early granite crosses in graveyard. May have been a church of the Ó Doráin, hereditary lawyers to the Uí Cheinnselaig. Circular enclosure *c.*70 metres diam. visible as band of subsoil when ploughed.

Kilgarvan, Taghmon. Sheet 36. No. 1252. Site of medieval parish church of same name, dedicated to St Garván. St Garvan's well *c.*250 metres east, pattern date not remembered (O'Donovan, 1840, ii, 20). Five St Garván's are listed in the Martyrology of Donegal, one of Kinsealy Co. Dublin, or Kinsale, Co. Cork, feast day 9 July, another of Dungarvan, Co. Waterford or Aghowle, Co. Wicklow, feast day 26 March. Only the feast days are given for the remaining three names. Circular bank of graveyard, *c.*60 metres diam. removed, but visible on an aerial photo.

Kilgorman, Castletown. Sheet 7. No. 1253. Site of medieval parish church of same name, dedicated to St Gorman, feast day 25 October. In the Martyrology of Donegal he is described as 'St Gorman of Kilgorman in the east of Leinster'. Kilgorman well is nearby to the church. Rectangular graveyard with earthen bank and raised central area. Slab with ringed cross in relief in graveyard.

Killabeg, Monagear. Sheet 20. 1166. Medieval parish of Clone. Remains of church walls, 15 x 6 metres, now grass-covered. Circular enclosure *c.*83 metre diam. Macalister (1945, vol. I, 49-50) has the following description of an ogham stone in this townland: 'A standing stone, 6'-3" by 3'-0" by 1'-8". The dexter angle of the principal face once bore an ogham inscription, but it has all been chipped away, leaving only the tip of an M, 3'-1" above the ground. The marks left by the processes of destruction are quite unmistakable. A cross, 1'-5" high and 1'-2" across the arms, which expand outwards, was cut on the principal face of the stone after the destruction of the inscription: it encroaches upon some of the new surface produced by the fractures'. Inscribing a cross on an ogham stone may have been a way of Christianizing a pagan monument.

Killag, Rathangan. Sheet 51. No. 1254. Site of medieval parish church of Ballymagir parish, dedicated to St Degumen, a Welsh saint, feast day 27 August (Flood, 1916, 176). Ballyconnick and Killiane Little are also dedicated to him. Rectangular graveyard.

Killagowan, Oulart. Sheet 27. No. 1255. Site of medieval parish church of Meelnagh, dedicated to St Cronán, also called Mochua Luachra, feast day 22 June. Holy well dedicated to St Cronán. Cronán is listed in the Martyrologies as abbot of Ferns. The Annals of the Four Masters give the year of his death as 654. O'Donovan (1840, ii, 38) gives the well dedication as Tobermaclura (Tober Mhic Lura, that is, Cronán) with the pattern on 22 June, abolished *c.*1810. Rectangular graveyard.

Killann, Rathnure. Sheet 18. No. 1167. Site of medieval parish church of same name. Pattern held at St Anne's well on 26 July, the feast day of St Anne, mother of the Blessed Virgin, until 1824, but still venerated. This was a post-Norman dedication which would have replaced an Early Christian one. Outside subrectangular graveyard are traces of an enclosure defined by scarp, *c.*120 metres diam.

Killannduff, Ballygarret. Sheet 22. No. 1393. No trace on map. Latin cross, in granite, now in County Museum, Enniscorthy. Incised circle, with cross in relief and Latin cross, in relief, on one face. An inscribed circle with marigold on the other side.

Killegney, Cloughbawn. Sheet 24. No. 1256. Site of medieval parish church of same name, dedicated to St Eigneach, whose feast day is given as 24 April in the Martyrologies of Tallaght and Donegal. Site of Lady's well *c.*50 metres southeast. D-shaped graveyard within larger, destroyed, enclosure, diam. *c.*250 metres, visible as cropmark on aerial photograph.

Killell, Bulgan td, Glynn. Sheet 36. No. 1162. Medieval parish of Whitechurchglynn. Cross-inscribed stone slab, with Greek cross, probably dating from the sixth or seventh century found on site (Kelly, 1988, 92-100). Now in County Museum, Enniscorthy. Roughly circular enclosure, now in forest, *c.*40 metres diam. defined by scarp and traces of fosse. No evidence of burial.

Killiane Little, Piercestown. Sheet 43. No. 1258. Site of medieval parish church of Killiane, dedicated to St Degumen, a Welsh saint, feast day 27 August.

Described in late 1600s as being 'ruinated latelie' (Hore, 1862, 67). Bullaun stone. Circular graveyard *c.*40 metres diam. Bank badly eroded, no fosse evident. Ballyconnick and Killag are also dedicated to St Degumen. Human bones were unearthed just below the surface during drainage work in the 1980s although there had been no previous indication of burials.

Killila, 'the church of the veiled one', that is, St Brigid. Glebe td, Blackwater. Sheet 27. No. 1240. Site of medieval parish church of same name, dedicated to St Brigid. St Brigid's well, pattern 1 February, until 1884 (O'Donovan, 1840, ii, 36) *c.*100 metres north. Oval graveyard, 52 x 40 metres.

Killincooley Beg, Kilmuckridge. Sheet 28. No. 1260. Site of medieval parish church of Killincooley, dedicated to St Mochonóc or Canóc, a Welsh saint. A church at Kilmuckridge was also dedicated to him. Flood (1916, 78) states that the old church was dedicated to a St Mochean, and lists a well dedicated to him adjoining the site, at which patterns were held on 28 September until 1825. O'Donovan (1840, ii, 81) gives a well dedicated to St Michael about 300 yards northwest of the old church, in the townland of Glebe, at which patterns were held on 28 September, the saint's feast day until about 25 years ago (1815). Granite stone, 0.5 x 0.32 metres, with perforation and petal-like decoration in relief on one side. Subrectangular, raised graveyard.

Killinick, Sanctuary td, Ballymore. Sheet 47. No. 1296. Site of medieval parish church of same name, dedicated to St Enóc or Inick. This may be St Fionóg or Mofhionóc Mac Cucha listed in the Martyrologies for 4 October. Kilscoran has the same dedication. Small, circular, raised graveyard *c.*45 metres diam.

Killisk, Oulart. Site of medieval parish church of same name. Sheet 27. No. 1261. St Brigid's well, 350 metres north, resorted to until 1820 (Flood, 1916, 151). Circular enclosure, 39 x 32 metres, with earthen bank.

Killurin, Glynn. Sheet 37. No. 1262. Site of medieval parish church of same name, dedicated to St Lurán. There are two saints of this name in the Martyrology of Donegal, Lurán, son of Cronán, feast day 2 June, and Lurán, bishop, of Doire-Luráin in Ulster, feast day 29 October. Holy well dedicated to St Laurence, a martyr who died in 258, feast day 10 August, pattern abolished *c.*1810 (O'Donovan, i, 129). Rectangular graveyard.

Kilmacot, Blackwater. Sheet 27. No. 1373. de Val (1994, 229) gives this as 'the church of Mochuda', the same as Kilmacud in Dublin. Mochuda is the hypocoristic or pet name form of Carthach, described in the Martyrology of Donegal for 14 May as 'bishop, abbot of Lismore' who died in 637. Site of church on map. Raised stony area.

Kilmakilloge, Clonatin td, Gorey. Sheet 7. No. 1219. Site of medieval parish church of same name, dedicated to St Sillóg (Mo-Sill-óg). In the Martyrology of Oengus he is called 'my Silóc, that is, of Cell Mo-Silóc, in Uí Dega, in Uí Chennsalaigh'. His feast day is 13 July. Carved stones in the Romanesque style once formed part of the door arch of the church. D-shaped graveyard, 82 x 60 metres, defined by earthen bank with stone revetment on outside.

Kilmallock, Crossabeg. Sheet 32. No. 1264. Site of medieval parish church of same name, dedicated to St Sillóg (Flood, 1916, 156). Hogan (1910, 201) gives Cill Mochellóc as the origin of the name. St Mary's well, pattern 15 August, *c.*350 metres south. Within raised, circular graveyard, 70 metres in diameter.

Kilmannon, Glebe td, Rathangan. Sheet 42. No. 1237. Site of medieval parish church of same name, dedicated to St Mannán. Bullaun stone now in Bannow church. The pattern date of 6 July indicates that the dedication was to St Monnena of Killevy, Co. Armagh, her feast day. She died around 517. The pattern was abolished around 1810 (O'Donovan, 1840, ii, 29). According to the Life of Monnena (Anon., 1980) this saint came to Wexford with a group of nuns to be under St Ibar but eventually had to leave. Rectangular graveyard. The following story is related in O' Donovan (1840,1,29): 'About one furlong south of the tower there is a holy well called after St Mannán, at which a pattern was held annually on the 6 July until about thirty years ago, when it was abolished.

'At a distance of two hundred paces from the site of the church there is just appearing above the surface of the field a rock called the "Bell Stone" about which the following little legend is told by the natives: St Munnu of Taghmon was one time on a visit to St Mannán of Kilmannan, and getting thirsty he called for a drink of water and St Mannán sent his servant man to the well for a pitcher of water. But in pulling up the pitcher out of the well the servant knocked it against a stone and broke it to pieces and, being afraid to return to the two saints, who were very irritable, especially St Munnu, he knelt down at this rock to pray to God to send him some vessel to bring the water in and lo! and behold you, a bell fell from heaven upon the rock and impressed its form on it, which remains to this very day. The servant fetched the water in the bell and when he appeared before the saints he told them what had happened to him and they pardoned him at once when they saw the beauty of the bell which was obtained "*coelitus missum*" instead of the rude earthen pitcher through the prayers of so humble an individual. This bell continued in the possession of the Harveys of Mountpleasant, in the parish of Mayglass, until a few years since when it was either taken up to Heaven whence it had originally fallen, or stolen by an antiquarian.'

Kilmokea (Cill Mac Aodha), Great Island, Suttons. Sheet 39. No. 1163. Site of medieval parish church of same name. Small high cross, with an inscription on one face described by Harbison (1992, i, 363) as follows: 'The small cross bears an inscription around the top of the present west face. It seems possible to read some letters, possibly NDMNA, on the upper left hand corner, but it has not proved possible to make any sense of the inscription. Although seemingly in Old Irish, its position could suggest that it may not be primary.' Two bullaun stones and a horizontal mill, within large enclosure, 330 x 260 metres, defined by earthen bank and fosse. There are no traditions attached to this site. Small graveyard. Originally an island.

Kilmore, Grange td, Kilmore. Sheet 52. No. 1243. Site of medieval parish church of Kilmore. St Patrick's well, pattern 19 (*sic*) March, 270 metres east southeast. Rectangular graveyard within possible circular enclosure, *c*.90 metres diam. revealed on aerial photograph.

Kilmuckridge, Kilmuckridge. Sheet 22. No. 1265. Site of medieval parish church of same name, dedicated to St Mochonóc or Canóc, pattern 11 February. Killincooley was also dedicated to him. St Bride's well *c*.450 metres southwest. O' Donovan (ii, 18) says site of old church occupied by modern church. D-shaped graveyard, 80 x 50 metres.

Kilmurry, Castletown. Sheet 7. No. 741. Medieval parish of Kilmakilloge. The Virgin Mary's church (murry=Muire=Mary). Another indication that this was probably an ecclesiastical site is shown by its circularity as described by Moore (1996, 75): 'Visible as a circular cropmark on an aerial photograph and visible on the surface as a vegetation mark, diameter c. 30 metres. Aerial photograph also shows cropmark of outer circular enclosure, diameter *c*.100 metres, overlain on east side by cropmark of D-shaped enclosure, diameter *c*.30 metres.'

Kilmyshall, Ryland Lower td, Bunclody. Sheet 9. No. 1290. Site of medieval parish church of same name, dedicated to St Colmán of Midísil, sometimes called St Columba Crossaire (Martyrology of Oengus, Stokes, 1905). Feast day 6 September. According to the Martyrologies he was son of Cathbhach, of Midísil, which Hogan places in Co. Cork. St Mary's well, at which the pattern was held on 22 July, the feast day of Mary Magdalene, until 1810, is 40 metres west.

Kilnahue (Aedh's church), Craanford. Sheet 6. No. 1266. Site of medieval parish church of same name, dedicated to St Aidán. Pattern known as Lamogue's (*lá Máedóg*) on 15 August (Flood, 1916, 67) until 1798 (O'D). Bullaun stone. Oval graveyard with stone-revetted earthen bank, 50 x 44 metres.

Kilnamanagh Lower (church of the monks), Oulart. Sheet 21. No. 1267. The medieval parish church of the same name was dedicated to St Moling (Flood, 1916,49). Flood also gives a well dedicated to St Moling. The name implies a monastic church, possibly an outlying church of St Mullins. No trace at ground level.

Kilpatrick, Saunderscourt td, Crossabeg. Sheet 37. No. 1297. Site of medieval parish church of same name. Hiberno-Norse doorway taken from St David's church, Ballynaslaney (Flood, 1916, 159). St Patrick's well nearby. D-shaped graveyard, 46 x 46 metres.

Kilrane, Churchtown td, Kilrane. Sheet 48. No. 1217. Site of medieval parish church of same name, dedicated to St Ruán of Lorrha, Co. Tipperary, died around 594, feast day 15 April. Rectangular graveyard. There was also a chapel at Hillcastle in the late 1600s dedicated to St Ruán (Hore, 1862, 68).

Kilrush, Ballynaberney td, Kilrush. Sheet 10. No. 1195. Site of medieval parish church of same name, dedicated to St Colmán of Midísil, also known as St Columba Crossaire, feast day 22 September (Flood, 1916, 34). This was later changed to St Brigid. Double bullaun stone in marshy ground outside circular graveyard, *c.*65 metres diam., defined by earthen bank.

Kilscoran, Tagoat. Sheet 48. No. 1270. Site of medieval parish church of same name, described in late 1600s as being dedicated to St Inick or Enóc (Hore, 1862, 68). Killinick and Rossminoge are also dedicated to this saint. Rectangular graveyard.

Kiltennel, Riverchapel-Courtown. Sheet 12. No. 1271. Site of medieval parish church of same name, dedicated to St Sinchell. The feast day of 15 June indicates St Sinell (Sinchell) Ua Liatháin the Younger, whose festival is given for this date in the Martyrologies. Two Sinchells, 'the elder' and 'the younger', were associated with the church of Killeigh (Cill-achid), near Tullamore, Co. Offaly. Sinchell the elder died in 549 according to the Annals of Ulster. D-shaped graveyard defined by earthen bank.

Kiltilly, Kilrush. Sheet 5. No. 1272. The church dedication was probably to St Teille, an Irish saint, whose feast day was celebrated on 25 June, according to the Martyrology of Oengus. The name is a hypocoristic or pet name of Ailill and it is under this form that the saint is commemorated in the Martyrology of Tallaght on 25 June (pers. comm. from Dónall Mac Giolla Easpaig). Tobermurry (*Muire*) well with modern granite cross nearby. Subcircular graveyard, 35 x 33 metres.

Kilturk, Glebe td, Kilmore. Sheet 52. No. 1239. Site of medieval parish church of same name, dedicated to St Cuán. It is given in the Tintern Charter of 1245 as Kenturc (Cionn torc) (Hore, 1901, ii, 32). Ó Muraíle (pers. comm.) suggests that Cionn became changed to Cill because of the church there. Pattern on 4 April until *c.*1820 (O'Donovan, ii, 70) for which date the Martyrology of Tallaght lists a St Mochuan, with no further information. Circular graveyard, 42 metres diam.

Kinnagh, Ballycullane. Sheet 45. Site of medieval parish church of same name.

Well dedicated to St Martin of Tours, France, feast day 11 November, 600 metres east. St Martin was venerated from as early as the mid-seventh century in the Irish church (Richter, 230, 1999). Colfer (1986, 46) suggests that the manor of Kinnagh, and presumably the church, were owned by the Church in pre-Norman times. Subrectangular graveyard.

Meelnagh. Sheet 27. See Killagowan

Middletown. Sheet 12. See Ardamine

Monamolin, Glebe td, Kilmuckridge. Sheet 16. No. 1234. Site of parish church of same name, dedicated to St Moling, pattern at well *c.*350 metres south, on 17 June, Moling's feast day. Triangular graveyard.

Monamolin, Rathnure. Sheet 24. No. 636. Medieval parish of Templeludigan. Circular church site, 46 x 44 metres, on map. The name indicates a dedication to St Moling.

Morrisseysland, New Ross. Sheet 29. No. 1168. Probable site of St Abbán's monastery. Two bullaun stones. St Stephen's well in southeast corner, feast day 26 December. Large subcircular graveyard, 155 x 140 metres diam. The connection of New Ross with St Evan of Monasterevan is spurious. The error was caused through confusion of Ros Glas and Ros Mhic Treoin by some early writers, Ros Glas being the site of St Evan's monastery at Monasterevan and Ros Mhic Treoin the site of St Abbán's at New Ross. Hore, however (i, 46, 74), claims that St Stephen's was Abbán's disert or place of retreat and that his monastery was located near the later site of the north gate of New Ross town.

Portersgate. Sheet 54. See St Brecaun's.

Rathaspick, the ráth of the bishop, Piercestown. Sheet 42. No. 1286. Site of medieval parish church of same name, listed as being dedicated to St Brigid in the late 1600's (Hore, 1862, 66)). Dutchman's well or St Brigid's well *c.*250 metres northeast. The Martyrology of Donegal gives Aed Glas and Oengus as bishops, both with feast days on 16 February.

The Book of Leinster gives seven bishops here, including Oengus of Uí Dega. There is a Rathaspick in Co. Laois where Oengus is also listed as bishop. Gwynn and Hadcock (1970, 401) suggested that these may have been two different people. Rectangular raised graveyard. Rathaspick was considered the mother church of St Patrick's church in Wexford town and the Church of Ireland rector of St Patrick's was first inducted there.

Rathmacknee Great, Glebe td, Piercestown. Sheet 47. No. 1287. Site of medieval parish church of same name, listed in late 1600s as being dedicated to St Martin of Tours (Hore, 1862, 67). St Martin's well *c.*100 metres west. The fact that this saint was venerated in the early Irish Church from the mid-seventh century (Richter, 230, 1999) indicates an Early Christian foundation. Subrectangular, raised graveyard.

Rossminoge North, Craanford. Sheet 11. No. 1289. Site of medieval parish church of same name, dedicated to St Enán. The Martyrology of Tallaght gives St Enán, son of Gemman, in Ros Mor, in Uí Dega, in Uí Cheinnselaig, feast day 30 January. O'Donovan (1840, i, 24-5) gives Ros Mionóg, Mo Innóc, as the origin of the name. Ringed but unpierced cross described by O'Donovan as follows: 'Cross 36 yards southeast of church, granite, pedestal 8" above ground, 1'-10' x 1'-3". From pedestal to top is 3'-6" and it was 3'-4" at the arms, one broken arm.' This high cross dates to the period 800 to 1200 (pers. comm. Peter Harbison). Rectangular graveyard.

Ryland Lower. Sheet 9. See Kilmyshall.

St Brecaun's church, Portersgate td, Templetown. Sheet 54. No. 1169. Medieval parish of Hook. In 1845 part of an ogham stone was found near the ruins of St Brecaun's church. A second part was found about 1930 (Macalister, 1930, 52-5): both parts are now in the National Museum. The inscription reads SEDANI MAQQU CAT TABBOTT AVVI DERCMASOC meaning 'of Sedan, grandson of Cattabott, son of Dermasoc'. Excavations at the site of the church in 1987 uncovered another fragment of the stone (Breen, 1988, 31).

That the early church was enclosed by a ditch and bank is indicated by the round-bottomed fosse, 1.06 metres deep, which was exposed at two points in the cliff face. No burials were found but local tradition locates the associated cemetery to the east of the church. Coastal erosion has washed it into the sea (Breen, 1988, 31).

St Dubhán's church, Churchtown td, Templetown. Sheet 54. No. 1213. Site of medieval parish church of Hook, dedicated to Dubhán, whose feast day is given for 12 February in the Martyrology of Donegal. According to Moore (1996, 124) the existing ruins contain part of an earlier nave, measuring 5.60 metres in length. The remains of this nave and antae on the east wall confirm a pre-Norman date for part of this church. Subrectangular graveyard. See p. 129, above.

St Kieran's, Ballycullane. Sheet 45. No. 1293. Medieval parish of Tintern. Dedicated to St Kieran, of Seirkieran, Co. Offaly, patron saint of the diocese of Ossory, feast day 5 March. Bullaun stone within church. No evidence of enclosure.

St Vauks, Lady's Island. Sheet 53. 1170. Medieval parish of Carne. Pattern held at well dedicated to St Vauk on 20 June (O'Donovan, 1840, i, 106). Saint also honoured on 15 June (Flood, 1916, 169). Excavation by O'Kelly, Cahill and Lynch (1975) revealed traces of a small, early, wooden oratory and hut site. Charcoal from post holes of the oratory gave uncalibrated Carbon-14 dates of AD 560 ± 80 and AD 660 ± 80. Even if calibrated the dates would not be significantly different. This is the earliest physical evidence for a church in the county. Wallace (1982, 24) calculated from the position of the post holes that the oratory measured about 4.50 x 3.25 metres. The present ruins may be seventeenth century (Moore, 1996, 119). Subcircular enclosure, 48 x 42 metres, defined by earthen bank. See p. 128, above.

Sanctuary. Sheet 47. See Killinick.

Saunderscourt. Sheet 37. See Kilpatrick.

Screen, Ballymore td, Castlebridge. Sheet 33. No. 1193. Site of medieval parish church of same name, dedicated to St Maelruan of Tallaght, feast day 7 July, who died in 792. Pattern abolished *c.*1820 (O'Donovan, 1840, i, 126). O'Donovan gives pattern at well for 27 September, but dedication unknown. According to Ranson (1949, 166) the name of the church was Screen Maelruain, meaning 'the shrine of Maelruan': 'This indicates that the church once contained a shrine of the saint, and that he was held in veneration there.' This was probably the fourteenth-century carved, oak statue of St Maelruan which stood 28 to 30 inches high. On the eve of the saint's feast day the people of the area bedecked the partly-gilded statue with flowers. The figure was in the possession of the Curran family of Ballinaleck until 1981, when it was stolen and never recovered (Nolan, 1997, 6). Raised rectangular graveyard.

Shelbaggan, Duncannon. Sheet 45. No. 1375. Medieval parish of Rathroe. Bullaun stone on site. St Agatha's well *c.*200 metres southwest. This saint, a Sicilian virgin, martyred at Catena, Sicily, in 251, is listed in the Martyrology of Oengus for 5 February, her feast day, showing that she was venerated in Early Christian Ireland. During her martyrdom her breasts were cut off; hence she was invoked by nursing mothers short of milk for their babies and by women with breast problems (Wilson, 1983, 18). Small oval enclosure on 1841 map.

Shemoge. Sheet 46. See Coolhull.

Tacumshin, Churchtown td, Lady's Island. Sheet 53. No. 1218. Site of medieval parish church of Tacumshin, but also of an earlier church dedicated to St Munnu or Fintan of Taghmon. This was described in the late 1600's as being 'latelie become ruinous' (Hore, 1862,68). Local tradition says that the bullaun stone, now at the roadside near the modern church, came from here. The later Norman church was dedicated to St Catherine, possibly of Alexandria, but O'Donovan (1840, i, 93) states that a pattern was held there on 21 October, the feast of St Munnu. A well dedicated to St Catherine is located *c*.150 metres east. Rectangular graveyard.

Taghmon-Poulmarl, Taghmon. Sheet 41. No. 1465. Site of early monastery founded by St Munnu. There were two churches dedicated to the saint. At St Munnu's well a pattern was held on 21 October, his feast day, until around 1800. Part of a high cross, now outside Church of Ireland church, may date to the eighth century (Harbison, 1992, 377). See pp 140-3, above.

Templeludigan, Rathnure. Sheet 24. No. 1300. Site of medieval parish church of same name, dedicated to St Lugidon (Flood, 1916, 53), son of Declán, bishop. In the Martyrology of Donegal his feast day is given as 6 January. No further information recorded. Church now dedicated to St Peter. St Patrick's well *c*.500 metres east, now dry. Subcircular graveyard.

Templeshanbo, Bola Beg td, Ballindaggan. Sheet 14. No. 1161. Site of medieval parish church of same name, dedicated to St Colmán, the founder of Kilmacduagh, Co Galway, whose feast day is 27 October. In the Martyrologies his church and well are stated to be at the foot of Mount Leinster. Bullaun stone in church doorway, another stone missing. Double-ditched circular enclosure, *c*.250 metres diameter, visible on aerial photographs. See p. 145, above.

Templeshannon, St Senán's. Sheet 20. No. 1301. Site of medieval parish church of same name, dedicated to St Senán, feast day 8 March. The bullaun stone and holy water vessel indicate an Early Christian site. According to Nicholls (1969, 90) the church was granted to the priory of St John's, Enniscorthy, by Gerald de Prendergast in 1230. D-shaped graveyard.

Tinnacross td. Sheet 20. See Kildenis.

Tomhaggard, Kilmore. Sheet 47. No. 1309. Site of medieval parish church of same name, dedicated to St Sacer or Mosachra, pattern 3 March, his feast day (O'Donovan, 1840, ii, 71-3). According to O'Hanlon (1875, iii, 100), 'he appears to have been called Sacer, from a Latin word which expresses holiness of life, by which he had been distinguished; and to this cognomen, the endearing term *Mo*, was prefixed. However, Sacer not being a name in use among the ancient Irish, we must suppose it, as only secondary to a previous and more national name. This holy man appears to have flourished, before or about the middle of the seventh century.' The Martyrology of Tallaght lists Mosachra of Findmag in Fotharta (Forth) in Uí Chennsalaig, near Cnamros (Camross) for 3 March. The Martyrology of Donegal gives Mosachra, abbot of Clonenagh, Co. Laois, Saggart, Co. Dublin and of Fionn Magh, in Fotharta, for 3 March. The life of Munnu shows that in the sixth and seventh centuries, at least, the Fothart territory extended to Camross and Taghmon and that Fionn Magh, 'the bright plain', was in that area and not in Tomhaggard as suggested by O' Donovan (1840).

The Normans rededicated the church and well to St Anne, the mother of the Virgin Mary, pattern day 26 July, her feast day. There is also a well dedicated to St

James, the apostle, *c.*200 metres southwest, but the pattern was abolished around 1820 (O'D). Rectangular graveyard.

Toome, Ballinclare td, Camolin. Sheet 11. No. 1178. Site of medieval parish church of same name dedicated to St Moling (Flood, 1916, 66). Bullaun stone. Rectangular raised graveyard.

Wexford Town

Pre-Viking church sites Based on the semi-circular street plan of the Selskar church area, Colfer (1990-1, 6) has put forward the plausible suggestion that Selskar may have been the site of an Early Christian monastery. It is quite possible, of course, that what was originally a small church may have later developed into a more sub-stantial foundation. Hadden (1968, 6) also suggested that in Early Christian times there was a small church where St Iberius' Church, dedicated to St Ibar of Beggerin, now stands.

Church sites within the Hiberno-Norse town The Vikings were Christianized about the middle of the tenth century and became devoted to certain saints such as the Norse St Olaf.

St Doologue's: This is a corruption of the name St Olaf, a saint-king who ruled Norway from 1015 to 1028. He died in 1030 and his cult spread quickly; by 1050 churches were being dedicated to him. Churches were dedicated to him at Dublin and Waterford as well as Wexford. The name was also spelled Tullock's and Tullogue's, which has led to suggestions that the dedication was to St Ellóc, as at Kerloge.

The Centenary Record of Wexford's Twin Churches (1958, 27) gives the following description: 'No trace of this church now remains except in legal documents of title. It was situated on the low-lying ground between the Castle (present Army Barracks) and the Bishopswater stream.'

Viking church sites outside the ramparts The Vikings usually located a graveyard out-side their towns. In Wexford's case they chose a steeply sloping site beside the mod-ern Kevin Barry Street, where they dedicated a church to St Michael the Archangel. The pattern was held up to recent times on 29 September, his feast day. The Norse had great faith in St Michael's protection of those at sea, and it seems likely that this church was specifically located on high ground, overlooking the sea. Thus, it would be the last thing they would see as they departed, and the first as they returned.

The Church of the Holy Trinity: As the *Centenary Record* (1958, 29) states there are no remains of this church, which stood at the foot of Wexford Castle. A well, also dedicated to the Holy Trinity, was marked on the 1840 Ordnance Survey six-inch map. Churches dedicated to the Holy Trinity were also erected by the Norse in Dublin and Waterford.

That by about 1210 to 1215 there was a plethora of churches in or around Wexford town is shown by the *Calendar of Pembroke Papers* (1891) which lists the churches of St John, St Patrick, St Brigid, St Mary Magdalene, St Mary and St Michael. However, it is not known exactly when all of these came into existence, but most would appear to postdate the arrival of the Normans.

APPENDIX 5: GAZETTEER OF POSSIBLE EARLY CHRISTIAN
ECCLESIASTICAL SITES IN CO. WEXFORD

Circular or subcircular enclosure

Ambrosetown, Rathangan. Sheet 46. No. 1172. Site of medieval parish church of
same name. Site of holy well 30 metres north, said to be dedicated to a St Ambrose,
but the area is called Ambrosetown after the Norman family of Ameroys or Ambrose
(Brooks, 1950, 108). Pattern date forgotten. Subcircular graveyard.

    Chapel, Cloughbawn. Sheet 31. No. 1211. Site of medieval parish church of
same name. St Francis's well *c.*500 metres southwest, pattern on 11 June until 1791
(O'D). But patron said to be St Clement (Harte, 1925, 106). Circular graveyard, 70
x 64 metres. According to O'Donovan (1840, ii, 19), 'In the townland of Clonroche,
about half a mile to the north of Chapel graveyard, there is a holy well called
Toberpatrick, at which *turases* were performed till about 20 years ago, but it has been
totally abandoned ever since.'

    Lady's Island, Sheet 53. 1274. Site of medieval parish church of same name,
listed in late 1600s as being dedicated to the Blessed Virgin Mary (Hore, 1862, 68).
That there was strong devotion to the Mary in Early Christian Ireland is well attested (O'Dwyer, 1988). The canons regular of St Augustine popularized the dedication
of churches to Our Lady in the twelfth and thirteenth centuries and may have taken
over an earlier church at Lady's Island in the twelfth century. Our Lady's well *c.*500
metres east. Subcircular graveyard.

    Lady's Island is first mentioned as a place of pilgrimage around 1607 among a
list of places to which Pope Paul V granted indulgences. But the pilgrimage may
have originated as early as the twelfth century when this form of religious practise
became popular.

Sites dedicated to early Irish and Welsh saints

Ballyboher, Ballymore. Sheet 47. No. 1181. Site of medieval parish church of
Ishartmon. Believed to be the 'disert' or hermitage of St Munnu of Taghmon, 'disert' becoming 'ishart' over time. Rectangular graveyard.

    Ballyconnick, Rathangan. Sheet 46. No. 1185. Site of medieval parish church
of same name, originally dedicated to St Degumen, a Welsh saint, feast day 27
August, later changed to St Anne (Flood, 1916, 176). Killag and Killiane Little
churches were also dedicated to him. Subrectangular graveyard.

    Ballynaslaney, Oylegate. Sheet 32. No. 1196. Site of medieval parish church
of same name, dedicated to St David, a Welsh saint who died in 601 (see p. 130,
above). St David's well, pattern on his feast day, 1 March, and bath house nearby.
According to O'Donovan (1840, ii, 39) 'about three paces to the west of the graveyard there was a holy well which was called St David's well which was enclosed by
a turret and its door locked: yea, and its water sold for money and the cure of diseases till about thirty years ago [1810] when it was stopped by the farmer on whose
land it was. The spot is now levelled with the ground but no grass grows upon it.'
Rectangular graveyard.

    Ballybrennan Big, Tagoat. Sheet 48. No. 1183. Site of medieval parish church
of Ballybrennan, dedicated to St Kevin of Glendalough, whose feast day is 3 June.
St Keevil's well, pattern 27 August, *c.*75 metres southeast. This is also the feast day
of St Degumen, a Welsh saint, to whom Ballyconnick, Killag and Killiane are dedicated. Subrectangular graveyard.

Burrow, Tagoat. Sheet 43. No. 1342. Medieval parish of Rosslare. Church listed in late 1600s as dedicated to St Brioc (Hore, 1862, 68). Hore states that this church was pulled down and a school erected on the site. There is a well dedicated to St Brioc, who, according to O'Hanlon (1845, v, 15) was a fifth- or sixth-century Welsh saint, who studied under St German of Auxerre, and who spent most of his life in France. He was buried in the cathedral of St Brieuc, in Brittany. He was venerated in France, Scotland, Wales and Ireland. His feast day is 1 May. See p. 130.

Chapel Carron, Bolabaun td, Glynn. Sheet 37. No. 1202. May have been associated with St Cairín, a Welsh saint. Possible site of medieval parish church. Foundations of small church, 6.25 x 3.65 metres. St Nicholas' well *c*.300 metres southwest. This was probably St Nicholas of Myra. Subrectangular enclosure, 26 x 10-14 metres.

Drinagh, Piercestown. Sheet 42. No. 1232. Site of medieval parish church of same name, dedicated to St Caomhán of Dairinis, in Wexford harbour, in late 1600s (Hore, 1862, 67). Rectangular graveyard. See p. 160, above.

Edermine, Glebe td, Oylegate. Sheet 26. No. 1236. Site of medieval parish church of same name, dedicated to St Cuarán (O'Donovan, 1840, ii, 39). The pattern date of 9 February confirms that the ancient church and well were dedicated to St Cuarán, otherwise called St Cronán, the Wise, whose feast occurs on this date according to the Martyrologies of Oengus and Tallaght. The pattern was abolished around 1810. The year of Cuarán's death is not known but he is said to have been a contemporary of St Columcille who died in 597. Rectangular graveyard.

Kilbegnet, Kilgorman, Castletown. Sheet 7. No. 1158. Churches in Dalkey and on Dalkey Island were also dedicated to this saint. No trace on map.

Kilmacoe, Castlebridge. Sheet 33. Medieval parish of St Margaret's. De Val (1994, 229) gives a church dedicated to St Mochua, feast day 22 June; this is the hypocoristic or pet name form of Cronán; hence the dedication may be to Mochuan Luachra, otherwise Cronán, abbot of Ferns, died in 654. No trace on map or ground. See Killagowan.

Kiltealy, Ballindaggan. Sheet 13. This church may have been dedicated to a St Téile, but no saint of that name can be identified in early ecclesiastical sources. No trace on map.

Mayglass, Glebe td, Ballymore. Sheet 47. No. 1238. Site of medieval parish church of same name, listed in late 1600s as being dedicated to St Fintan (Hore, 1862, 67). Well dedicated to St Fintan, pattern on 17 February, abolished *c*.1820 (O'Donovan, i, 102). This date shows that the saint venerated here was St Fintan of Clonenagh, Co. Laois, and not St Munnu, or Fintan, of Taghmon whose feast day is on 22 October. Rectangular graveyard.

St Iberius, or **St Ivor's**, Lady's Island. Sheet 48. No. 1291. Site of medieval parish church of same name, listed in late 1600's as being dedicated to St Ibar (Hore, 1862, 68). Subrectangular graveyard.

Mention in the literature

Ballyanne, Cushenstown. Sheet 29. No. 1180. Site of medieval parish church of same name. According to Brooks (1950, 109-10) the pre-Norman name of this place was Disertmachen, which indicates an isolated place, possibly an eremetical foundation. Lady's well *c*.100 metres northeast. Rectangular graveyard.

Camaross, Taghmon. Sheet 36. Medieval parish of Kilgarvan. According to the life of Abbán (Plummer, 1910, i, 24) the saint had a church at Find Magh, in

Camaross, which was plundered by Cormac Mac Diarmata, the king of Uí Cheinnselaig. The Martyrology of Oengus gives 16 December as 'the feast of my excellent Beooc, from lustrous Ard Cainross'. Stokes (1895, 240) suggested that Ard Cainross is a variant of Ard Camross. A note on the margin in the Martyrology of Garmán mentions 'MoPhioc from Ard Camross, on the brink of Loch Garman, in Uí Cheinnselaig'. Although not close to Wexford harbour, Camaross seems the most likely location of this place, but Ardcandrisk has also been suggested. Camaross is also mentioned in the Martyrologies of Tallaght and Donegal, which list ' Mosachra of Find Magh, near Cnamros' (Camaross). This may have led Flood (1916, 78) to have Mosachra succeeding Abbán at Camaross. The exact location of Abbán's church is not known but there is a strong tradition in the area that it was in a field near Camaross Cross Roads.

Glascarrig North, Ballygarret. Sheet 17. No. 1319. Medieval parish of Donaghmore. The Genealogies, Tribes and Customs of Hy Fiachrach (ed. O'Donovan, 1844, 37) describes how a saint, Fiodghus Ó Suainaigh, settled here and died in 763. The monks of the French Order of Tiron established a priory there in 1199 (Gwynn and Hadcock, 1970, 112).

Inch, Castletown. Sheet 3. 1245. Site of medieval parish church of same name, occupied by nineteenth-century Church of Ireland church. Subrectangular graveyard. Originally Inis Mo-Colm-Og or Colman's Island. According to the Martyrology of Donegal 'Colman of Inis Colm-Og in Hui Enechglais in the east of Leinster' is commemorated on 14 November. The term island or inis was sometimes applied to a portion of land enclosed by two branches of a river.

Limerick, Killinierin. Sheet 3. Medieval parish of Kilcavan. According to Chronicum Scotorum (Hennessy, 1866) Finachda, king of Connacht for twelve years, withdrew to a retreat at Limerick in the nineth century (see Hore, vi, 651). This was also reputed to be the stronghold of Dubthach moccu Lugir, chief poet of Leinster.

Bullaun stone on possible site

Ballymaclare, Suttons. Sheet 34. No. 1191. Bullaun stone found in 1970. Faintly enclosing feature on 1841 map.

Ballynastraw, Oylegate. Sheet 29. No. 1197. Possible site of parish church of Ballyhuskard. Bullaun stone in graveyard. Site of St Peter's well, pattern 29 June, until around 1800 (O'Donovan, 1840, ii, 39). *c.*100 metres east. Rectangular graveyard.

Coolstuff, Taghmon. Sheet 41. No. 1225. Site of medieval parish church of same name. Bullaun stone. Site of Lady's well *c.*90 metres east, pattern 15 August (O' Donovan, i, 130)). Rectangular graveyard.

Courthoyle Old, Newbawn. Sheet 35. No. 1226. Medieval parish of same name. Bullaun stone and pointed slit window. Site of Tobermurry (Mhuire) *c.*100 metres north. Rectangular graveyard.

Garraun Lower, Rathnure. Sheet 25. No. 1366. Marked site of chapel on 1940 map. Faintly marked circular enclosure on 1841 map. Bullaun stone lost since 1940s. No evidence of burial.

Killowen, Suttons. Sheet 34. No. 740. Site of medieval parish church of same name. Bullaun stone described by Westropp (1918, 13) as consisting of a rock, 3 ft x 18 x 14 inches, with an oval, shallow basin ground into it, 11 x 10 inches. Subrectangular area, 102 x 97 metres, defined by earthen bank, with external fosse.

Killynann, Laighnan's church, Gorey. Sheet 7. No. 1417. Bullaun stone now lost. May have been the church of the O'Laighnen family (now Lynam) who retained the abbacy of the monastery of Ferns over a long period. Former burial place.

Kilmacree, Piercestown. Sheet 42. No. 1263. Site of medieval parish church of same name. In the late 1600s it was dedicated to All Saints (Hore, 1862, 67) but Flood (1916, 171) says it was earlier dedicated to St Caomhán of Dairinis but gives no reference. Bullaun stone from site now in possession of Nicholas Furlong of Drinagh Lodge. Subrectangular graveyard.

Tradition

Ballinaleck, Crossabeg. Sheet 33. Medieval parish of Artramon. There is a strong tradition in this area that St Maelruan, abbot of Tallaght, who died in 792, founded a monastery in this place. his feast day is 7 July. He was a strong supporter of the eighth-century Céli De movement. According to Ranson (1949,166) the site was formerly known as Leck Maelruain, St Maelruan's Stone. 'Local tradition says that St Maelruan's Stone was built into Ballinaleck Bridge, but no one can tell where the stone formerly stood, nor can anyone tell which stone in the bridge is his.' St Maelruan's well is a few yards below the bridge. A carved, wooden statue, said to represent St Maelruan, which was in the possession of the Curran family of Ballinaleck for over 100 years, was stolen in 1981 and never recovered (Nolan, 1997, 6). See Screen.

Cross-inscribed pillarstone

Millquarter, Cushenstown. Sheet 30. 1276. Site of medieval parish church of Old Ross, dedicated to St Mary (Hore, i, 2). Cross-inscribed pillarstone in rectangular graveyard.

APPENDIX 6: EARLY PLACE-NAMES FROM WRITTEN SOURCES, WITH MODERN VERSIONS AND TOWNLAND NAMES WHERE KNOWN
Abbreviations B. Arm. = Book of Armagh, B. Lein. = Book of Leinster

Place-names in the martyrologies and annals

Ancient name	Modern name	Modern parish
Airbre (MO)	Kilcowan	Rathangan
Ard Cainross (MO)	Ardcandrisk?	Glynn
Ard Coluim (AFM; MG)	Ardcolm	Castlebridge
Camros (MT; MD)	Camaross	Taghmon
Cell Mo-Silóc (MO)	Kilmakilloge	Gorey
Disertmachen (Brooks, 109)	Ballyanne	Cushenstown
Domnach Mor (B. Arm.)	Donaghmore	Riverchapel/Courtown
Inis (MD)	Inch	Castletown
Cill Gormáin (MD)	Kilgorman	Castletown
Rath An Easpaig (B. Lein.)	Rathaspick	Piercestown
Rossminoge (MT)	Rossminoge	Craanford
Finmagh	unknown	
Fotharta	Forth	

Place-names in the Lives of the saints

ABBÁN

Achadh Huabhair	Unknown
Ath Daimh dha Cheilt	unknown
Beg Eire	Beggerin
Camros	Camaross
Disert Cendubháin	unknown
Druim Cain Ceallach	unknown
Loch Garman	Wexford
Magh Arnaidhe	Adamstown
Magh na Taibhse	unknown
Ros Mhic Treoin	New Ross
Senboith Ard (Templeshanbo)	Bola Beg

AIDÁN

Achel	unknown
Ard Ladrann	Ardamine
Disert nDairbre	unknown
Fearna	Ferns
Teach Munnu	Taghmon
Teampall na Sean Botha (Templeshanbo)	Bola Beg

FINNIAN

Cill Caireni	unknown
Dairinis	North Slob
Inis Cortaigh	Enniscorthy

MOLING

Cluain Caoin	Clongeen
Fearna	Ferns

MUNNU

Achadh Liathdrom	unknown
Airbriu (Airbre?)	Kilcowan
Ard Crema	Artramont ?
Inis Liacháin	unknown
Inis Tobairri	unknown
Loch Eachtach	unknown
Teach Munnu	Taghmon

Place-names mentioned in Diarmait Mac Murchada's charter to Ferns abbey, 1160 (Hore, vi, 180)

Old name	Modern name	Modern parish
Baliculum	unknown	–
Balinafusin	unknown	–
Balilacussa	unknown	–
Balisifin	unknown	–

Balligery	unknown	–
Borin	unknown	–
Ferneghenan (Fearann-na-gCenél)	Shelmalier East	Castlebridge
Fearna	Ferns	Ferns
Forth	Barony of Forth	–
Kilbride	Ballymore	Camolin
Munemethe	unknown	–
Roshena	unknown	–

Place-names listed in foundation charter of Tintern abbey, 1200 (Hore, ii, 19)

Akitiper	unknown	–
Auanduff	Owenduff	Ballycullane
Baliennen	Balliniry?	Ballycullane
Balicross	Ballycross	Kilmore
Dunmethan	Dunmain	Ballycullane
Karuel?	Campile	Suttons
Rathubenai	Rathumney	Ballycullane
Ross	Ross	New Ross
Wexford	Wexford	Wexford

Place-names listed in foundation charter of Dunbrody abbey, 1207-13 (Hore, iii, 37)

Norman name	*Modern name*	*Modern parish*
Ardfithan	unknown	–
Balistrage (Ballystraw)	Ballyvaroge	Suttons
Ballygoue	Ballygow	Bannow
Calatrum	Campile	Suttons
Crossgormos	unknown	–
Cusduff	Coolstuff	Taghmon
Drunculip	Dungulph	Templetown
Dunbrodik	Dunbrody	Suttons
Dunmechanan	Mersheen (Duncannon)	Duncannon
Kempul	Campile	Suttons
Koillache	Coole	Ramsgrange
Kuilleskard	Killesk	Suttons
Lescullnum	unknown	–
Malpas	unknown	–
Raidcru	Rathroe?	Ramsgrange
Theachmun	Taghmon	Taghmon
Urbegan	Shelbaggan	Duncannon
Urgueron	unknown	–

Place-names in bishop's grant from Henry III, 1226

Enniscorthy, Ferns, Templeshanbo (Hore, vi, 342)

Place-names in bishop's agreement with Canterbury, 1228-32 (Hore, iv, 311)

Banew	Bannow
Fethard	Fethard
Kilcogan	Kilcowan
Kilmor	Kilmore
Kenturc	Kilturk
Thamagr	Tomhaggard

Place-names in bishop's agreement with Prendergast, 1230 (Hore, vi, 342)

Ballyregan	Ballyregan
Clon	Clone
Kilanegry	Killegney
Killalethan	Killalligan
Lishote	unknown

Place-names listed in forest charter for Ross and Taghmon, 1231-34 (Orpen, 1934)

Accefade	Aughfad	Taghmon
Acchedre	Harperstown	Taghmon
Adhangene	unknown	–
Admoinger	Aughermon	Taghmon
Alislenam	unknown	–
Astrut	unknown	–
Auene Duf	Owenduff	Ballycullane
Baligram	Ballylane	Cushenstown
Balifistlan	unknown	–
Bannow	Bannow	Bannow
Bruncunri	unknown	–
Carneuath	Carnagh	Cushenstown
Clonmen	Clonmines	Ballycullane
Cockeswode	unknown	–
Colari	unknown	–
Colp	Collop's Well	Newbawn
Cnocrod	Knockroe	Cushenstown
Cnoklithan	Lacken Hill	Cushenstown
Crouath	unknown	–
Deriardcolman	unknown	–
Dernegilath	unknown	–
Dunrodgel	unknown	–
Glanbothar	unknown	–
Glenroban	unknown	–
Hoge or Sutan	Ballyhoge	Bree
Karrothobren or Hoel	Carrigbyrne	Newbawn
Karrech-castle of	Newtown	Glynn
Karrchogan	Carrigadaggan	Newbawn
Kerrechonal	unknown	–

Kulbore	Coolboy	Clongeen
Kyldouan	unknown	–
Matherneyuin (Magh Arnaidhe)	Adamstown	Adamstown
Moendermot	unknown	–
Radbredmath	unknown	–
Radcrotheri	Templenacroha?	Newbawn
Raddiniskerd	unknown	–
Radmochelath	unknown	–
Sceter	Skeetarpark	Rathangan
Taouchmune	Taghmon	Taghmon
Thauchkoynoch	Boss Rock?	–
Wexford	Wexford	Wexford
Ynnell or Clondelef	unknown	–

Place-names from knights' fees (Brooks, 1950; Colfer, 1987, 95-9)

Balimalgir	Ballymagir (Richfield)	Rathangan
Baliregan	Ballyregan	Camolin
Balkwynch	Ballywitch (Ballywith)	St Helen's
Ballicarnall	Ballicarnall	Craanford
Balliduykin	Ballyduskar	Ballymore
Ballikermuth	Ballydermot	Cushenstown
Ballikeroch	Ballykeeroge	Suttons
Balliregan	Ballyregan	Ballymore
Balliregan	Ballyregan	Craanford
Ballybrennan	Ballybrennan	Tagoat
Ballically	Galgystown?	Templetown
Ballyconway	Ballycanew	Camolin
Ballyconyng	Ballyconnick	Rathangan
Ballydufathely	Ballyhealy	Kilmore
Ballyfistelbane	Ballyfistlane	Lady's Island
Ballygavereth	Ballygarvey	Tagoat
Ballymaccarne	Ballycarran	Tagoat
Ballymakaterine	Ballymacane	Lady's Island
Ballymacktorny	Ballytory	Lady's Island
Ballyranchan	Ballyrankin	Kilrush
Ballythayk	Ballyteige	Kilmore
Balybrazil	Ballybrazil	Suttons
Balyhelol	Ballyell	Tagoat
Carne	Carn	Lady's Island
Duncormok	Duncormick	Rathangan
Duferth	Duffrey	Enniscorthy
Glaskerec	Glascarrig	Ballygarret
Karecbren	Carrigbyrne	Newbawn
Kilcogani	Kilcowanmore	Bree
Kilcouegan	Kilcowan	Bannow
Kilkevan	Kilcavan	Bannow
Kilcolky	Kilcorkey	Camolin
Kilmucres	Kilmuckridge	Kilmuckridge
Kilrothane	Kilrane	Kilrane

Kylluskerd	Killesk	Suttons
Leskine	Leskinfere	Camolin
Mowmayn	Mackmine	Bree
Molranchan	Mulrankin	Kilmore
Slefcolter	Slievecoiltia	Suttons
Tillocdovan	Tilladavin	Kilmore
Torkhill	Tarahill	Castletown
Trumered	Trimmer	Tagoat

Sources

Anderson, A.O. and Anderson, M.O., ed. and trans. 1961. *Adomnán's life of Columba*, Oxford.

Andrews, J.H. 1955-6. The Wexford civil survey, 1655-8, as a source for historical geography (unpublished).

Annals of Clonmacnoise, ed. and trans. D. Murphy, 1896. Reissued, Lampeter, 1993.

Annals of the Four Masters, ed. and trans. by J. O'Donovan, 1851. Reissued, Dublin, 1990.

Annals of Inisfallen, ed. S. Mac Airt, 1951. Royal Irish Academy, Dublin.

Annals of Tigernach, ed. W. Stokes, 1896-7, *Revue Celtique*. Facsimile reprint, Lampeter, 1993.

Annals of Ulster, ed. S. Mac Airt and G. Mac Niocaill, 1983, Dublin.

Anon. 1921. 'St Palladius and the diocese of Ferns', *The Past* 2 (1921), 100-12.

Anon. 1980. 'The life of St Monenna by Conchubranus', edited by the Ulster Society for Medieval Latin Studies, *Seanchas Ard Mhaca* 10:1 (1980) 117-41.

Armagh, Book of: extracts in L. de Paor, *Saint Patrick's World*, 1993, Dublin, 154-97.

Armstrong, E.C.R. 1915. 'Catalogue of silver and ecclesiastical antiquities in the collection of the Royal Irish Academy by the late Sir Wm Wilde', *Proc. RIA* 32 (1914-16) C, 287-312.

Bennett, I. 1989. 'The settlement pattern of ringforts in Co. Wexford', *RSAI Jn.* 119 (1989) 50-61.

Best, R.I. and Lawlor, H.J. 1931. *The martyrology of Tallaght*, Henry Bradshaw Society, London.

Bieler, L. 1963. *The Irish Penitentials*, Scriptores Latini Hiberniae, V, Dublin.

Binchy, D.A. ed. 1941. *Crith Gablach*, Medieval and Modern Irish Series, XI, Dublin.

Bourke, E. 1988-89. 'Two eleventh-century Viking houses from Bride Street, Wexford, and the layout of properties on the site', *Jn. Wexford Hist. Soc.* 12 (1988-89) 50-61.

Bourke, E. 1995. 'Housing and domestic economy in Viking and medieval Wexford', *Archaeology Ireland* 8: 3 (1995) 33-36.

Bowen, E.G. 1969. *Saints, seaways and settlements in the Celtic lands*, Cardiff.

Bowen, E.G. 1970. 'Fair gwelygordd santaidd ynys prydain', *Studia Celtica* 5 (1970) 10-14.

Breen, T.C. 1988. 'St Brecaun's church, Portersgate'. *Excavations*, ed. Isobel Bennett, Dublin, 30-1.

Brooks, E. St John, 1950. *Knights fees of counties Wexford, Carlow and Kilkenny*, Stationery Office, Dublin.

Byrne, F.J. 1967. 'Early Irish society (first-ninth century)' in *The course of Irish history*, ed. T.W. Moody and F.X. Martin, Cork, 43-60.

Byrne, F.J. 1973. *Irish kings and high kings*, London.

Byrne, F.J. 1984. 'Heads of churches to 1200' in *A new history of Ireland*, ix, ed. T.W. Moody, F.X. Martin and F.J. Byrne, Oxford, 237-46.

Byrne, F.J. 1987. 'The trembling sod: Ireland in 1169' in *A new history of Ireland*, ii, *Medieval Ireland, 1169-1534*, ed. A. Cosgrove, Oxford 391-42.

Calendar of ancient deeds and muniments preserved in the Pembroke estate office, 1891, Dublin

Carney, J. trans. 1967. *Medieval Irish lyrics*, Dublin.

Centenary record of Wexford's twin churches, ed. M.J. Berney, 1958, Wexford.

Colfer, B. 1978. *The promontory of Hook*, Wexford.

Colfer, B. 1987. 'Anglo-Norman settlement in Co. Wexford' in *Wexford history and society*, ed. Kevin Whelan, Dublin.

Colfer, 1990-91.' Medieval Wexford', *Jn. Wexford Hist. Soc.* 13 (1990-91) 5-29.

Colgan, J. 1947. *The Acta Sanctorum Hiberniae of John Colgan*, Irish Manuscripts Commission, Reflex Facsimiles No. 5, Dublin

Comerford, M. 1883. *Collections relating to the diocese of Kildare and Leighlin*, i, p. 1.

Corish, P.J. 1972. *The Christian mission*, in *A history of Irish Catholicism*, Dublin, 65-96.

Culleton, E. 1984. *Early man in Co. Wexford*, Dublin.

Culleton, B. 1994. *Treasures of the Wexford landscape*, Wexford.

Culleton, E. and Mitchell, G.F. 1976. 'Soil erosion following deforestation in the Early Christian period in Co. Wexford', *RSAI Jn.* (106), 120-3.

Dalton, J. P. 1921. 'St Vauk's of Carne', *The Past* 2 (1921) 1-37.

de Paor, L. 1993. *St Patrick's world*, Dublin.

de Val, S. 1994. 'The origin and meaning of townland names in Co. Wexford', in B. Culleton 'Treasures of the Wexford landscape', Wexford.

Dinneen, P.S. ed. 1927. *Foclóir Gaedilge agus Béarla*, Irish Texts Society, Dublin.

Doble, G. H. 1971. *Lives of Welsh saints*, ed. D. Simon Evans, Cardiff.

Doherty, C. 1980. 'Exchange and trade in early medieval Ireland' *RSAI Jn.* (110) 67-89.

Doherty, C. 1982. 'Some aspects of hagiography as a source for Irish economic history', *Peritia* 1 (1982) 300-28.

Doherty, C. 1986. 'Saint Máedóg and Saint Molaise', *Bréifne* 11:24 (1986) 363-74.

Doherty, C. 1987. 'The Irish hagiographer: resources, aims, results' in *The writer as witness: literature as historical evidence*, ed. T. Dunne, Historical Studies 16 (1987) 10-22, Cork

Dolley, R. M.H. 1966. *The Hiberno-Norse coins in the British Museum*, London.

Dugdale, J. 1673. *Monasticon Anglicanum*.

Dunn, E.C. 1989. *The Gallican saints and the late Roman dramatic tradition*, Washington DC.

Edwards, N. 1990. *The archaeology of early medieval Ireland*, London.

Etchingham, C. 1994. 'Bishops in the early Irish church: a re-assessment', *Studia Hibernica* 28 (1994) 35-62

Expugnatio Hibernica: the conquest of Ireland, by Giraldus Cambrensis, Scott, A.B. and Martin, F.X. (eds) 1978, Dublin.

Fitzpatrick, E. 1997. 'The practice and siting of royal inauguration in medieval Ireland', PhD thesis, Trinity College, Dublin, 2 vols.

Flanagan, D. 1981-2. 'Some guidelines to the use of Joyce's Irish names of places', *Bull. Ulster Place-Name Soc.* (2nd series) 4 (1981-2) 61-9.

Flanagan, D. 1984. 'The Christian impact on early Ireland: place-name evidence' in *Ireland and Europe*, ed. P. Ní Chatháin and M. Richter, Stuttgart, 25-81.

Flanagan, D. and L. 1994. *Irish place names*, Dublin

Flood, W.H. Grattan. 1916. *The history of the diocese of Ferns*, Waterford.

Furlong, N. 1973. *Dermot, king of Leinster and the foreigners*, Tralee.

Gardiner, M.J. and Ryan, P. 1964. *Soils of Co. Wexford*, Agricultural Institute, Dublin.

Geary, P. 1964. *Living with the dead in the Middle Ages*, Ithaca, New York.

Graham-Campbell, J. 1976. 'The Viking-age silver hoards of Ireland', Seventh Viking Congress, ed. B. Almquist and D. Green, Dublin, 39-74.

Grant, M. 1956. *Tacitus, the annals of imperial Rome*, London.

Grosjean, P. 1959. 'Deux textes inedits sur S. Ibar', *Analecta Bollandiana* 77 (1959) 426-50.

Gwynn, A. 1945. 'The first synod of Cashel', *Irish Ecclesiastical Record* 66 (1945) 82-92.

Gwynn, A. and Hadcock, R.N. 1970. *Medieval religious houses: Ireland*, London.

Gwynn, E. 1913. *Metrical dindsheanchas*, 5 vols, Dublin.

Hadden, G.W. 1968. 'The origin and development of Wexford town', *Jn. Old Wexford Soc.* 1 (1968) 5-16.

Harbison, P. 1988. 'Exotic ninth to tenth century cross decorated stones from Clonmore, Co. Carlow and Beggerin, Co. Wexford', *Keimelia: Studies in medieval archaelogy in memory of Tom Delany*, ed. G. Mac Niocaill and P. Wallace, Galway.

Harbison, P. 1992. *The high crosses of Ireland: An iconographical and photographic survey*, 3 vols, Bonn.

Harte, L. 1925. 'The parish of Cloughbawn', *The Past* 3 (1925) 100-106.

Heist, W.W. 1965. *Vitae Sanctorum Hiberniae e Codice olim Salmanticensi nunc Bruxellensi*, Subsidia Hagiographica, 25.

Heist, W.W. 1976. 'Over the writer's shoulder: St Abbán', *Celtica* 11 (1976) 76-84.

Hennessy, W.M. 1866. *Chronicum Scotorum*, Dublin.

Henry, F. 1970. *Irish art in the Romanesque period, AD 1020-1170*, London.

Herbert, M. and Ó Riain, P. ed. 1988. *Betha Adamnáin. The Irish Life of Adomnán*, Irish Texts Society, 54. London

Herity, M. 1987. 'A survey of the royal site at Cruachan in Connacht, III. Ringfort and ecclesiastical sites', *RSAI Jn.* 117 (1987) 125-41.

Hodnebo, F. 1985. 'Who were the Vikings?', *Tenth Viking Congress*, ed. J.E. Kinirk and C. Blindheim, Oslo, 43-54.

Hogan, E.I. 1910. *Onomasticon Goedelicum*, Dublin.

Hore, H.F. 1862. 'An account of the barony of Forth, in the County of Wexford, written at the close of the seventeenth century', *Kilkenny and Southeast of Ireland Archaeological Society Jn.* 4 (1862-3) 53-92.

Hore, P.H. 1901-11. *History of town and county of Wexford*, 6 vols, London.

Hore, P.H. 1920. 'The barony of Forth', *The Past* 1 (1920) 62-106.

Hughes, K. 1954. 'The historical value of the Lives of Saint Finnian of Clonard', *English Historical Review* 69 (1954) 353-72.

Hughes, K. 1959. 'On an Irish litany of pilgrim saints, around 800', *Analecta Bollandiana*, 77 (1959) 305-31.

Hunt, J. 1970, 'The Life of St Munnu, otherwise Fintan, abbot of Taghmon', translated from the Latin Life in *Vitae Sanctorum Hiberniae*, Plummer, 1910, ii, Oxford, 226-38.

Hurley, V. 1979a. 'The early church in southwest Ireland: settlement and organization' in *The early church in Britain and Ireland*, ed. S.M. Pearce, BAR British Series No. 102, 297-330.

Hurley, V. 1979b. 'The distribution, origins and development of temple as a church name in southwest Ireland', *Cork Historical and Archaeological Soc. Jn.* 84 (1979) 74-94.

Kelly, D. 1988. 'Cross-carved slabs from Latteragh, Co. Tipperary', *RSAI Jn.* 118 (1988) 92-100.

Kelly, F. 1997. *Early Irish farming*, Early Irish Law Series, iv, Dublin Institute for Advanced Studies, Dublin.

Kenney, J.F. 1929, *The sources for the early history of Ireland*, i: *ecclesiastical*, New York and Dublin.

Kinahan, J.H. 1872. Communication on Beggerin, *Jn. Royal Historical and Archaeological Assoc. Ireland* 11:2 (1872) 435.

Mac Airt, S. ed. 1944. '*Duanaire Aodha mhic Sheaáin*', in *Leabhar branagh*, Dublin Institute for Advanced Studies, 62.

Macalister, R.A.S. 1920. 'Beg-Eire', *The Past* 1 (1920) 5-14.

Macalister, R.A.S. 1938-56. *Lebor Gabala Erenn: the book of the taking of Ireland*, i-v, Irish Texts Society, Dublin.

Macalister, R.A.S. 1945. *Corpus Inscriptionum Insularum Celticarum*, 2 vols, Stationery Office, Dublin.

Mac an Bhaird, A. 1991-3. 'Ptolemy revisited', *Ainm* 5 (1991-3) 1-20.

Mac Giolla Easpaig, D, 1996-97. 'Breccán Cathe, a forgotten Derry saint', *Ainm* 7 (1996-7) 75-88.

Mahr, A. 1941. 'The Early Christian epoch' in J. Raftery, *Christian art in ancient Ireland*, ii, 152-4, Stationery Office, Dublin.

Mac Lean, D. 1983. 'Knapdale, dedication to a Leinster saint: sculpture, hagiography and oral tradition', *Scottish Studies* 27 (1983) 49-65.

Mac Lysaght, E. 1980. *The surnames of Ireland*, Dublin.

Mac Néill, M. 1962. *The festival of Lughnasa*, Oxford.

Mac Niocaill, G. 1971. '*Tír cumaile*: on land classification in Early Christian times', *Ériu* 22 (1971) 81-6.

Mac Niocaill, G. 1972. *Ireland before the Vikings*, Dublin

McCormick, F. 1995. 'Cows, ringforts and the origins of Early Christian Ireland', *Emmmania* 13 (1995) 33-7.

McErlean, T. 1983. 'The Irish townland system of landscape organization' in *Landscape archaeology in Ireland*, ed. T. Reeves-Smyth and F. Hammond, BAR British Series No. 116, 315-39

Moore, M.J. 1996. *Archaeological inventory of Co. Wexford*, Stationery Office, Dublin.

Murphy, G. 1956. *Early Irish lyrics*, Oxford.

Mytum, H. 1992. *The origins of Early Christian Ireland*, London.

Nicholls, K.W. 1969. 'Some place-names from *Pontifica Hibernica*', *Dinnseanchas* 3:4 (1969) 85-98.

Nicholls, K.W. 1972. *Gaelic and gaelicised Ireland in the Middle Ages*, Dublin.

Nicholls, K.W. 1984. 'Celtic Leinster, a review', *Peritia* 3 (1984) 554-8.

Ní Chatháin, P. 1979-80. 'Swineherds, seers and druids' *Studia Celtica*, 14-15 (1979-80) 200-11.

Ní Gabhláin, S. 'The origin of medieval parishes in Gaelic Ireland' *RSAI Jn*. 126, 37-61.

Nolan, B. 1997. 'St Maelruan'. *The Bridge* (Castlebridge parish newsletter), ed. Rev. W. Forde, 2:1 (1997) 6.

O'Brien, E. 1988. 'Churches of southeast Co. Dublin; seventh to twelfth century', *Keimelia: Studies in medieval archaeology in memory of Tom Delaney*, ed. G. Mac Niocaill and P.F. Wallace, Galway.

O'Brien, M.A. 1962. *Corpus genealogiarum Hiberniae*, i, Dublin Institute for Advanced Studies, Dublin.

Ó Broin, G. 1983-4. 'The holy wells of Wexford', *Jn. Wexford Historical Soc.* 9 (1983-4) 27-35.

O'Connor, N. 1983. 'Cross slab' in *Treasures of Ireland, Irish art 3000 BC-1500 AD* ed. M. Ryan, Dublin, 142-3.

Ó Corráin, D. 1971. 'Irish regnal succession: a reappraisal', *Studia Hibernica* 2 (1971) 7-39.

Ó Corráin, D. 1970-1. 'The career of Diarmait Mac Maél na mBó, king of Leinster, Part 1', *Jn. Old Wexford Soc.* 3 (1970-1) 27-35.

Ó Corráin, D. 1972. *Ireland before the Normans*, Dublin.

Ó Corráin, D. 1981. 'The early Irish churches, some aspects of organization' in *Irish antiquity: essays and studies presented to Prof. M.J. O'Kelly*, ed. by D. Ó Corráin, 327-341, Cork.

Ó Corráin, D. 1983. 'Some legal references to fences and fencing in early historic Ireland' in *Landscape archaeology in Ireland*, ed. T. Reeves-Smyth and F. Hammond, BAR, British Series, No. 116, 269-80, Oxford.

O'Donovan, J. 1840. Letters containing information relative to the antiquities of Co. Wexford collected during the progress of the Ordnance Survey in 1840, 2 vols, compiled by M. O'Flanagan, 1933, Bray.

O'Donovan, J. 1844. *The genealogies, tribes and customs of Hy Fiachrach*, Dublin.

O'Donovan, J. 1862. *The topographical poems of John Ó Duibhagáin and Giolla na Naomh Ó hUidhrin*, Irish Archaeological and Celtic Society, Dublin.

O'Donovan, J. 1868. ed. W. Stokes, *Sanas Chormaic; Cormac's Glossary*, Calcutta.

O'Dwyer, P. 1988. *Mary: a history of devotion*, Dublin.

Ó Floinn, R. 1998. 'The archaeology of the early Viking age' in *Ireland and Scandinavia in the early Viking age*, ed. H.B. Clarke, M. NÍ Mhaonaigh and R. Ó Floinn, Dublin, 131-65.

Oftendal, M. 1976. 'Scandinavian place-names in Ireland', *Seventh Viking Congress*, ed. B. Almquist and D. Green, Dublin, 123-125

O'Hanlon, J. 1875. *Lives of Irish saints*, 9 vols, Dublin.

O'Keeffe, J. G. 1904. 'The rule of Patrick', *Ériu* 1 (1904) 216-24.

O'Keeffe, T. 'Diarmait Mac Murchada and Romanesque Leinster', *RSAI Jn.* 127, forthcoming.

O'Kelleher, A. and Schoepperle, G. 1918. *Bethe Colaim Cille*, by Manus O'Donnell, Urbana, Illinois.

O'Kelly, M. J., Lynch, A. and Cahill, M. 1975. Archaeological survey and excavation of St Vogue's church, enclosure and other monuments at Carnsore, Co. Wexford. Unpublished Electricity Supply Board report.

O'Leary, P. 1913. *Saint Mullins*, Graignamanagh.

Ó Lochlainn, C. 1940. 'Roadways in ancient Ireland' in *Féil-sgribhinn Eoin Mhic Néill*, ed. J. Ryan, Dublin, 465-74.

Ó Maidín, U. 1996. *The Celtic monk: rules and writings of early Irish monks*, Kalamazoo.

O' Meara, J. 1951. *The topography of Ireland by Giraldus Cambrensis*, Dundalk.

Ó Riain, P. 1983. 'Cainnech, alias Colum Cille, patron of Ossory' in *Folia Gadelica*, ed. P. de Brún et al., Cork

Ó Riain, P. 1985. *Corpus genealogiarum sanctorum Hiberniae*, Dublin Institute for Advanced Studies, Dublin.

Ó Riain, P. 1986. 'St Abbán: the genesis of an Irish saint's life' in *Proc. Seventh Internat. Congress of Celtic Studies*, ed. D. Ellis Evans, J.G. Griffith and E.M. Jope, Oxford, 159-70.

Orpen, G. H. 1982. *The song of Dermot and the earl*, Oxford.

Orpen, G. H. 1894. 'Ptolemy's map of Ireland', *RSAI Jn.* Fifth Series, 4 (1994) 115-28,

Orpen, G.H. 1911. 'Croghans and Norman motes' *RSAI Jn.* 41 (1911) 270-1.

Orpen G.H. 1913-16. 'Rathgall, Co. Wicklow, Dun Gallion and the dunum of Ptolemy', *Proc. RIA* 33 (1913-16) C 41-57.

Orpen, G. H. 1934. 'Charters of earl Richard Marshal of the forests of Ross and Taghmon', *RSAI Jn.* 64 (1974) 54-63.

Otway-Ruthven, A.J. 1964. 'Parochial development in the rural deanery of Skreen', *RSAI Jn.* 94 (1964) 111-22.

Plummer, C. 1910. *Vitae Sanctorum Hiberniae*, 2 vols, Oxford.

Plummer, C. 1922. *Bethada naem nErenn*, 2 vols, Oxford.

Plummer, C. 1925. *Irish litanies*, Henry Bradshaw Society, London.

Ranson, J. 1948. 'Ancient crosses in the barony of Ballaghkeen', *The Past* 4 (1948) 93-104.

Ranson, J. 1949. 'Saint Maelruan', *The Past* 5 (1949) 161-7.

Richter, M. 1999. *Ireland and her neighbours in the seventh century*, Dublin.

Reeves, W. 1857. *The life of saint Columba written by Adomnán*, Dublin.

Roche, R. 1985-6. 'Two decorated headstones from Gibberwell' *Kilmore parish journal* 14 (1985-6) 33.

Ryan, J. 1931, *Irish monasticism*, Dublin.

Sharpe, R. 1989. 'Irish saints before St Patrick' in *Sages, saints and storytellers. Celtic studies in honour of Prof. James Carney*, ed. D. Ó Corráin et al., Maynooth, 376-99.

Sharpe, R. 1991. *Medieval Irish saints' lives*, Oxford

Sharpe, R. 1992. 'Churches and communities in early medieval Ireland; towards a pastoral model' in *Pastoral care before the parish*, ed. J. Blair and R. Sharpe, 81-109.

Shearman, J. F. 1875. 'On Patrick and Iserninus', *RSAI Jn.* vol. iii, Part 11, Fourth Series, 381-7.

Simington, R.C. 1953. *The civil survey, AD 1654-6*, ix, *Co. of Wexford*, Stationery Office, Dublin.

Simms, A. 1983. 'Rural settlement in medieval Ireland: villages, farms and frontiers, in *Studies in European rural settlement in the medieval and early modern periods*, ed. B.K. Roberts and R.E. Glasscock, BAR International Series No. 185, 133-152, Oxford.

Smyth, A.P. 1982. *Celtic Leinster*, Dublin.

Stokes, M. 1893. 'St Beoc of Wexford and Lan Veoc of Brittany', *RSAI Jn.* 22 (1893) 380-5.

Stokes, W. 1887. *Vita tripartita*, the tripartite life of Saint Patrick, with other documents relating to the saint, Rolls Series, London.

Stokes, W. 1890. *Lives of saints from the Book of Lismore*, Oxford.

Stokes, W. 1892. 'The borama (from Book of Leinster)', *Revue Celtique*, 13 (1892) 32-124.

Stokes, W. 1895. *The martyrology of Gorman*, Henry Bradshaw Society, London.

Stokes, W. 1905.*The martyrology of Oengus the culdee*, Henry Bradshaw Society, London.

Stokes, W. 1907. *The birth and life of Moling*, Specimens of Middle Irish Literature, No. 1, privately printed, London.

Stout, G. 1987.' Wexford in prehistory, 500 BC to 300 AD' in *Wexford; history and society*, ed. K. Whelan, Dublin.

Stout, M. 1997. *The Irish ringfort*, Dublin.

Swan, B. 1972-3. 'The manor of Rosslare', *Jn. Old Wexford Soc.* 4 (1972-3) 80-7

Swan, D.L. 1988. 'Enclosed ecclesiastical sites and their relevance to settlement patterns in the first millennium AD' in *Landscape archaeology in Ireland*, ed. T. Reeves Smith and F. Hammond, 269-280, BAR British Series No. 116, Oxford.

Thomas, C. 1994. *And shall these mute stones speak*, Cardiff.

Thomas, C. 1995. 'Cellular meanings, monastic beginnings' *Emmania* 13 (1995) 51-67.

Todd, J.H. and Reeves, W. 1864. *The martyrology of Donegal*, Irish Archaeological and Celtic Society, Dublin.

Ussher, J. 1639, *Britannicarum ecclesiarum antiquitate*, Dublin

Wallace, P. F. 1982. 'Irish early "wooden churches" – a suggestion' *North Munster Antiquarian Jn.* 24 (1982) 19-28.

Walsh, J. R. and Bradley, T. 1991. *A history of the Irish Church, 400-700 AD*, Dublin.

Warner, G. 1906, 1915. *The Stowe Missal, I and II*, Henry Bradshaw Society, London.

Watson, W. 1926. *The history of Celtic place-names of Scotland*, Edinburgh.

Watt, J. 1972. *The Church in medieval Ireland*, Dublin.

Westropp, T. J. 1918.'Five large earthworks in the barony of Shelburne, Co. Wexford', *RSAI Jn.* 48 (1988) 1-18.

Wilson, S. 1983. *Saints and their cults*, Cambridge.

Index

Abbán, 18, 32, 75, 79, 97-101, 155
Abingdon, England 99
Adamstown 18, 97, 101, 159, 184, 203
Adomnán 75
Agatha, St 213
Aghade, Co. Carlow 67, 191
agriculture 28-9
Aidán, St 15, 18, 33, 101-7, 155, 180
Airbre 113, 207
Ailbe, St 84
Allóc, *see* St Ellóc
Ambrosetown 160, 184, 216
Anglesey Wales 41
Annagh 179
Anne, St 208, 214
Ardamine 50, 52, 104, 134, 159, 186, 203
Ardcandrisk 18, 72, 128, 159, 203
Ardcavan 126, 153, 159, 165, 203
Ardcolm 147, 153, 159, 165, 203
Ard Ladrann, *see* Ardamine
Ard Lemnacht, *see* Forth mt
Arklow, Co. Wexford 168, 169
Arklow, Co. Wicklow 48, 170
Arnestown 30
Askinvillar, *see* Kildoran
Aughclare 177
Aughermon 30, 112, 177
Aughfad 30, 177
Augustine, St 70
Augustinian canons 19, 138-40
Auxilius, St 66

Baginbun 27, 194
baile 173-4, 183-4
Ballagh 31
Ballaghablake 31

Ballaghboy 31
Ballagh Burrow 31
Ballaghkeen 31, 32, 194, 196
Ballinacoola 69
Ballinaleck 18, 72, 161, 219
Ballindaggan 192
Ballingly 183
Ballinvalley 31
Ballyanne 160, 184, 217
Ballyandrew 64
Ballybeg 64
Ballyboher 64, 111, 160, 216
Ballybrazil 19, 150, 159, 174, 184, 204
Ballybrennan, Tagoat 19, 160, 174, 184, 216
Ballybrennan, Bree, *see* Kilcowanmore
Ballybuckley 16, 37, 39
Ballycanew 127, 153, 159, 161, 174, 184, 204
Ballyconnick 130, 160, 174, 184
Ballycullane 168
Ballydoyle 168, 169
Ballygarvey 174
Ballyhealy 174
Ballylane 174
Ballyleigh 37, 42
Ballymacane 174
Ballymaclare 161, 218
Ballymagir 174
Ballymore 68
Ballynabarney 64
Ballynaberney, *see* Kilrush
Ballynaslaney 69, 130, 160, 216
Ballynastraw, Oilgate 161, 218
Ballynestragh Demesne 161
Ballyorley 192, 204